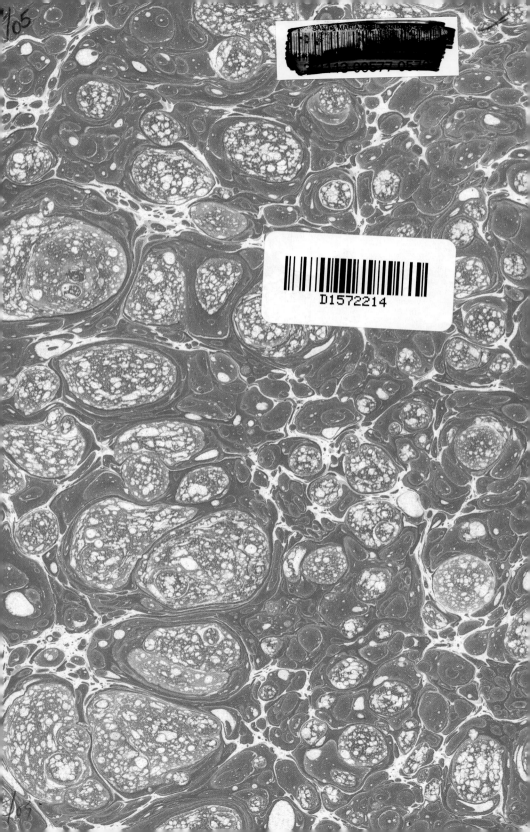

The World's First Jet Fighter Unit 1944/1945

JG 7

Manfred Boehme

Translated from the German by David Johnston

Schiffer Military History
Atglen, PA

Dust Jacket Artwork by Jerry Crandall, Sedona, AZ
Courtesy of Eagle Editions Ltd.
Prints Available through Eagle Editions Ltd.
P.O. Box 1830, Sedona, AZ 86336

The Painting:
This colorful machine was flown by Rudi Sinner, III Gruppe JG 7 *Kommandeur*. A few aircraft were equipped with Wgr. 21 cm. rockets, but proved unsuccessful. In March 1945, Wolfgang Späte took over the duties leading this prominent jet unit, III./JG 7.

Translated from the German by David Johnston.

Copyright © 1992 by Schiffer Publishing Ltd.
Library of Congress Catalog Number: 92-60364

Printed in the United States of America.
ISBN: 0-88740-395-6

This book was originally published under the title,
Jagdgeschwader 7, Die Chronik eines Me 262-Geschwader 1944/45,
by Motorbuch Verlag, Stuttgart.

We are interested in hearing from authors with book ideas on related topics.

Published by Schiffer Publishing, Ltd.
77 Lower Valley Road
Atglen, PA 19310
Please write for a free catalog.
This book may be purchased from the publisher.
Please include $2.95 postage.
Try your bookstore first.

We are interested in hearing from authors
with book ideas on related subjects.

Foreword

The author of this book belongs to a generation that did not experience the war as soldiers. He therefore possesses the great advantage of being free to examine the subject critically. The author was able to meticulously compile all that he learned in countless discussions with surviving participants and in documents held by the survivors of those who have died or in archives.

During his years of research he contacted designers directly involved in the Me 262 project, technicians from factories and industry, former Luftwaffe pilots who flew the Me 262, from leading aces to the most inexperienced, and even the enemy, who met the first jet aircraft in air combat over Germany.

As a result this book is not one-sided, rather it seeks to depict the truth about the development of the Me 262 from the viewpoint of a third party.

We ourselves believe that this should be emphasized, as we flew not only the Me 262, but many other types of aircraft as well, and have read a great number of books on various aircraft, their designers, the Luftwaffe and the war.

Transferred from various fighter units to join the Me 262 Test Unit (Nowotny) at Lechfeld in the autumn of 1944, we experienced the jet's relative quietness in flight, the enormous thrust of its engines, its speed and combat flying with JG 7. It was the beginning of a new era, the era of the jet aircraft, but it was also one filled with initial difficulties – technical, piloting and military. In addition to design shortcomings, which were of concern to us pilots as well, there were supply shortages caused by the war. Rational training of pilots was out of the question and there was no tactical concept for the employment of the few machines available.

Even experienced pilots sometimes failed to return from missions for technical reasons, lack of experience on the type or the numerical superiority of the enemy, and the number of candles burning in front of the empty places in the evening was increased by the loss of young pilots who had received an introduction to the Me 262 but no conversion training.

One had to be young, to have grown up in such a time and been enthusiastic about flying, to fly under those conditions. But in retrospect one also recognizes the madness in first testing such an inspired invention for military purposes in order to shoot at others, men who would most likely have preferred to sit around a table in friendship had the situation been different.

This book, which presents both sides, the positive and the negative, praises and criticizes, and in so doing seeks to stand alone, will surely find its share of readers.

Alfred Ambs
Hellmut Detjens
Ernest Giefing

JG 7 Pilots

Contents

January — The Waiting Is Over, III. Gruppe Operational — I. Gruppe
Hobbles Along Behind — Problems with the Engines — Deficiencies in
Conversion Training — Fuel Shortages — Bomber Pilots Become Fighter
Pilots — Lack of a Two-seat Trainer — Development of the Two-seater —
The Ergänzungsgruppe — Operations by the two Gruppen in February

Chapter IV - March 1945 — The Crucial Test   107

The First Large-scale Operations — Development of the R4M Air-to-air
Rocket — First Use of the R4M on 18.3.1945 — Oblt. Wegmann Is Put out
of Action — Catastrophe at Kaltenkirchen — Formation of I. Gruppe Is
Further Delayed — II. Gruppe Exists Only on Paper — Only the Me 262 Can
Stand up to the Overpowering Enemy — First Encounters with the US 15th
Air Force — Kommando Stamp — Hitler Is Pleased with the Success —
Bloody 31st of May for the RAF — Balance for the Month of March — With
III./EJG 2 — Heinz Bär, the Great Role Model

Chapter V - Toward the End   145

I. Gruppe Evacuates Kaltenkirchen — Major Sinner is Shot Down and Fired
Upon in His Parachute — The Death of Major Heinrich Ehrler — "Kommando
Elbe" — The Gyro Gunsight — The 8th Air Force Smashes the Jet Bases —
The Great Me 262 Massacre — The Geschwader Is Ordered to Move to
Bavaria — The Flying Unit Gets Stuck at Prague-Ruzyne — Scattered to the
Four Winds — Close-support Operations — The End in Prague — A Pilot
of JG 7 Scores the Last Victory of the War

Chapter VI - A Look Back   177

Surrender — JV 44 — The Pilots of JG 7, A Cross-section of the Entire
Luftwaffe — Foreign Jet Fighter Developments — The Legend of the Me
262 as a Possible War-Winning Weapon — Criticism of Previous Literature
on the Me 262 Fighter — There Was No Jet Fighter Tragedy and No Stab
in the Back — The Me 262, One Armaments Problem of Many — A Word
from the Author

Appendixes   191

Introduction

The Battle for Air Superiority over the Reich – Attacks on Schweinfurt – The Americans Learn an Expensive Lesson – The Second Front in the Air Becomes a Reality – "Big Week" – The Pendulum Swings – A Change through the Me 262?

Schweinfurt! The announcement of this target on the morning of October 14, 1943 left the American bomber crews sitting in stunned silence. Since August 17 the city had been known as "Killer Town." That was the day the US Army Air Force had made its first attempt to penetrate deep into Germany to destroy a vital industrial target through precision bombing. But the attempt had failed with terrible losses. Twenty-four Flying Fortresses were shot down in the attack on the Messerschmitt works in Regensburg, and no fewer than thirty-six smoldering wrecks littered the path of the bomber force assigned to attack and destroy the ball-bearing factories in Schweinfurt.

The American air command was deeply worried. Were the British, who had warned of insupportable losses in daylight attacks, to be proved right? The effects of the debacle were such that it was about three weeks before the Americans again appeared in the skies over Germany. On September 6 they risked another deep penetration. The German fighter arm's response was similar: 55 bombers were shot down in the raid on Stuttgart. The Americans called off their bombing offensive against Germany again, this time for three weeks. They returned to German skies in early October with catastrophic results. A series of raids on Frankfurt, Bremen, Anklam, Marienburg and Münster resulted in the loss of 104 four-engined bombers. However the climax of the air battles of 1943 was yet to come. On the morning of October 14, 1943, 291 Flying Fortresses of the 1st and 3rd Bombardment Divisions of the US 8th Air Force assembled over southern England. Their target: Schweinfurt. P-47s screened the bomber stream as far as Germany's western frontier. There, at the limit of their range, the escort fighters were forced to turn back. It was then that the German fighters struck; as the American fighters were turning for home they could see the first heavy bombers spinning toward the ground trailing long banners of black smoke.

The next few hours were a nightmare for the B-17 crews. Attacking in waves, the Focke-Wulfs and Messerschmitts shot down bomber after bomber. October 14, 1943 went into the annals of the 8th Air Force as "Black

Thursday." Fifty-eight bombers fell victim to German fighters and two more to anti-aircraft guns. Five badly-damaged Boeings crashed during the return flight over England; a further twelve were written off in crash-landings. More than 100 B-17s landed with more or less severe battle damage. More than 600 superbly-trained pilots, navigators, bombardiers and gunners were killed or captured. This was a blood-letting which even the Allies, with their nearly inexhaustible reserves of manpower, could not endure. What was more, even the temporary paralysis inflicted on the Fichtel & Sachs, Kugelfischer and VK factories and the reported destruction of 199 German aircraft and the probable destruction of another 28 could not make up for this unparalleled loss of qualified aircrew.

Probably influenced by these fantastic figures and trying to calm a shocked American public, General Arnold, Commander-in-Chief of the US air forces, confidently declared: "The efforts of the Luftwaffe were the death throes of a monster. The Germans suffered a fatal defeat on October 14." This illusion burst like a soap bubble a few days later. After careful analysis of the combat reports the euphoric victory claims could no longer stand up. But even the official Allied figure of 104 German aircraft destroyed did not correspond to the facts. The German forces which engaged the American incursion lost no more than 35 machines.

In mid-October 1943, after these convincing defensive successes, the German fighter and *Zerstörer* arms stood at the zenith of their fighting power. Their pilots had overcome the initial shock produced by their first meetings with the heavily-armed Flying Fortresses over France. Following the introduction of new tactics their own losses were being held within acceptable limits. A satisfactory resurgence of the aircraft industry, the generally good level of training, the outstanding morale of the crews and not least the climbing victory totals buoyed hopes that air superiority could be maintained over occupied western Europe and the Reich.

The responsible personalities in the RLM saw their single-minded efforts of the previous year confirmed. They continued to pin their hopes on new, more capable versions of the Bf 109 and Fw 190 as the main weapons of the air defense, without, however, losing sight of or even neglecting their replacement with more capable defensive weapons. It seemed that sufficient resources were available to meet coming burdens. However *General der Jagdflieger* Galland and other far-sighted leaders continued to stress that very soon the Allies were bound to turn their nearly limitless development and production potential to the production of a long-range fighter which could escort the bombers during deep penetrations over the Reich. The resulting consequences for the German fighter arm were incalculable in the long run.

December 30, 1943

The US 8th Air Force launched its heaviest raid yet against a target in Germany. 710 four-engine bombers set out on an hours-long flight over enemy territory. But this was to be no Schweinfurt. This time the bombers were accompanied by 463 P-47, 79 P-38 and 41 P-51 fighters, which guarded the bombers all the way to Ludwigshafen and back.

American calculations were proved correct. Only 23 bombers failed to return to their bases. Losses during the Schweinfurt raid had been 25% of the aircraft committed; this time they had only been about 4%.

However, long-range fighter escort was only one of the measures adopted by the Americans in answer to October 14, 1943. Two days later, on October 16, they decided to form two further bomber fleets, to be equipped with a total of 3,000 medium and heavy bombers. The strategic heavy bomber units of the 8th and 15th Air Forces would smash the German armaments industry, while the tactical medium bomber units, the 9th and 12th Air Forces, destroyed the transportation system and the German defensive positions in the West in preparation for the planned invasion of France.

With the formation of a strategic air fleet in Italy the worst nightmare of the German air command become a bitter reality: a second front in the air. The units based in southern Italy could now reach any target in southern Germany and Austria as well as in Hungary. Previously these targets could only be attacked by the 8th Air Force with considerably reduced bomb loads.

The Luftwaffe attempted to counter this double threat by withdrawing forces from Russia and reorganizing its fighter units in the West. The objective of the American strategic measures was to split the German air defense and thus directly reduce the number of German fighters defending against each incursion. Nevertheless, the thinly-spread units were initially able to withstand the increased pressure and during the initial weeks of 1944 inflicted considerable losses on the US Air Force over France, Germany and southern and southeastern Europe.

The defensive front was still holding and, in spite of almost ceaseless operations, there was no sign of a decimation of the German fighter units. In mid-February 1944, therefore, General Spatz, Commander-in-Chief of US strategic air forces, decided to put an end to this "spook." On February 20 more than 1,000 heavy bombers opened "Big Week," a series of destructive attacks against the aviation industry and airfields in southern, central and northern Germany.

But "Big Week" failed to produce a decisive reversal in fortune in favor of the Allies. On the contrary; in only six days the German defenses brought down 250 heavy bombers, while another 19 crashed in England. German successes continued to mount in early March. During its first major daylight raid on Berlin on March 6 the US Army Air Force suffered its highest single-day loss of the war: 69 bombers and 11 escort fighters. Two days later, on March 8, a further attack on the Reich capital resulted in the loss of another 37 heavy bombers.

The Americans were faced with the threat of losing control of the air war. Their reaction was immediate. The number of escort fighters was raised from 800 to 1,300! The Germans had nothing with which to answer apart from spirit and courage. Their personnel and material reserves were nearly exhausted.

What was more, the task of the defenders had been rendered more difficult by Allied developments in navigation and target-finding methods, which permitted a growing level of all-weather attacks.

The Luftwaffe also had to meet this demand, but the all-weather capabilities of its units were limited. Under the pressure of the prevailing situation the fighter units were forced to operate in weather conditions for which the crews had not been trained and which were beyond the capabilities of the navigational equipment installed in its aircraft. The results were predictable. Their pilots unused to instrument flying and bad-weather landings, large numbers of fighters crashed, further lowering the already reduced fighting strengths of the units.

The Germans resisted the swelling flood of bombers from east and west with the courage of desperation. American losses during the first months of the year were disastrous. The 8th Air Force alone lost 213 bombers in January, 287 in February, 342 in March, 420 in April and 373 in May. The loss of 1,635 bombers in the space of five months meant that the 8th Air Force had to replace its complete complement nearly twice. The air fleet lost 814 fighters in the same period!

However, from June 1944 the pendulum began to swing. The sacrificial efforts of the fighter and *Zerstörer* arms could not prevent the loss of air superiority over the occupied western territories and the Reich. At a sitting of the Aircraft Development High Commission Professor Tank summed it up bluntly:

> "The development of the Luftwaffe has in no way kept pace with the systematic buildup of the enemy air forces; the German fighter arm is no longer equal to its task of defending the homeland and engaging the enemy in strategic and tactical missions."

It was at this time that the Luftwaffe accepted the first examples of a new design, whose outstanding speed and armament tempted responsible personalities with the pipe dream that this weapon could lead to a change in the hopeless air situation. It was an illusory hope which did not, and could not have, come true.

This aircraft was the subject of the most audacious stories even during the war years. Rumors of its "imminent mass employment" were carefully fomented at the highest levels right up to the bitter end. The alleged "reasons" for the failure of this "mass employment" to materialize swelled to dozens – and were believed.

These rumors proliferated after the war, spun into sensational stories, "disclosures" and myths of "stabs in the back" by writers and plagiarists. Until now little of the published material has come close to the truth, often for quite transparent reasons.

The author admits that it was not always easy to free himself from and steer clear of well-worn cliches and his own version of events. All too often time-consuming investigations, contradictory documents or opposing statements tempted him to follow more comfortable paths and neglect the foremost duty of the historian, finding the truth.

Sincere efforts to do justice to this requirement delayed the completion of the work at hand by nearly three years. Over a period of five years the author assembled thousands of documents and questioned former pilots, mechanics, technicians and designers. In the end this enabled him to trace for the first time the history of the Me 262 and JG 7 as it really happened.

Chapter I
Origins & Development of the Me 262

New Engines, New Possibilities – Setback in Power Plant Development – Beginning of Project Work on the Me 262 – First Flight 1941 – The Junkers T 1 Engine – The Me 262 is Assigned a Priority Level – Development of the He 280 is Abandoned – Testing the Me 262 Prototypes – Endless Problems – Galland Flies the V4 and Declares It Ready for Front-line Service – Milch Orders Series Production – Messerschmitt "Dawdles" – No Delivery of First Pre-production Aircraft before January 1944 – Flight Tests Not Entirely Satisfactory – Göring Asks if the Me 262 Can Carry Bombs – Hitler at Insterburg, Demand for Me 262 as a Fighter-Bomber Comes As No Surprise – May 25, 1944, Hitler Loses Patience – Bombers Temporarily Receive Priority

November 1941

During a briefing held in Göring's special train, *General der Jagdflieger* Adolf Galland was brought up to date on the state of new developments in the fighter field on which Heinkel and Messerschmitt had been working on since 1938. The developments in question were "very high-speed pursuit fighters" which might one day decide the air war in Germany's favor. Perhaps, if the engine industry succeeded in preparing the necessary power plants in the near future. But there was very little hope of that at the time. The power plants which were to endow the new fighters with speeds never before achieved were not sophisticated and well-tried engines of the usual kind, instead they were a new type of engine, examples of which were being developed on the test stands of various manufacturers: jet engines. These differed in their mode of operation from the engines previously used to power aircraft, which developed their thrust through a propeller. The

turbojet engine operates on another principle: air streaming into the front of
the engine is compressed, heated by burning fuel, increased in volume and
ejected rearward with increased speed through the decrease in pressure to
the level of the outside air pressure. The reaction to these accelerated air
masses results in forward thrust. Although less efficient than piston engines
at low speeds, the jet engine is superior at higher speeds, as the efficiency
of the propeller drops off as speed increases while that of the jet engine
climbs. The jet engine is therefore more suitable for high-speed flight.

Development of the jet engine had started about two-and-a-half years
earlier and in spite of systematic efforts on the part of the designers was still
in its infancy. This was understandable. It was a completely new technology
which posed new problems for the engineers and technicians. Overcoming
these problems was a slow, time-consuming process.

One of the firms pursuing development of the gas turbine in Germany
was Junkers. Its work on this new generation of aero engine had begun in
autumn 1939. After extensive mathematical analyses and tests in principle
with axial compressors, combustion chambers and ejector nozzles, a design
team under the direction of Dr.Ing. A. Franz created the groundwork for the
design and construction of the first test unit. Completed in early October
1940 and designated the T 1, the first prototype was installed on a test bench
for mechanical and thermal analyses, measurement of mass air flow and
determination of the operating limits and efficiency of the compressor,
combustion chamber and turbine as well as the necessary starting capacity.
Operating experience with the full-scale model during the following weeks
fully lived up to expectations. The following is a document from the Special
Power Plant Department from 9.12.1940:

"After the first disassembly of the T 1 revealed no significant damage,
it was possible to continue test runs. The rotational speed was increased
from 5,000 to 7,000. The evaluations of these test runs, which were carried
out at 5,000, 6,000 and 7,000 revolutions, suggest that the design level of
operating efficiency has been reached. No damage was discovered during
the second disassembly which followed these runs. There was no evidence
of corrosion or scaling on the combustion chamber parts or the turbine
diffuser. The turbine blades were also undamaged. No loosening of the
blade seating was observed. The power plant logged 18 hours and 30
minutes between the first and second disassemblies."

A design breakthrough appeared to have been achieved with the first prototype engine. In January 1941 a manufacturing plan and timetable were drawn up for the prototype engines to be completed in the coming months: "... V4 and V5, the first two power plants cleared for flight, will probably be delivered to Messerschmitt at the beginning of July this year."

The optimistic deadline laid down on January 21, 1941 could not be met however. Only seven days later, on January 29, the compressor of the second prototype engine was destroyed. This was the first of a series of setbacks which was to drive the engineers to the verge of desperation. Mechanical difficulties with the axial arrangement of the compressor, damage to the impeller and diffuser (fractures due to vibration) and unequal temperature distribution in the combustion chamber were only several of the problems encountered which forced the redesign or rearrangement of individual power plant assemblies. There were further delays while the time-consuming process of testing materials was carried out, the result of an RLM decree to economize on scarce raw materials. Testing and selection of auxiliary equipment such as fuel pumps[1], fuel injection nozzles, ignition mechanisms, speed governors, temperature regulators and engine fuel flow controls also took longer than anticipated.

The Junkers deadline for delivery of flight-cleared engines was pushed back from month to month. Not until July 1942, a year after the initial deadline, had the prototype engines reached a level of technical maturity sufficient to justify their delivery to Messerschmitt at Lechfeld.

In the meantime Messerschmitt had completed two airframes for an aircraft whose concrete development had started with the beginning of project work on April 1, 1939, based on the following technical guidelines:

Purpose:	High-speed fighter for use against aerial targets
Number and Type of Engines:	2 jet engines
	Installation of various types of engine must be possible without major structural changes
Crew:	1
Armament:	4 MG 17 each with 800 rounds
	2 MG 131 each with 400 rounds
Gunsight:	Revi C 12 C
	Installation of weapons in fuselage nose
Signals and	1 FuG 18
Equipment:	Identification 1 flare pistol with six rounds
Fuel Tank	Forward removable protected tank, rear

Requirements:	removable metal or sealed riveted tank.
Electronic Equipment:	Aircraft must be capable of being operated at night
Performance:	Maximum speed as high as possible. Landing speed not to exceed 140 kph. Takeoff run not more than 600 meters to altitude of 20 meters. Endurance of approx. 1 hour at 85% power at an altitude of 6,500 meters (Fuel quantity 2,000 liters). Time to climb to 6,000 meters not to exceed 8.5 minutes.
Flight Characteristics:	Flight characteristics must satisfy E-Stelle Rechlin guidelines for the assessment of flight characteristics for the required role.
Stress Limit:	H 5
Airframe:	The aircraft is to be of all-metal construction. Simple and cheap design is required.

On June 7, 1939 the Messerschmitt firm submitted a project proposal to the RLM under the running number P 65, which had been drawn up to meet the specification. The design was an all-metal, low-wing monoplane with a retractable undercarriage. The fuselage was of triangular cross-section.

Specifications:

Landing speed at landing weight	130 kph	
Landing speed at maximum weight	164 kph	
Wing area	22 m²	
Landing weight with ammunition and fue	13,196 kg	
Maximum gross weight	4,321 kg	
Fuel supply sufficient for	1 min. takeoff at	130%
	climb	100%
	5 min. combat	130%
	55 min. flying time	85%
Armament:	1 MG 151 with increased calibre and 200	

	rounds
	2 MG 151 each with 400 rounds
Equipment:	FuG 18 with D/F
	Cockpit lighting for night flight
	Pressure cabin

Performance:

| Time to climb to 6,000 meters at 100% thrust | 6.16 min. |
| Time to climb to 6,000 meters at 130% thrust | 3.98 min. |

Takeoff run required to reach 20 meters at 100% thrust	800 m
Maximum speed at 3,000 meters at 100% thrust	840 kph
at 130% thrust	950 kph

This Messerschmitt design was the first stage in the development of what years later would become the Me 262, an aircraft which was to revolutionize air warfare.

In the following months new findings led to revision of the project. Messerschmitt submitted its improved Project Proposal I on 9.11.1939, and in early December began construction of a visual mockup. Work on the cockpit mockup started on January 15, 1940, followed at the end of the month by the structural mockup.

Favorable reports by the *Technische Amt* and the *E-Stelle Rechlin* led the RLM to issue a contract for three prototype aircraft on March 1, 1940. The prototypes were to be designed to take P 3302 jet engines built by BMW, which was working on jet engine development concurrently with Junkers.

The placing of the order was the signal for Messerschmitt to begin construction, and the first airframe was completed in late January 1941. The intervening ten months saw Messerschmitt submit Project Proposal II on May 15, 1940, and Project Proposal III on November 1, 1940. These addressed an ongoing series of changes, some resulting from new requirements from the *Technische Amt* and the *E-Stelle* such as air brakes and a braking parachute. At that time it was already certain that neither the Junkers nor BMW jet engines would be ready for delivery before July of that year. The Me 262 V1 was therefore fitted with a Jumo 210 G piston engine in the fuselage nose weapons bay to allow the airframe to be flight tested while awaiting delivery of the jet engines. All necessary work was completed by mid-April 1941. Initial taxying trials were carried out on April 17 and the following day the aircraft, which had received the series designation 8-262 in February of that year, made its first flight with *Flugkapitän* Wendel at the controls.

Although flight tests with the Jumo-powered prototype allowed only limited conclusions to be drawn over the aircraft's characteristics in the high speed range, on July 25, 1941 the RLM issued a contract for the construction of 5 V-Series and 20 0-Series aircraft.

As the deadlines for delivery of the BMW and Junkers engines were repeatedly set back, in the autumn of 1941 consideration was given to equipping the Me 262 with other high-performance power plants. A Walter rocket installation was considered and a pulse-jet (Argus-Schmidt) fighter version was planned. Performance figures for the pulse-jet version were as follows:

Version with	2 X 500 kg	4 X 500 kg
Max. speed at zero altitude	680 kph	960 kph
Rate of climb at zero altitude with half fuel	17 m/s	42 m/s
Low altitude climb speed	380 kph	450 kph
Range at		
0 m	500 km	
4,000 m	610 km	
8,000 m	760 km	

However none of these projects was accepted by the RLM, which continued to back the jet engine as the means of propulsion for the Me 262.

In early March 1942 the long wait finally appeared to have been rewarded, when BMW delivered the first pre-production P 3302 engines. These were fitted under the wings of the Me 262 V1, fuel lines and pumps installed in the wings and fuselage and additional instruments added to the cockpit. On March 30, 1942 Fritz Wendel took off on the first flight with partial jet power. The entire affair proved a disappointment:

> "The units accelerate too slowly. Power can only be increased slowly, especially above 6,400 rpm. The takeoff run itself was very long. At speeds of 400-500 kph engine speed could not be reduced below 7,000 rpm with an injection pressure of 16-18 atm in spite of pulling the throttle levers all

the way back . . . At a fuel reading of 100 liters a major fluctuation of the left injection pressure was observed and at the same time the left unit began to run roughly. The throttle lever was moved to idle, whereby the right throttle lever was inadvertently moved back so far that both units died. No special attention could be paid to the aircraft's characteristics due to lack of time. Aileron forces felt noticeably heavier than before. The overall impression was not satisfactory. It can already be said that average pilots will not be able to master this aircraft with such a high wing loading."

It was to be the only flight with the BMW P 3302 engines. The units were removed and sent back to BMW for redesign.

At the end of May 1942 the fate of the Me 262 hung by a slender thread. The RLM had drawn its conclusions from the completely failed dress rehearsal. It now made series production contingent upon the satisfactory testing of the V3, which was to be fitted with Junkers jet engines in the near future. Their state of development was summed up in a Junkers report from June 30, 1942:

Development of the Axial Compressor

Fluidic tests were carried out on compressor T 1, likewise the compressor underwent thorough mechanical testing. Initial difficulties (blade fractures, questions of clearance) were partially overcome through design changes.

Construction was of equipment to test individual wheels was started and the first tests with the dynamic pressure compressor were begun. In view of the expected difficulties with the testing of high-altitude behavior with the model compressor these tests were postponed. The high-altitude behavior of axial compressors is to be clarified at a later date.

Combustion Chamber Development

Ignition of the combustion chambers was considerably improved as a result of joining the individual chambers through interconnecters. Preliminary tests with igniting the combustion chambers with the aid of an igniter in place of spark plugs were carried out. Preliminary testing of air injection of fuel (better performance at high altitude) was carried out with favorable results.

Turbine Development

Design of an air-cooled turbine blade was concluded and preparations made for its manufacture. Preliminary tests with soldering these blades to the wheel demonstrated the practicality of this method. The amount of cooling air required to cool the blades was determined through tests on a turbine wheel segment.

Development of Auxiliary Equipment
Extensive test runs were carried out with the Leisritz firm's fuel pump, which was initially planned for use. Tests with a fuel pump from the Barmag firm produced better results, and this pump will be used in the O-Series of the T 1. Comparative tests with various starters demonstrated the superiority of the Ardie motor.

General Development Work on the Whole Machine
Engine duration trials (up to 50 hrs.) and operational tests were carried out on the test bench and in the Bf 110 test bed.

Construction materials development
Tests with molybdenum alloy heat-treated steel led to a switch from the previously used high-alloy Cr-Ni steel to a Cr-Mo steel for the turbine wheel. Further duration trials have begun in order to replace the Mo content entirely with Vanadium and reduce the Cr content. Tests were begun to explore the usability of low-alloy sheet metal (partially chromed) for the ejector nozzles. The fatigue lives of various turbine blade – wheel disk connections were tested. The great dependability and toughness of the hardening of Tinidur, the presently used turbine blade material, was determined, establishing this as the most favorable heat treatment."

In early July 1942 power plants V9 and V10 were delivered to Messerschmitt in spite of some concern as to their reliability under flight loads. It was not difficult to foresee what the RLM's reaction to a failure of these units would have been. But fortunately the historic first flight of an Me 262 on pure jet power took place without significant complaints:

> **"July 18, 1942**
> V 3 Flight No. 1   Takeoff 0840   Landing 0852
> All-up weight was 4,600 kg. In contrast to the V1 the rudder is ineffective during the first 500-600 meters of the takeoff roll due to the absence of the propeller slipstream, a brief activation of the brakes is required to raise the tail. The rudder becomes effective immediately and the machine can soon be lifted off.
> Elevator and rudder forces and effectiveness are satisfactory, aileron forces are too high, effectiveness inadequate.

Landing is comparatively simple. Touchdown speed is approximately 190 kph.

During the second flight at 1205 a stick vibration was felt at high speeds (from Va = 550 kph) dependent on dynamic pressure and rudder position.

The wing slat was deflected 15 mm between the inner bearings during high-speed, horizontal flight.

The engines worked well."

A relieved Junkers firm also commented on the gratifying way in which their engines had functioned:

"On 18.7.42, following two ground runs on 17.7., Me 262 V3 with Jumo T 1 engines took off from Leipheim airfield for the first time with Flugkapitän Wendel at the controls.

The flight was trouble-free.

Altitude = 2 km

Vmax = 600 kph

Duration about 10 min.

Assessment of pilot:

Satisfied with engines

Control and acceleration performance satisfactory,

practically the same as flying with one engine.

Machine difficult to brake on roll-out

(Idling thrust! Lack of propeller braking effect)

A second flight was conducted in the afternoon:

Climb from 2.5 to 3.5 km altitude

Airspeed 720 kph (airspeed indicator not calibrated)

Rate of climb 5-6 m/sec

The second flight was also trouble-free."

The favorable results achieved on the two flights were probably responsible for the RLM's decision on August 12 to expand the testing base by a further five machines, and on December 2 to increase the number of V-Series aircraft to 30 by the end of 1943.

Available records do not reveal any corresponding plans by the Messerschmitt firm, however. Not until November 15, 1942 does a company document mention the designing of production facilities having started and the first steps being taken to procure materials for the pre-production series. Initial plans were for production of ten aircraft, however, not the thirty specified in the contract.

Discussions took place on December 2, 1942, presumably at the instigation of the RLM, over planning questions relating to the V- and 0-Series. The atmosphere was cool, and concrete decisions foundered on unreasonable demands by Messerschmitt: in response to an RLM request to advance the first flight date of each of the V-Series aircraft by one month "to permit the conducting of a trouble-free flight test program during the summer of 1943," Messerschmitt replied that he would only be able to do so if a further 20 designers were made available "immediately." He also stated that the V- and O-Series programs could be carried through as planned only on condition that he receive assurances that 600 workers and 200 specialists could be transferred to his company within four weeks. Messerschmitt's demands were utopian; further, they were seen as a protective measure to cover up his own failures and errors in planning, which led to a steady deterioration in relations with the RLM. In late 1943 Göring even ordered an investigation by a court martial to explain the company's failure to meet deadlines and ordered: ". . . that an interview with Messerschmitt may only take place in the presence of witnesses, in particular of a stenographer."

On December 10, 1942, eight days after the first planning discussions over production of the Me 262, Milch ordered an urgency classification for certain promising developments:

> "The absolute demand for qualitative superiority of German air force equipment over that of enemy countries has led me to order the creation of an urgent development and production program under the code word 'Vulcan.'
>
> Operations proceeding under this code word have absolute first priority within the Luftwaffe.
>
> The program encompasses jet-propelled aircraft and guided weapons, including associated equipment and the ground organization necessary to support these activities.
>
> A request has been made of the Reich Minister for Armaments and Munitions to extend the legal force of the code word 'Vulcan' throughout the entire armaments field. Development of some of the following equipment is already taking place under priority DE. Through the code word 'Vulcan' priority will also apply to procurement of this equipment, for which extensive preparations will have to be made as before.
>
> The program encompasses the following equipment:
>
> (A) Aircraft: Me 163, Me 262, He 280, Me 328, Ar 234.

(B) Guided weapons: Hs 293, Hs 294, Fritz X, Fi 103.

(C) Jet engines: Jumo 004, BMW 003, 018, He 011, DB 007.

Other equipment, for which project work has not yet been completed, will be designated subsequently to supplement this program. The projects in question are high-speed bombers and heavy fighters with jet propulsion as well as further guided weapons."

This document corrects all the lies which continue to maintain, often in the face of knowledge to the contrary, that the people responsible failed to recognize the significance of jet aircraft in time, treated them with indifference, or even stood in their way.

Messerschmitt's task for the new year with the implementation of the "Vulcan" Program was clear: accelerate efforts to ready the Me 262 for series production. The project bureau applied for the manpower necessary to meet this demand. Existing design drawings were brought up to the latest standard based on new information and experience from the test program, and cockpit, structural and visual mockups of the production version were built.

A Messerschmitt document from March 4, 1943 summarized the construction configuration of the Me 262 as follows:

Armament:

The previously planned fixed armament of 3 MG 151 is no longer adequate to meet present demands.

The General der Jagdflieger demands:

(a) Standard armament: 6 X MK 108 or 4 X MK 108 + 2 X MG 151/20

(b) Alternative solution: In the event that the MK 108 cannot be made available in time an armament of 3 X MG 151 + 4 X MG 131 is foreseen.

Ammunition Capacity

Planned: if possible 100 rounds for each MK 108
                  250 rounds for each MG 151/15 or MG 151/20

Bomb Racks

As per an order from the Führer, every fighter must henceforth be capable of performing in the fighter-bomber role. An installation capable of carrying 500 kg of bombs is foreseen for the Me 262. The number of fixed weapons can be reduced for fighter-bomber missions.

Bomb-aiming Installation

Initially it is planned to use the normal Revi sight on a folding mount as bomb-aiming device.

Tires:

In view of the heavy armament and the requirement for the fighter-bomber role, 840 X 300 tires will be installed on the main landing gear in place of the previously planned 770 X 270 tires.

Air Brake:

Inclusion of an air brake would entail such a great technical expenditure that its installation will initially be dispensed with. Development work continues, however.

Radio Equipment

Radio equipment consists of: FuG 16 ze, FuG 25a.

Ejector Seat

Production aircraft will not receive an ejector seat.

Performance and Weight Specifications:

Messerschmitt AG provides a provisional summary of performance figures and weights. Definitive data will follow by 25. 3."

The promised figures reached the RLM by the specified date:

Basic equipped weight	3,280 kg
Crew	100 kg
Ammunition	220 kg
Fuel	1,330 kg
Gross Weight	5,470 kg
Maximum Speed:	805 kph at 0 km altitude
	880 kph at 6 km altitude
	875 kph at 9 km altitude
Rate of Climb:	22.0 m/sec at 0 km at 100% thrust
	12.0 m/sec at 6 km at 100% thrust
	6.0 m/sec at 9 km at 100% thrust
Time to Climb:	to 6 km at 100% thrust 5.9 min

	to 9 km at 100% thrust 11.5 min
Service Ceiling:	12.2 km
Range:	235 km at 100% thrust at 0 km (1,800 l)
	460 km at 100% thrust at 6 km
	540 km at 100% thrust at 9 km
Flight Duration:	0.29 hrs at 0 km at 100% thrust
	0.60 hrs at 6 km at 100% thrust
	0.79 hrs at 9 km at 100% thrust

With the receipt of this information the RLM was able for the first time to make an accurate comparison with the projected production version of the Heinkel jet fighter, the He 280. This aircraft was initially favored by the *Technische Amt* and the *E-Stelle Rechlin* and possessed an undeniable lead in development over the Me 262. The aircraft flew for the first time long before the Me 262, on September 22, 1940, and the first flight powered by HeS 8 A jet engines took place on March 30, 1941. Flight testing had been generally satisfactory, however two shortcomings were revealed which were finally to settle the fate of the He 280: limited endurance and vibration of the tail unit at high speeds, a problem which Heinkel was unable to overcome. On December 11, 1942 Professor Heinkel ordered some fundamental changes in his efforts to eliminate existing problems and find the definitive design configuration for his aircraft: a thicker fuselage to accommodate more fuel, an improved wing profile, a central fin and rudder and an extension of the fuselage by 50-60 cm.

At the end of March 1943 none of the planned changes had been realized, much less tested. The RLM had no choice but to decide in favor of the Me 262:

Berlin, 27. III. 1943

Dear Herr Heinkel,

Regretfully I must inform you that I have dropped the He 280 from the development program in favor of the Me 262. As you know, the war situation no longer permits us to allow two types to run side by side. However, I would like to ask you to complete the prototypes up to and including the V9, as these are being considered as flying test-beds for various jet engines.

All further work on the type, especially that relating to design changes and preparation of production drawings, is to be stopped.

25

For the work you have done and the new findings resulting from your initiative in the field of jet aircraft, I express to you my sincere thanks.

I remain, with warmest greetings,

your Milch

The Me 262 was flown for the first time by a service pilot, Hptm. Späte of Ekdo. 16, on April 17, 1943. Five weeks later, on May 22, *General der Jagdflieger* Galland flew the aircraft. The opinion of both officers: "The state of development of the machine is such that it could be used in action immediately!"

Was it really? Let us look back at the testing of the prototypes during the previous months.

Following the successful first flight of the Me 262 V3 on pure jet power on July 18, 1942, the machine carried out a total of only six calibration flights to investigate control column and wing vibration before crashing on takeoff on August 11. At the controls was *Fliegerstabsingenieur* Beauvais of the *E-Stelle Rechlin*. The second Jumo-powered Me 262, the V2, was not ready until about six weeks later, on October 1, 1942. Testing had to be discontinued after three manufacturer's test flights on October 1 and 2. "Testing had to be halted for four weeks owing to the training of Italian night fighter pilots." Testing resumed with flight number 4 on October 29. All eight flights carried out by December 16 served to investigate control surface forces, stability and the continuing problem of control column and wing vibration. From December 17 the aircraft was unserviceable "owing to the addition of the inboard leading edge extensions, new power plants, and so on."

The limited number of flights conducted during the last half of 1942 had contributed little to the aircraft's development and it was still too immature to commit to series production. In general the situation was unchanged from that of July 1942.

The pace of testing continued to drag during the first weeks of 1943. Between January 1 and February 7, 1943, the V2, which at the time was the only serviceable prototype, made out just four flights. The following report described the results:

"Flight Characteristics:
In spite of minor modifications aileron forces are still too high, in addition a restlessness in the control column is noticeable above 680 kph. The

rudder begins to flutter at large deflections. Rudder and elevator forces are good up to the speeds that have been flown.

Performance:
An accurate measurement of performance could not be carried out as the wing and aileron vibration prevents the aircraft from being flown to the limits of its performance.

Airframe:
Other than very poor wing manufacturing standards, especially on the trailing edge, and the overly-sloppy ailerons, no significant complaints have arisen.

Power Plants:
Repeated breakdowns of the left engine. Cause appears to be overheating in climbing flight. The engine will have to be changed.

Messerschmitt's testing program was increasingly hindered by a growing number of complaints about the airframe and engines. Every one of the 14 flights carried out by Messerschmitt pilot Ostertag in the period to March 20, 1943 encountered some sort of problem:

Test Report No.12 from 22.2. – 28.2.43:

Flight Characteristics:
Wing and aileron vibration appeared again in spite of securing the leading edge slats with bolts and locking them in the retracted position with 5 butt straps.

Preliminary evaluation of the machine with locked slats revealed that the slats can scarcely be dispensed with.

Single-engine flight is possible without difficulty, the rudder trimmer range is easily adequate.

Performance:
Because of the vibration investigations no performance measurements could be carried out.

Power Plants:
Rapid closing of the throttles results in both engines flaming out, a

situation which will definitely have to be corrected. Restarting in the air is possible, but is not successful every time.

Airframe:
In spite of securing the slats with bolts there was still shifting of the slats (play and suppleness in the roller tracks and mountings). Even after locking the slats with four butt straps there was bending between the inner bearings at high speed (Va = 680 kph), and a fifth butt strap had to be added."

"Test Report No.14 from 8.3. – 14.3.43:

Following the conclusion of ground vibration tests and test runs to readjust the engines, as well as the completion of modification work, the machine was sent back to Lechfeld.

In spite of the modifications the machine once again could not be flown at higher speeds as the wing and aileron vibration reappeared.

The engines likewise gave cause for complaint (flame-out on throttling back, fluctuations of fuel pressure, continued burning after engines switched off):

12.3.43 Flight No.29. Duration 12 min. Pilot Ostertag. Transfer flight. The pilot complained of considerable engine thrust fluctuations while climbing, which resulted in a pitching motion.
Subsequent ground running revealed no clues as to the cause, the engines ran trouble-free."

13.3.43 Flight No.30. Duration 10 min. Pilot Ostertag.
Both engines again flamed out when the throttles were pulled back. The left engine started again with no problem, however the right one refused to start. The pilot thereupon returned and landed.

During ground running it was determined that injection pressure was too low. As the flight had taken place quite late in the day and darkness was approaching, it was possible to observe that the engines kept burning for some time after being shut down. If the machine is parked in the hangar in this condition a fire could easily result. The cause of the burning will have to be investigated."

"14.3.43. Flight No.31. Duration 10 min. Pilot Ostertag. While warming up, the left engine began to exhibit the fluctuations observed on flight 29, accompanied by fuel pressure fluctuations.

The throttles were opened repeatedly and the problem disappeared. As a heavy mixing of lubricating oil and fuel takes place up to that point, perhaps very thin lubricating oil causes a malfunction in the fuel regulator, therefore the fluctuations in fuel pressure and, as a result, engine thrust. A change of lubricating oil is being undertaken."

Repairs to the Me 262 V3, which had been damaged in a takeoff accident, were completed by March 20, 1943 and the aircraft was ferried to Lechfeld to resume flight testing. Serious complaints were raised following the aircraft's first flight: "Aileron loads are still not acceptable." "Vibration occurs at speeds above 700 kph." "For the first time the V3 experienced a flame-out of the right engine in minimum speed gliding flight with throttles at idle. Attempts to restart the engine were made at various revolutions and speeds but without success."

The problems continued. From Test Report No.17 from 29.3. – 4.4.43:

"Tests to investigate engine flame-outs were carried out on V2. Uncoupling the fuel cocks had no effect. (It was suspected that the fuel cocks were not fully open when the throttles were at idle.)

During a takeoff by V3 the fuel boost pump of engine 002 seized, whereby the unit mounting shaft broke. As well steel fragments were found in the oil pump, probably from a ball-bearing cage. The engine was stripped down and is being inspected. Filling the rear tank through the sloped canopy section is unsuitable for continuous service and must definitely be changed for the production version. The solenoid-operated switch for the starter generator no longer functions and was replaced with a new one. There was a leak in the emergency compressed air bottle where the lines joined. The joint was resealed."

Difficulties had been expected in the testing of a new aircraft and a new propulsion system, but certainly the plethora of technical problems which now faced the technicians. Naturally, certain progress had been made, but could the machine be "placed in the hands of any good fighter pilot in its present condition, without hesitation," as Hptm. Späte concluded in his working report? Späte's and Galland's enthusiasm over the performance of the Me 262 is understandable. Späte expressed it as follows: "In assessing flight performance, the increase in speed over the fastest existing fighter is striking. Having finally been measured, the maximum speed at low level of 780 kph should not be reduced considerably by the installation of weapons and radio equipment, especially since a significantly more powerful engine is available for production aircraft. Its superior level and climbing speeds should allow the aircraft to operate successfully against a numerically-superior enemy fighter defense even in small numbers. As a fighter-bomber it promises to be faster than any enemy fighter even while carrying bombs."

Like Späte, Galland was enthusiastic about the Me 262. He summarized his impressions and recommendations in a teletype message to Milch:

> "On the 22nd of this month I flew the Me 262 at Augsburg in the presence of Oberst Petersen and various officers of the department.
>
> Regarding the Me 262 may I submit the following:
> (1) The aircraft represents a great step forward, which assures us an unimaginable advantage in operations should the enemy adhere to the piston engine.
> (2) The flying qualities of the airframe make a very good impression.
> (3) The engines are completely convincing, except during takeoff and landing.
> (4) The aircraft opens completely new tactical possibilities.
>
> May I make the following suggestion: We have the Fw 190 D under development, which should be roughly equal to the Me 209 in all areas. Neither aircraft's performance will exceed that of the enemy types, especially at altitude. Advances will be made only in armament and speed.
>
> Therefore: (a) drop the Me 209
> (b) switch fighter production to Fw 190 with BMW 801 and Fw 190 with DB 603 or Jumo 213
> (c) immediately transfer freed-up design and production capacity to the Me 262."

The claims made after the war by numerous authors that the Me 262 was ready to enter production in May 1943, based mostly on this document, are not supported by the facts, ". . . the officers were quite enthusiastic," so said a Messerschmitt report from May 23, 1943. However Messerschmitt test director Caroli assessed the state of the Me 262's construction and development somewhat more dispassionately:

> –"aileron forces are still too high in spite of the addition of slots
> – elevator and rudder forces are too high
> – directional stability is inadequate

– machine demonstrates poor stall behavior in a turn

– engines run irregularly. Traceable to insufficient fuel injection pressure. Resulting insufficient atomization and incomplete combustion of fuel increase consumption,

– major buildup of flame during stationary running,

– constant sticking of starter fuel solenoid valve (solution requires design modification)."

To repeat, the enthusiasm of the fighter officers over the new aircraft was understandable and justified. Of course, ". . . the aircraft represented a great step forward . . .", and naturally it, ". . . opened completely new tactical possibilities . . ." No one would want to contradict Galland's opinion. But the advantages offered by the new weapon could be utilized only once it had reached a level of operational maturity, and this had certainly not been achieved by the early summer of 1943.

Conjecture as to "what might have happened if?" is inevitable, but visions of hundreds of jet fighters sweeping the enemy from the skies over Germany – if only Hitler had desired it – must be consigned to the realm of fantasy. Series production of the Me 262 would undoubtedly have commenced sooner had the jet engine reached maturity earlier, allowing potent jet units to be formed and trained. In the fighter role (fighter-bomber as well) they would certainly have inflicted serious losses on the enemy. They might even have forced a temporary halt to the strategic bombing offensive; but they couldn't have decisively changed the outcome. Hostilities would have been ended in August 1945 at the latest through the dropping of atomic bombs on Berlin, Munich, Hamburg or Frankfurt.

Milch reacted immediately to Galland's teletype message. The same day the subject of the Me 262 was discussed at length during a conference of department heads in Berlin. A résumé of the May 25 meeting summarized the discussion as follows:

"General der Jagdflieger advised by teletype that the Me 262 has performed extremely well in its flights to date. Oberst Petersen stressed that, apart from difficulties with takeoff and landing, the aircraft made an exceptionally gratifying impression. On average its speed is 200 kph higher than the contemporary Bf 109 G fighter. It is the only aircraft capable of catching the Spitfire and the high-flying reconnaissance aircraft. The Me 209, which is supposed to replace the Bf 109, has a poorer climbing performance than the existing Bf 109.

"The Generalfeldmarschall decided that the Me 262 will be placed in production immediately, the Me 209 will be dropped. The Me 262 will receive the Me 209's Wehrmacht priority number. Until production of the Me 262 begins the shortfall in aircraft will be made good through continued production of the Fw 190 and possibly the Bf 109.

"Another engine besides the BMW 801 will have to be retained for the Fw 190; whether priority given to Jumo 213 or DB 603 must be decided. The Generalfeldmarschall himself will brief the Reichsmarschall (Göring) on the Me 262.

"The Generalfeldmarschall underlined the importance of achieving production of the Me 262 and named Oberst Petersen as commissar for this project. It is considered desirable not to involve the General der Jagdflieger in purely production matters, so that he remains unbiased in assessing the fighter. The final shape of the aircraft and deadlines for delivery of production stage blueprints and production facility drawings are to be determined as quickly as possible."

The latest state of development of the Me 262 incorporating new findings and requirements had in the meantime been summarized in Project Submission IV. The specification for the "Me 262 fighter and fighter-bomber" drawn up on May 9, 1943 largely determined the shape of the aircraft from then on.

The following is a brief outline of salient points of the improved version:

- strengthened armament of 4 X or 6 X MK 108 cannon,
- strengthened undercarriage with larger wheels,
- auxiliary tanks for 650 l and 125 l,
- bomb-carrying installation for 1 X 500 kg, BT 700 or 2 X 250 kg bombs,
- cockpit heating,
- improved armor protection,
- expanded radio installation.

The first point of Milch's demand had thus already been met. Far more problematic was fixing a deadline. As early as April 10 the commander of the *E-Stelle*, *Oberst* Petersen, had written to the Commander-in-Chief of the Luftwaffe and suggested that, ". . . Messerschmitt be instructed to begin construction at once of an O-Series of 100 Me 262s under priority 'DE' so as to create a broad experience and testing base in the field as quickly as possible."

It is highly unlikely that Messerschmitt learned of Petersen's suggestion. Company documents also give no indication of considerations or measures relating to such a plan. Not until May 29, 1943 was the "general situation" discussed by Messerschmitt, resulting from Milch's decision to begin series production of the Me 262.

After clearing up various technical questions, Messerschmitt drew up a planning chart for the production of pre-production and series aircraft, which was based on three basic conditions:

(a) Assigning the Me 262 a higher classification than all existing programs (as well as engines and associated requirements).
(b) Total protection of the labor force, including its leaders
(c) Acceptance of all risks associated with such a short buildup to production by the RLM.

The detailed planning chart was shown to Milch at a development conference on June 17, 1943:

Milch: "This is all madness. Who made this chart?"

Alpers (Senior Engineer GL): "The chart is from the Messerschmitt firm. Herr Bley prepared it and it is signed by Herr Kokotaki as manager. The conditions are grouped as follows . . ."

Milch: "We don't need that now. We just have to see what is justified and what we can do."

Alpers: "It hasn't been studied yet."

Milch: "Of course we'll have to do that. When we have we'll order everyone to come here, including Messerschmitt, Bley and Kokotaki. Then I'll speak with them."

Vorwald: "The main thing is the ordering of materials. We'll have to keep an especially close eye on that."

Milch: "Hopefully they've already ordered everything."

Alpers: "That I can't say."

Milch: "Then call at once and ask whether orders have been placed for everything Messerschmitt will need and find out if anything hasn't been ordered yet. I want a report on your findings. And if the gentlemen back down later, have them provide you with purchase documents. I am convinced that Messerschmitt hasn't ordered a thing yet, although they've known for four weeks that they're to produce the Me 262. They've dawdled for four weeks and now we're supposed to make up for it by applying for DE priority . . . Vorwald, I don't trust those people."

Milch's skepticism was well-founded. Messerschmitt had in fact "dawdled." Orders for materials for the pre-production series did not go out until late June 1943. In connection with this it should not go unmentioned that Messerschmitt kept the *Technische Amt* largely in the dark over the true state of development and testing of the Me 262. The RLM was literally thunderstruck when, at the end of May 1944, or a year later, the Lechfeld Test Detachment's reports of the shortcomings of the initial production machines were submitted. The ministry found itself forced to involve the *E-Stelle Rechlin* deeply in the testing of the Me 262 to support Messerschmitt. At different times more than 20 machines of this type were detached to the *E-Stelle* for various technical tasks.

On June 29, about 14 days after presentation of the production chart, the representatives of the Messerschmitt firm who had been summoned to Berlin met with Milch and Vorwald:

> *Messerschmitt*: "All I have to say is that most of the drawings for the aircraft will be delivered by the middle of next month. Then construction of assembly jigs can get into full swing. I have no demands to make from the design side."
>
> *Milch*: "Now the preparations for construction!"
>
> *Bley*: "Delivery of drawings will take place by 15.7., followed by the construction of temporary plant facilities for the first batch of 100 pre-production aircraft. From the beginning we have planned a further monthly production of 60 machines to bridge the gap to full series production. Construction of plant facilities will be completed four weeks after delivery of the design work sheets. The first section of the production line for the pre-production series will be completed by us by mid-September. We therefore have a span of two months between completion of design work and completion of the first section of the production line in our factory. In order to speed up the beginning of production we have divided construction of the pre-production series between Regensburg and Augsburg. We have decided that Augsburg will handle the wings and final assembly and Regensburg the production of the entire fuselage, including the tail unit, together with equipment where possible. If we harness all our forces and certain conditions are met, we can have delivery of the first pre-production aircraft in January 1944. Deliveries of pre-production aircraft will then climb to eight in the second month, to 21 in the third, in April to 40 and in May to 60 aircraft. We will reach the requested figure of 100 in mid-May, then run at 60 aircraft per month until November 1944. Series production will be starting in November and the pre-production series will be phased out."

Despite involving a large number of licensees and subsidiary firms, Messerschmitt's deadlines and production numbers were never to be met. First of all, completion of the drawings and the construction of plant facilities was delayed by about two months. Messerschmitt advised the Commander-in-Chief of the Luftwaffe but not those responsible in the RLM; an omission which resulted, as mentioned, in court martial proceedings against him. Further delays resulted from bomb damage to the company's tool manufacturing facility at Kottern, difficulties in assembling materials, delays in production of components and the large-scale use of unskilled labor. A not inconsiderable loss of time resulted from a limited revival of the Me 209. Only a week after Milch's order to delete the Me 209 in favor of the Me 262 the topic came up again. From a discussion on June 4, 1943:

> "With the decision reached last week both the Me 209, at the time planned as a high-altitude fighter, and the high-altitude version of the Me 155 carrier aircraft were dropped. The K.d.E.[2] agreed completely with the decision to support the Me 262. However enemy aircraft development forces us to ensure that we have a high-altitude (14 km) intercept capability at the earliest possible date. For this we should have another look at starting the Me 209 program – as a high-altitude version only. The entire high-altitude fighter question, including the Me 209, with regard to the capacity situation is to be brought up again as soon as possible."

On August 13, 1943, following consultation with Messerschmitt, the Me 209 was in fact reinstated in the program on Milch's direct order: "Work on the Me 209 is to resume immediately to the extent previously envisaged. The Me 262 program is not to be allowed to suffer as a result." Naturally this notion was illusory. Work on the Me 209 tied down considerable development and construction capacity until the type was dropped for good on November 26, 1943 as a result of Göring's personal intervention.

It is uncertain at which point in time and in what form Hitler was first informed of the RLM's intention to place the Me 262 in series production. A statement by Milch in August 1943 allows us to conclude, however, that this must have taken place quite early on, probably at the end of May 1943. According to Milch, Hitler spoke out clearly against dropping the piston-engined fighter in favor of the Me 262, "The Führer sees too great a danger in that."

This was all too correct, as the progress of flight testing at Lechfeld showed emphatically. One day after Späte's first flight in the Me 262, the V2 prototype crashed while being flown by Ostertag. The cause of the accident was clearly established after inspection of the wreckage – a spontaneous change of tailplane incidence – but in spite of all their efforts the technicians were unable to get a complete grip on this frequently-appearing problem. By the end of the war between 20 and 30 pilots had lost their lives "due to an increasing nose-down trim situation."

With the loss of V2 and with V3 out of commission (since April 12), all test activity ground to a halt. It was not until weeks later, on May 17, 1943, that testing could be resumed with the rebuilt V3 and the V4, which had just been placed in service. With the arrival of V5, the first Me 262 with a nosewheel undercarriage (albeit a fixed one), for the first time three aircraft were available for a limited flight test program. This state of affairs lasted six weeks. Then, on July 25, V4 crashed on takeoff at Schkeuditz, and on August 4 prototype V4 came to grief at Lechfeld during braking trials. As a result V3 remained the only test machine until October 17, when V6, the first aircraft with a retractable nosewheel undercarriage, arrived. It was followed two months later, on December 20, 1943, by the Me 262 V7.

A thorough and comprehensive test program, vital in developing the definitive form of the aircraft, was thus also out of the question during the second half of 1943. Valuable information had undoubtedly been gained from the previous flight tests and design changes had been made, but as 1943 gave way to 1944 the machine was not yet ready for use by front-line units. Control surface forces were still unacceptably high, the production under-carriage had proved unsuitable, the planned armament package of 4 X MK 108 cannon had just undergone initial firing trials, the radio equipment had not yet been installed or tested and the aircraft had not been flown at speeds above 850 kph, thus the handling characteristics and behavior of the aircraft at high mach numbers were completely unknown. In addition to all this, problems associated with the immaturity of the engines gave cause for serious concern:

"July 5, 1943: Inconsistencies again appeared in engine performance. The investigation is not yet completed. The engines of V3 and V4 repeatedly continue burning after being shut down, and on occasion the fires have to be extinguished with carbon dioxide.

August 18, 1943: A horizontal stage could not be flown, because on leveling off with a partial load after the second climb both engines simultaneously began to burn between the engine and cowling and then flamed out, restarting in flight was not possible . . . It must be assumed that leaking fuel is sufficiently atomized by the intensive air circulation beneath the engine cowling to allow the mixture to be ignited by the hot combustion chambers.

October 3, 1943: On occasion it turned out that the necessary diagrams for adjustments based on outside air pressure and temperature provided us by Junkers did not coincide with the actual behavior of the engines during changes in external conditions. As a result adjustments were frequently required prior to takeoff.

December 13, 1943: On several occasions diffuser failures have occurred as a result of the turbine running after the engine has been shut down. This especially applies to the first B-engines. Experience with the B-engine has also shown that the Riedel starter does not work satisfactorily. It has been necessary on occasion to change the Riedel engine as many as six times to prepare a machine of the test series for delivery. Difficulties with the Riedel engine mainly concern jamming of the fuel pump, shorting and difficulties with freewheeling."

These four damage reports filed by the flight test department, selected from dozens of similar documents from the period July-December 1943, give some idea of the susceptibility to trouble and the general unreliability of service which presented the technicians and pilots with new problems day in day out. The commander of the *E-Stelle*, *Oberst* Petersen, summed up his assessment of the Junkers engines in one sentence in a letter to the *Technische Amt* on December 24, 1943: "The present state of the engine does not justify speaking of the 004 being fully developed."

Dr. Franz, the responsible designer, openly conceded the slow development of the 004 during a visit by Milch and Göring to Dessau on November 5:

"In principle, development has now reached a stage where functionally the various parts of the engine are in order. However, due to the haste with which this development was carried out it is impossible to claim that there will be no more difficulties and that development is concluded. The difficulties we still have involve individual components of the engine and I would like to select only two from this group. One is the turbine. Recently we have had certain difficulties with the turbine wheel, with unexpected failures in the turbine blades due to vibration. The second component is the control system, and here I will touch on the problem of opening and closing the throttles, which was raised by the *Reichsmarschall*. I mentioned in Regensburg that we had things under control up to 8 km. Beyond that we are still somewhat unsure. But we have already flown to over 11 km. However it cannot be guaranteed with certainty that we will have the problem at upper altitudes rectified by the time series production begins, so that the pilot will be able to open and close the throttles without worrying about a flame-out."

In fact Junkers failed to eliminate this shortcoming before the engine entered production. Controlling the engine remained the great weakness of the 004 until the end of the war.

Dessau was the final stop on a trip which had taken Göring and Milch to all the important aircraft manufacturers: Arado, Dornier, Heinkel and, naturally, Messerschmitt.

On November 2 at the company's Regensburg works Göring came right to the point without beating around the bush:

Göring: "Gentlemen! Today I would like to clarify the situation concerning the Me 262, and in two directions. One, with regard to the rate of production of this machine, as this is planned at this time and appears assured. Two, what things can eventually be done to produce this aircraft more quickly and in greater numbers while cutting back in other areas. But the main question is a very important technical question, namely is the 262 jet fighter capable of carrying one or two bombs so as to be able to operate as a surprise fighter-bomber. Here I would like to convey the train of thought of the Führer, who spoke to me about these matters several days ago and who would very much like to see this issue settled. When the enemy attempts a landing in the West and the first signs of confusion appear on the beach as tanks, guns and troops are unloaded and a terrific traffic jam ensues, these fast machines, even if only a few of them, should be able to race through the heavy enemy fighter screen, which the Führer expects in the event of such an attack, and drop bombs into this confusion. He is aware that there can be no question of precision, but this will be the first appearance of these fast machines provided the enemy gives us enough time until then. I told the Führer that we would also try to accomplish this task with existing fighter-bombers and that they would be able to carry it out to some degree in spite of the fighter defenses as they will have no difficulty in finding the enemy. The bombs will be dropped frightfully quickly and then the fighter-bombers must fly away at once to get more.

I would now like to steer this discussion in another direction and speak first not of production and so on, but rather discuss in detail the technical possibilities of the Me 262 carrying bombs externally – any other way is probably impossible – and what weight of bombs we are talking about in two configurations: one bomb in the center and in the other case two bombs right and left. The machine was designed by Professor Messerschmitt and I would therefore like to ask for your view."

Messerschmitt: "Herr Reichsmarschall! It was intended from the beginning that the machine could be fitted with two bomb racks so that it could drop bombs, either one 500 kg or two 250 kg. But it can also carry one 1,000 kg or two 500 kg bombs. But for the time being the bomb racks and necessary electrical circuits are not being installed, as the machine is about to enter production."

Göring: "That answers the Führer's main question. He is not thinking of 1,000 kg, indeed he once said to me that he would be extremely grateful if we could carry even two 70 kg bombs. Naturally he will be very pleased to hear that two 250 kg bombs can be carried.

Now on to the second question: When would it be possible to retrofit the machines now under construction, meaning the first ones, with these racks?"

Messerschmitt: "The design work has not yet been done. I must first design the bomb racks and electrical circuits and then retrofit the first machines with them."

Göring: "You said that it has already been planned, therefore you must have given it some thought . . . How long do you estimate for the design of the racks and circuits if it really becomes a matter of do or die?"

Messerschmitt: "It can be done relatively quickly, in 14 days. The installation isn't much. It's just a matter of fairing the bomb racks."

Göring: "Has construction begun on the first series, is it already laid down?"

Messerschmitt: "Yes, some components have been made in the workshop. The plan is for the first machine to come in mid-January, 8 in February, 21 in March, 40 in April, 60 in May and 60 in June."

Diesing: "That is the plan!"

Göring: "But if that's the plan they must have given it some thought. It could be that some things necessary for the plan are still missing at present and I'm here to put things straight if necessary. In any case the plan must have a substantial basis, and they must be able to tell me in the very near future what is still missing and what must be done to ensure that the plan is carried out . . . I must make a concrete proposal to the Führer as soon as possible. Therefore a commission must be formed in the very near future, in about eight days, in which Messerschmitt and several of his officers, officers from your office (Milch) and from the Junkers firm will be represented, which will then settle the engine question and once again thoroughly discuss the whole thing, including the fighter-bomber concept. That is the decisive issue!"

Of the planned use of the Me 262 as a fighter-bomber, Adolf Galland states in his book *Die Ersten und die Letzten:*,

> "When I took part in a demonstration of the Luftwaffe's latest developments at Insterburg air base in East Prussia in December (actually November 26), I knew nothing of the consideration being given to possibly using the Me 262 in other than the fighter role." But he must have known that the idea was being talked about. Indeed the minutes prove that he was a participant in the discussions at Regensburg! Galland continues: "Hitler had come from his nearby headquarters. The Me 262 jet fighter attracted special attention. I was standing right beside Hitler when, out of the blue, he directed the question to Göring: 'Can this aircraft carry bombs?' Göring had already discussed the question with Messerschmitt and therefore left it to the latter to answer. 'Jawohl, mein Führer, in principle yes. It will be possible to carry 500 kg for certain, possibly even 1,000 kg.' Hitler gave Messerschmitt and us no chance to elaborate, rather continued: 'For years I've been demanding a high-speed bomber from the Luftwaffe which, ignoring the enemy fighter defence, can reach its target with certainty. In this aircraft, which you present to me as a fighter, I see the *Blitzbomber* with which I will smash the invasion in its first, weakest phase. Regardless of the enemy fighter screen it will strike the masses of troops and materiel which have just landed and spread panic, death and destruction. This is the *Blitzbomber* at last! Naturally none of you thought of that! Hitler was right. In fact none of us had thought of it."

But why not? A Führer Order had been on the table since February of that year which unequivocally required that all fighters – including the Me 262 – should be able to carry bombs. Hitler never withdrew from this requirement. Accordingly Messerschmitt had planned bomb-carrying installations for almost every one of his Me 262 variants. Even if Hitler's order was forgotten in the meantime or pushed into the background, all of the participants were reminded of it emphatically on November 2 at the latest. And finally, several days later, Hitler even involved the Luftwaffe Operations Staff in the question of using the Me 262 as a fighter-bomber. After giving the matter consideration the latter reached the following conclusions on November 18:

"For technical reasons use of the jet aircraft as a *close-support* aircraft does not promise the same high probability of success tactically (. . . as in the fighter role). Should it be used as a close-support aircraft we will be consciously negating two of the advantages of the jet aircraft:

(1) Operations at low altitude will seriously reduce the aircraft's range due to excessive fuel consumption.

(2) Low-altitude flight will to a certain extent give the enemy the opportunity to attack from a superior altitude, from which he can make up speed, thus preventing the jet aircraft's advantage in horizontal speed from being exploited to the full.

This fact must clearly be taken into consideration in case such a type should be given preference over the other two basic types (jet bomber, jet fighter). It would be better to develop jet fighters and jet bombers and use these in the battle for the coast in the event of an invasion than to postpone their development in favor of a jet fighter-bomber which would not take full advantage of the new technical possibilities and tactically would be of little use in other roles. Also to be taken into consideration is the production situation of the German industry, which cannot permit further new developments to begin, in addition to those projects already under way but not assured.

As the carriage of bombs by the Me 262 fighter is already in the planning and the potential in fact exists, the demand by the Führer for a jet aircraft for bombing missions against ground and sea targets during a coastal battle can be fully met by retaining the aircraft's high production priority without disrupting development or production as would be the case if priority were shifted from bomber to fighter or if special production of a jet fighter-bomber was to begin.

in the event that enough of these aircraft could be produced this solution has an advantage in that this aircraft would probably also be capable of restraining the numerically far superior enemy fighters and clearing the skies to a degree that existing bombers would be able to operate effectively along our own coast. Based on these considerations it is recommended that:

Series production of the Me 262 fighter be accelerated. Preparation of conversion kits for use of the Me 262 in the fighter-bomber role."

The signs were all there that it was intended that the Me 262 be used as a fighter-bomber initially, but apparently no one knew or suspected anything at Insterburg on November 26. Reference should be made to the claims by many authors that Hitler sowed the seeds of the German fighter arm's demise that day. What was the immediate effect of the "Führer's inspiration," as it is often called: absolutely nothing! Operational testing as a fighter or fighter-bomber was simply not feasible with the prototypes. Such a program could not begin until after series production had begun, and no measures were initiated by Messerschmitt, such as the designing of conversion kits, to accommodate Hitler's demand. Everyone kept quiet about the fact that production planning was still focused on the pure fighter version.

The bomb burst on May 25, 1944. Under pointed questioning by Hitler Milch was forced to admit that none of the machines built so far could be employed as fighter-bombers. Hitler's reaction to the disregarding of his order was predictable and found its logical sequel in Göring's statements to representatives of the Luftwaffe, the *E-Stelle Rechlin* and Messerschmitt four days later:

> "I have had to call you gentlemen here as the matter of the Me 262 must be cleared up once and for all . . . The Führer is rightly quite upset and says that everything he ordered has not been carried out . . . First, so as to eliminate any error, we want to stop referring to the aircraft as a 'fighter-bomber' and call it a 'high-speed' bomber instead, and second we want the General der Kampfflieger to assume responsibility for it. The Führer wants the aircraft as a high-speed bomber and not as a fighter at first. Nevertheless, he does not want further development as a fighter to be completely halted . . . He only wants all production aircraft to be bombers until further advised and that all emphasis be placed on the bomber sector . . . The Führer is aware that this aircraft cannot hit pinpoint targets, therefore it will not be used like a close-support aircraft or dive-bomber. The Führer envisages the aircraft releasing its bombs against large targets from an altitude of several thousand meters . . . The machine may be a splendid fighter and may be flown as such, all very well, but he has doubts as to how, tactically, it can be used in the fighter role."
>
> *Petersen*: (as to the question of fighter operations): "There is still a problem relating to operations, and it involves the engines. The bugs have not been worked out of the engine controls and the throttles cannot be closed above 9,000 m without the engines flaming out immediately. Combat above 9,000 m therefore poses difficulties.
>
> *Galland*: "That's true."
>
> *Göring*: "Therefore it is clear that at present the aircraft can best be used

as the Führer proposes. I will say it once again so that we all understand: the Führer does not want a complete paralyzation of the Me 262 as a fighter. It is just that he needs the aircraft for other purposes at this time, and as it is not ready to be used as a fighter, as we now hear again about the 9,000 m altitude, he says correctly: at 4,000 or 6,000 meters I have the full advantage of the machine as a high-speed bomber which cannot be caught. I hope to God that the 262 will be an outstanding fighter, and the Führer earnestly hopes that as well. But, as I have said, at the present point in time, or as production begins, we can get the machines more quickly as a bomber than as a fighter, and this is the main thing, can employ them with greater success.It is decisive, as it will be on the channel, that I have a machine with which I can strike at the enemy. Thus in the final analysis practically everything centers around getting a machine which can drop its bombs on enemy concentrations without worrying about insane losses . . . When the day comes that I can tell the Führer that the first Staffel of high-speed bombers is ready and that production is in full swing, then the Führer will authorize the machine as a fighter. I must now be able to rely on you to carry out this order with zeal and not frustrate my aims."

Hitler's decision to divert the bulk of Me 262 production from the fighter role is still controversial. However, discussions on the subject are rarely characterized by factual arguments. The last thing the author wishes to do is pour new oil on a smoldering fire. However if one makes an unbiased assessment of the prevailing situation, then Hitler's conclusion that the temporary use of fast jet aircraft in the bomber role against the masses of troops and materiel during the decisive invasion of France promised a more effective operational result than their employment as fighters in the defense of the Reich cannot be dismissed out of hand.

All discussions of this theme are basically academic: the Allied landings took place before an operational unit had been formed. Thus history must be responsible for proving or disproving Hitler's thesis.

For months Hitler held onto the hope that he could decisively intervene in the land battle with the Me 262 high-speed bomber. The thoroughly disappointing results achieved in operations by numerically-weak bomber units, as well as the disappearance of the supposed opportunities which had led him to adopt this interim solution – bomber instead of fighter – finally resulted in a gradual loosening of his May 25 directive. On August 20 he authorized the diversion of every twentieth Me 262 coming off the production lines to the fighter arm, on September 20 he agreed to a proposal by Speer to shift the bulk of production back to the fighter sector – the formation of *Kommando Nowotny* a few days later was a direct result – and this was followed on November 4, 1944, by authorization for the production of the Me 262 solely for the fighter role, "... under the express condition that every aircraft must be capable of carrying at least one 250 kg bomb if need be."

About six months after the beginning of the failed *"Blitzbomber"* operation, all production of the Me 262 was, for the first time, allocated to the fighter arm.

The question must now be asked as to the possible course of the air war had all the machines built between May 25 and November 4, 1944 been incorporated into Germany's air defence. Absolutely reliable sources show a production of 239 Me 262s during this period. But only about 60 (!) aircraft were in fact delivered to KG 51. This is the figure that must be used in any calculations or speculations. These 60 Me 262s would undoubtedly have been a great advantage in the careful retraining of fighter pilots and in a logically-designed front-line testing program; but no one will seriously contend that they could have brought about a decisive change in the air war. Had the experience gained by the end of October 1944 in operational testing justified the euphoric expectations which had been generated by Galland's first flight in May 1943? Let us look back one year, to December 1943.

Notes:

[1] "17 fuel pumps were checked for delivery capacity. It was determined that delivery capacities varied greatly (from + 10% to - 35% of rated output). Endurance tests with these pumps resulted in failures in 30-40% of the pumps through seizures."

[2] *Kommando der Erprobungsstellen*. The body which oversaw the Luftwaffe's testing establishments, or *E-Stellen*. The most well-known is *E-Stelle Rechlin*, which was responsible for general testing, but there were others which tested aircraft, weapons, radars, radio equipment and even winter equipment.

Chapter II
Testing the Me 262 as a Fighter Aircraft

Formation of Erprobungskommando Thierfelder — III./ ZG 26 Is Retrained — Complaints about the Me 262 — Hauptmann Thierfelder Is Killed in a Crash — First Air Victories by the Me 262 — Me 262 Operational Testing Detachment is Formed — Major Nowotny Takes Command — Me 262 Still Barely Fit for Front-line Use — Initial Success — Kommando Nowotny in Action — Fritz Wendel s Critical Assessment — Nowotny s Death — Back to Lechfeld for Retraining — Change of Fortune: The Fighter Version Now Has Priority — Reasons for Delays in development and Production — Engines, the Weak Point

At Galland's request, on December 9, 1943 the Quartermaster-General's independent Department 2 ordered the formation of *Erprobungskommando Lechfeld*, the first Me 262 test detachment. Galland had considered forming a small detachment of 12 machines as early as October 1943, but no concrete steps were taken pending series production of the Me 262. In December 1943 this was still some way off, nevertheless on the 15th of the month Hptm. Werner Thierfelder, who had been named to command the detachment, took up quarters at Lechfeld. As "vanguard" he was to work closely with Messerschmitt to pave the way for all the steps necessary for the formation his unit. Thierfelder, who had been seconded to the staff of the *General der Jagdflieger* from ZG 26 to advise in matters concerning heavy fighters, had already flown the Me 262 several times and probably influenced Galland's decision to initially give priority to *Zerstörer* pilots in converting to the Me 262.

The arguments in favor of Bf 110 pilots were plausible: their basic training was more suited to the job at hand and because of their experience flying twin-engined aircraft they were quicker to "convert" than Bf 109 or Fw 190 pilots.

The first "students" arrived at Lechfeld in early January 1944. There were three veteran F*eldwebel* pilots: Helmut Baudach and Erwin Eichhorn from JG 2 *Richthofen*, and Helmut Lennartz of JG 11. They were, so to speak, the first fathers of JG 7. Conversion of these pilots to the Me 262 could not begin right away, as there were no aircraft available for training. Finally, on April 19, 1944, the prototype aircraft V8 was withdrawn from the test program and made available to Hptm. Thierfelder.

With the acceptance by the Luftwaffe of the first production Me 262s in early May 1944, orders went out to the III. *Gruppe* of *Zerstörergeschwader* 26 based at Königsberg-Neumark to transfer elements of the *Gruppe* to southern Germany for conversion to the Me 262. The war diary of III./ZG 26 recorded the details:

9.5.1944: Gruppenstab and H.Q. Company transferred by rail to Lechfeld. 8. and 9. Staffeln to follow next day.

10.5.1944: Advance detachment at Lechfeld

11.5.1944: H.Q. Company and Gruppenstab arrive at Lechfeld. Temporary accommodations on base. H.Q. Company in barracks, Stab and office staff in houses on base.

12.5.1944: Arrival at base. Discussion with the Me 262 test detachment's CO, Hptm. Thierfelder. Fourteen of the Gruppe's crews are to come to Lechfeld. The headquarters company ground personnel and other ranks are to learn to service the Me 262 at Lechfeld. Ground personnel of 8. Staffel at Leipheim and 9. Staffel at Schwäbisch Hall are to participate in the construction and assembly of the Me 262 to support industry on the one hand and to get to know the machine on the other.

13.–17.5.1944: The headquarters company and Gruppenstab moved into a barracks installation about 3 km from the base. Fourteen crews from the entire Gruppe have been assigned to the test detachment, which is housed at the base.

Despite intensive research only 10 of the 14 pilots who began conversion training on production aircraft S3 and S4 on May 15 have been identified: Oblt. Günter Wegmann, Oblt. Paul Bley, Oblt. Hans-Günter Müller, Lt. Joachim Weber, Lt. Alfred Schreiber, Ofw. Göbel, Ofw.

Recker, Ofw. Strathmann, Fw. Herlitzius and Uffz. Flachs.

Thierfelder's cautiously-formulated concept for the methodical formation of his fighter test detachment was undone only 14 days later as a result of Hitler's decision to employ the Me 262 as a high-speed fighter-bomber at first. The delivery of new machines was stopped and the small unit's personnel were dispersed. The leaders of 8. and 9. *Staffeln*, Oblt. Müller and Oblt. Bley, took over duties as acceptance and delivery pilots at Leipheim and Schwäbisch-Hall, respectively, where the ground crews of both *Staffeln* were employed in the production of the Me 262. Fw. Herlitzius and Uffz. Flachs were assigned to the test department at Lechfeld, while Ofw. Strathmann and several other pilots were transferred back to ZG 26.

Hptm. Thierfelder was left with six to eight aircraft and about eight pilots with which to carry out his assignment: evaluating the suitability of the Me 262 for front-line use.

Conditions were less than favorable. The pilots were not yet sufficiently acquainted with the aircraft and the state of the first production aircraft on delivery was shocking:

- loose rivets at ribs and trailing edges
- inner landing flaps deformed
- torn fuselage panels
- faulty undercarriage position indicator
- leaky hydraulic cylinder for landing flaps
- oil level in main undercarriage too high
- oil level in nose gear too low
- elevator chafing against outer bearing
- cracks in elevator push rods
- misaligned landing flaps
- no engine generator ventilation
- terminals of radio elements not tightened – poor contact
- flanged spools not fastened
- faulty spot welding on trailing edge of landing flaps, and so on and so on.

Complaints of this nature, registered after acceptance of the aircraft, could be corrected in a relatively short time by the detachment's ground crews under the direction of the unit's technical officer, Hptm. Kiefer, even if it meant hours of extra work. However the shocking design flaws which appeared in the course of daily flying were not so easy to remedy. In fact the rectification of these problems was often delayed for months. One of many such problems has been selected to illustrate this point. The control surfaces of the first production machines delivered in April 1944 were fabric covered. At high speeds, above approximately 750 kph, the fabric began to flutter or puff up, resulting in a strong buildup of vortices at the control surface's trailing edge and a separation of airflow. At this point the aircraft began to oscillate uncontrollably about its lateral axis; the control column would be torn from the pilot's hands, and he would be tossed about in the cockpit. Only through extreme concentration and physical effort could the pilot reach the throttles and cautiously close them. Once 100-150 kph of airspeed had been lost, control returned and the amplitude of the oscillations slowly eased. It was hoped that a change to metal-skinned control surfaces would quickly and effectively eliminate this phenomenon, but this was not to be the case. The technicians encountered other problems. A Messerschmitt document dated August 10, 1944 observed:

> "Clearance for front-line use of the aircraft is not assured at this moment, as difficulties have arisen with the installation and testing of metal-skinned control surfaces which have not yet been completely overcome. The utmost energy is being devoted to this task at the present time.
>
> Concerned are:
> 1. Elevator flutter
> 2. Restlessness around the yaw axis
>
> Overcoming both points is important operationally. The complaint first appeared during acceptance flights of aircraft with metal-skinned control surfaces. What we are dealing with are complications involving high-performance aircraft with speeds attained for the first time by the Me 262 and which are associated with insufficient knowledge of aerodynamic processes in this speed range . . . It can be said that conditions at high mach numbers are still unclear at this time and that we must therefore proceed with great caution. There is still considerable uncertainty, in that too little is known about control surface effectiveness and forces (free-floating position angle) at high mach numbers . . . The possibility cannot be excluded that control surface effectiveness disappears in the high mach range and that the control surface may move out of its normal position at the same or another mach number.
>
> What is desireable is proof that the aircraft can be pulled out of a dive

at speeds up to 1,000 kph and 6 G. There is agreement that all resources should be committed to fulfilling this requirement . . . Given what we know now, this cannot be guaranteed . . ."

For the men of the Lechfeld *Erprobungskommando*, carrying out their assignment under such unfavorable omens was extremely dangerous, laborious and wearisome. However, their knowledge, determination and enthusiasm for the new aircraft allowed them to overcome most obstacles. The valuable practical knowledge and new findings gleaned from airframe, weapons, electronics and engines testing were applied to design improvements to the airframe, equipment and engines, which were incorporated into production aircraft in the months that followed. This pioneering accomplishment made by Erprobungskommando Thierfelder is deserving of the highest recognition and appreciation.

The *Erprobungskommando* suffered its first loss in mid-July 1944. Details of the incident appear in the war diary of ZG 26 under July 18, 1944: "The Kommandeur took off in an Me 262 against enemy formations. He made contact with about 15 enemy fighters and was subsequently shot down in the vicinity of Lechfeld (near Kaufering). Hptm. Thierfelder – Kommandeur – killed in action."

This official version is disputed by at least four former members of the K*ommando*: Hans-Güther Müller, Horst Geyer, Helmut Lennartz and Dr. Viktor Preusker. According to their recollections Thierfelder did not make contact with the enemy on his last flight, rather he crashed due to a technical fault with the aircraft. Dr. Preusker even believes that he can remember the exact cause: the ripping away of the stator rings on both engines. It was during those days in July that the final phase of the testing of the new type began with live actions against high-flying reconnaissance aircraft. The hope for quick success was disappointed, however. Previous fighter control methods proved useless with the Me 262. The aircraft's high speed resulted in many unsuccessful interceptions, its range with a fuel capacity of 1,800 liters was inadequate and when contact was made the nimbler propeller-driven aircraft were able to avoid being shot down by out-maneuvering the jets.

The spell was broken in late July 1944, when the Me 262 downed its first enemy aircraft. The successful pilot was "Bubi" Schreiber and his victim was a Mosquito, shot down over the Alps on July 26. A few days later Schreiber scored a second success, destroying a Spitfire reconnaissance aircraft on August 2, 1944.

In early August Galland ordered several personnel changes within the *Erprobungskommando*. Once again the war diary of ZG 26:

> "Hptm. Geyer assumed command of the Gruppe on 5. 8. 1944.
> Major Neumayer, Hptm. Kiefer and Waffeninspektor Wassermann left the Gruppe on 9.8.1944. They were transferred to JG 10 at Parchim. Hptm. Richter of JG 10 took over the duties of the Ia Officer, Oblt. Wiing (JG 10) those of the T.O. and Waffeninspektor Tietze (JG 10) Dept. Ib/Wa.

> This resulted in the following roster:

Kommandeur:	Hptm. Geyer
Adjutant:	Oblt. Wegmann
Staff Major:	Hptm. Richter
Technical Officer:	Oblt. Wiing
Signals Officer:	Oblt. Leitner
Ib/Wa:	Oberinspekteur Tietze
IVa:	Oberzahlmeister König
8. Staffel:	Oblt. Müller
9. Staffel:	Oblt. Bley"

Galland's measures involved personnel only. Planned deliveries of aircraft to bring the unit up to its authorized strength, which had been approved by Göring, were delayed several times by enemy action. Air attacks on July 19 destroyed 5 aircraft on the ground at Lechfeld and 7 at Leipheim. At least one aircraft was also lost during a combat mission at that time. The following is a report submitted on July 30, 1944 by *Fähnrich* Herbert Kaiser, who had joined the *Kommando* in June with several other pilots:

> "I took off on a combat sortie at 0958 in Me 262 *Werknummer* 170 058. Takeoff was normal and I climbed out at 650 kph and 8,200 rpm. Engine instruments were normal. At 1010 at an altitude of 3,000 meters the starboard engine suddenly began to vibrate and at the same time began to burn from back to front beneath the cowling.
> "I immediately shut down the engine and tried to extinguish the fire by diving steeply. This was unsuccessful and the fire spread over the wing and neared the cockpit. My vision was seriously impaired by smoke, and as the heat was unbearable I decided to bail out. At 1,500 meters I pulled up slightly at 550 kph and pulled the canopy jettison lever, however the canopy failed to release. I then moved the canopy lock to the rear and pulled the canopy jettison lever again. This time the canopy separated

cleanly. Afterward I slowed to 400 kph, rolled the machine onto its back and released the seat belt. I exited cleanly from the machine, let myself fall for five seconds and pulled the parachute release handle . . . I landed smoothly in a marshy meadow, 1 km southwest of Biberbach. The machine crashed in a field 1 km south of Biberbach and was completely destroyed."

The limited number of aircraft and the absolute priority given technical testing prevented the *Kommando* from conducting any methodical and controlled operational activity. In addition to Schreiber's kill only two other victories are known to have been scored in the first half of August: a Mosquito shot down at 8,000 meters over the Ammersee (at 1536) by Lt. Weber, and a Flying Fortress, the first four-engined bomber of the US 8th Air Force to fall victim to the guns of the Me 262. The successful pilot, Helmut Lennartz, described the event 37 years later:

"Airframe and weapons testing had yet to be concluded, but we pilots were burning to fly this machine in action. Finally we received authorization to go after reconnaissance aircraft. Each morning there was a dispute as to which pilot would be permitted to take off if enemy aircraft approached. August 15, 1944 was the day I was to see action. There were no reconnaissance aircraft in the air, but we received a report that a single Boeing B-17 was flying up the Rhine, attacking shipping with its machine guns. I took off from Lechfeld at 1254 with my wingman, Ofw. Kreutzberg. Flying at staggered altitudes, we tried to track down the enemy aircraft, but initially had no luck. After about 40 minutes in the air my wingman, who was flying close to the ground, informed me that he had to land immediately as he was running low on fuel. I decided to drop down and follow him. After some time I was able to make out a dot at extreme range. As I got closer I realized that it was not Kreutzberg's Me 262 but the Boeing we had been seeking. I had to attack quickly, as my fuel was also running low. I approached the aircraft from behind but failed to get off even a single burst, because at a range of at least 800 meters the Boeing went into a steep turn and reversed course. I made my second approach from behind and below. By now we had reached Stuttgart. The anti-aircraft guns stationed there opened up with everything they had. Perhaps for this reason the crew failed to notice my approach. I scored hits on the left wing. The effect of the cannon shells was devastating. The wing broke away immediately. When I looked at the fuel gauges both indicators were showing zero. I had to get down. Before me lay Stuttgart-Echterdingen airfield. Although a series of red flares was fired off while I was on approach to land – the airfield had been carpet bombed hours before – I was very lucky and missed the craters. After 56 minutes flying time my fuel tanks were completely empty. Several hours later a lane was marked off for me to take off, and at 1600 I departed for Lechfeld. In the meantime Professor Messerschmitt had been informed that the first four-engined bomber had been shot down by an Me 262. The professor was the first to congratulate me on my success after I landed."

It was the fourth air victory since the beginning of operational suitability testing in May, hardly an impressive balance and one unlikely to convince Hitler to allow the Me 262 to be produced exclusively as a fighter. Hitler did, however, deviate from his directive of May 25 for the first time, allowing Galland to form the first Me 262 operational testing detachment. The following is an entry from the war diary of ZG 26: "On August 21, 8. Staffel transferred to Lärz. It is the first operational detachment to employ the Me 262 against enemy reconnaissance aircraft. The pilots are being provided by Erpr.Kdo. 262. The Gruppe is being assigned a steady flow of technical personnel."

The entry in the war diary is imprecise. The *Kommando*'s pilots, Oblt. Müller, Lt. Weber and Fw. Lennartz, had already transferred from Lechfeld to Lärz on August 18. Lt. Preusker followed several days later as fighter controller.

No preparations had been made at Lärz to receive the small unit. The base commander was taken completely by surprise and initially assigned the men makeshift accommodations on the south side of the airfield. An immediate commencement of operations was impossible as there was no means of controlling the fighters. In early September Lt. Preusker drove to Berlin. Oblt. Müller was astonished when his signals officer returned a few days later with a complete *Würzburg* radar installation. When asked by his *Staffelkapitän* where he had got the equipment at such short notice, Preusker replied with a grin: "Following a bombing raid I reported a set destined for the Eastern Front as destroyed, and subsequently diverted the equipment here."

Sorties against enemy reconnaissance aircraft began on about September 10. They led to two victories over Mosquitoes by Lt. Weber on September 14 and 18.

Further kills had meanwhile been scored by Me 262s flying from Lechfeld. On August 24 Ofw. Baudach shot down a Lightning. This was followed on August 26 by a Spitfire downed by Lt. Schreiber and a Mosquito by Ofw. Recker. Lt. Schreiber destroyed a Spitfire on September 5, while Ofw. Göbel brought down a Mosquito on the 6th and Ofw. Baudach a Mustang on the 12th.

War Diary of III./ZG 26:4

"The advance detachment of a new operational testing detachment under the command of Oblt. Wegmann left for Erfurt-Bindersleben on 20. 9. 1944. The detachment itself transferred by rail on 22. 9.

On an order from the General der Jagdflieger dated 26. 9. 44, III./ZG 26 has been renamed III./JG 6. The detachments at Schwäbisch Hall, Leipheim, Erfurt-Bindersleben and Lärz, as well as elements of the H.Q. Company, the entire signals platoon and elements of Erpr.Kdo. 262 will form the new Gruppe commanded by Major Nowotny. On 27. 9. 44 the detachments will transfer from their former bases to Achmer.

The remaining elements of III./ZG 26 and Erpr.Kdo. 262 will be combined into one unit which, with the assignment of new personnel, will form the new testing detachment."

With 256 kills, Walter Nowotny, who had been promoted to the rank of *Major* on September 1, was at the peak of his fame. Galland considered this young, successful officer and wearer of the Oak Leaves with Swords and Diamonds especially capable of building up an Me 262 fighter *Gruppe*. He hoped that by achieving an eye-catching number of victories he could succeed in convincing Göring and Hitler of the Me 262's worth as a fighter.

As is generally known today, the overly hasty operation failed for various reasons:

– The majority of the pilots had received insufficient conversion training; training in tactics and formation flying was totally lacking,
– the aircraft was neither technically mature nor sufficiently tested for front-line use,
– the choice of airfields was wrong.

We will now examine each of these points more closely. The initial establishment of the Nowotny *Jagdgruppe* was set at three *Staffeln* with 16 aircraft each and four machines belonging to the *Gruppenstab*, a total of 52 Me 262s. For the unit to be effective an appropriate number of pilots would have to be extensively and thoroughly trained. Immediate measures to ensure this absolutely vital requirement were not taken. When combat operations commenced on October 7, 1944, the only pilots equal to the task were the approximately 15 members of the Lechfeld *Erprobungskommando*. The remaining pilots, who had been transferred from various *Jagdgeschwader* to *Kommando Nowotny* beginning September 20, 1944 and then to Lärz several days later, among them the *Kommandeur*, *Major* Nowotny, had completed perhaps two or three "check flights" in the new aircraft on arriving at Achmer.

At the risk of being drawn into an unnecessarily pessimistic evaluation of the aircraft as a notorious "know it all," the author cannot avoid the conclusion that, in spite of being cleared for fighter operations by the *E-Stelle Rechlin* on September 12, 1944, the Me 262 was only conditionally suitable for front-line fighter operations. The following problems still remained:

– The engines still tended to flame out if the throttles were closed above 8,000 meters,

– high temperatures during start-up and acceleration often led to overheating of the stator rings resulting in damage to the compressor,

– leaking fuel lines frequently led to engine fires,

– performance of the Riedel starters was generally unsatisfactory,

– improperly adjusted engines led to a large performance loss in high-speed flight,

– in spite of considerable improvements compared to the first production machines, functioning of the weapons installation was still unsatisfactory. Disintegrating gun barrels, the tearing out of skinning around the cannon muzzles, bursting weld seams, poorly-designed ammunition feeds and ejector chutes and unsuitable disintegrating ammunition belts considerably reduced the combat value of the Me 262. The lack of heating in the weapons bay, which was technically feasible but was not considered necessary by *E-Stelle Tarnewitz*[1], frequently led to grounds through frost buildup in the weapons bay during high-altitude sorties which, given the electrical firing system, resulted in an immediate weapons failure.

– Undercarriage failures with deformation of the undercarriage leg and attachment point, burst tires and high tire wear showed that the entire undercarriage installation was not equal to the demands placed on it by the aircraft's high landing speeds and the unique undercarriage layout. (Joint investigations by the DVL and the manufacturers of the oleos and tires were supposed to eradicate these problems. A series of minor modifications, such as raising tire inflation pressures and hydraulic fluid levels, installation of recoil damping and redesign of the nosewheel steering arrangement, finally made it possible to make the undercarriage operationally suitable without major changes. High tire wear made it necessary to check thoroughly not only the design of the undercarriage leg, but the mounting of the tire as well. A significant tire improvement was achieved by changing over to a greater number of layers of thin rayon and thin cord as well as the reinforcement and profiling of the protector. Another source of complaint was the inadequate brakes. Improved, more heat-resistant linings were developed and tested in cooperation with the 'Brake and Coupling Linings' working group and the brake industry.)

– The compass installation was still unreliable. The cause lay on the one hand in the use of non-magnetized steel parts. On the other tests showed that the behavior of magnetic compasses was poorer in high-speed aircraft than in slower, conventional aircraft. Deviations in inclination occurred at relatively low turn rates, resulting in inaccurate compass readings. A usable compass indication was possible only when the aircraft was flown at a constant speed for at least 15 seconds. As ground orientation was more difficult at low level due to the aircraft's great speed, this compass shortcoming increased the danger of getting lost. (The K 22 fighter autopilot was developed to simplify navigation. After extensive testing it was released for service use in February 1945. However this device was only installed in three production aircraft before the end of the war, together with more extensive radio equipment, with the FuG 125 supplementing the FuG 16zy for airborne homing. These three aircraft were prototypes for a planned all-weather fighter version with the designation Me 262 A-1a/U2.)

This description of the type's technical shortcomings is in no way intended to question the potential worth of the Me 262 in the air defense role or present an overly-negative picture of the state of production jet aircraft in the autumn of 1944. It is merely intended to counter much of what has been written about the aircraft, which irresponsibly ignores the realities and in doing so contributed to the formation of the legends around the Me 262. Even in September 1944 the Me 262 was a deadly weapon in the hands of an experienced, thoroughly trained pilot, one capable of dealing with the new technology and its inevitable teething problems. Its performance was far greater than that of the standard fighter or *Zerstörer*. The following is an extract from a report by *E-Stelle Rechlin* from 1. 9. 1944:

"Type testing of the Me 262 A-1 (fighter). Preliminary performance measurement of Werk.Nr. 130 170. Condition of machine: aerodynamic condition poor, corresponding to previous production machines. Results of performance measurements: at a takeoff weight of 6,100 kg the aircraft reached a maximum speed of 740 kph at ground level and 810 kph at an altitude of 9 km. Rate of climb was 14.7 m/sec at an altitude of 2,000 meters and 1.3 m/sec at 12,000 meters. The best speeds in the climb were obtained in step climbs. These were 420 kph at ground level and 400 kph at 10,000 meters.

As the special power plants still vary in performance due to variations in the working of the controls, these figures cannot be considered to represent the ultimate performance of the Me 262."

Another assessment, made from a different viewpoint, by Helmut Lennartz, a pilot in *Kommando Nowotny*:

"In spite of the engines' teething troubles, these performed with scarcely a problem if handled properly. After all a race horse has to be handled more gently than a plow horse. One needed a certain fine touch. Understandably this was difficult or impossible in combat. But one could not handle the throttle roughly as in the Bf 109. This fine touch was also needed on landing. It was known that the undercarriage had weaknesses, but I never had a tire blow out during my many landings and takeoffs. As to the aircraft's performance I can say only one thing: one felt like Münchhausen on the cannonball."

Nowotny had at most a dozen pilots who possessed the patience and ability to master the aircraft's technical shortcomings. This was just too few. This combination of inadequately trained pilots and technical shortcomings had to have catastrophic consequences.

Nowotny tackled the job of quickly bringing the *Jagdgruppe* to operational readiness, as was expected by his superiors, with youthful enthusiasm and energy. Most of his initial efforts were concentrated on building up the ground organization. From the *Gauleiter* of Osnabrück he obtained the immediate detachment of labor forces to prepare Achmer and Hesepe airfields for jet operations, while Messerschmitt and Junkers dispatched technical teams to support his ground services.

The command post, which was situated in a *Gasthof* in Penterknapp, in the vicinity of Bramsche, became operational on October 2, with Lt. Preusker as fighter controller. Thanks to the efforts of all concerned, the ground elements of the former III./ZG 26, which arrived at Achmer and Hesepe on September 30, were soon able to assume responsible for servicing the aircraft.

The transfer of the bulk of the pilots to the new bases took place on October 3 and 4, 1944. In the process the *Kommando* suffered its first casualty, Oblt. Alfred Teumer. Teumer, who was seen by Nowotny as the successor to Müller ("What? You're *Staffelkapitän* and haven't scored a kill yet in the Me 262? Look for another job in the RLV!"), was one of the pilots who had transferred from Lärz to Braunschweig on October 3. The following is an entry in Helmut Lennartz' diary:

> "As we prepared to taxi out at Braunschweig on October 4 in preparation for the flight to Hesepe, the starboard engine of Oblt. Teumer's aircraft refused to start. Teumer summoned me by radio and I climbed out and went over to his aircraft. I managed to get the engine running. One could not place the throttle fully in the idle position, otherwise the engine would quit again. I offered to fly Oblt. Teumer's aircraft, but he refused. He crashed and burned while trying to land at Hesepe. I can imagine that the engine flamed out again while on approach. An instinctive turn onto base leg at low speed with one engine out probably led to the crash."

At about 1345 on October 7, 1944 the command post reported the approach of heavy bomber formations with strong fighter escort. Although the conditions necessary to begin operations did not yet exist, Nowotny gave the order to take off. At Hesepe Lt. Schall, who had taken over the *Staffel* following Teumer's death, and Fw. Lennartz taxied out for takeoff, while Oblt. Bley, Lt. Kobert and Obfhr. Russel prepared to scramble from Achmer. While Schall and Lennartz took off from Hesepe without incident and scored the *Kommando*'s first victories by downing a Liberator each, at Achmer the Me 262s were jumped by enemy fighters which appeared without warning. Lieutenant Urban Drew and the rest of the 361st Fighter Group were screening the bomber formations against attacks by German fighters as they returned to England following an attack on Naumburg. Shortly after 1400, while flying at 5,000 meters, Drew spotted aircraft preparing to take off from Achmer. He and his squadron mates descended at once and attacked the German aircraft in a dive as they were taking off. Russel was lucky. As the Mustangs roared over the airfield they only hit his aircraft's tires. The undercarriage collapsed and the Me 262 slid along the runway on its engines until it came to a stop. Kobert and Bley were not so fortunate. Barely off the ground, they were helpless against the P-51s. Drew's altimeter was showing 300 meters when he acquired the two Me 262s, which were flying in line astern, in his gunsight reticle. Kobert flew right through the hail of bullets from Drew's machine guns. His aircraft caught fire and seconds later exploded in a ball of fire. Oblt. Bley, who was flying the leading machine, spotted the onrushing Mustang and tried to increase speed and climb away, but the slow acceleration of the jet engines was his undoing. His Me 262 took numerous hits in the wings and fuselage. The *Oberleutnant* jettisoned the canopy and bailed out at the last second, before the fatally-wounded Messerschmitt, its controls shot away, rolled over onto its back and spun away in a steep spiral.

These bitter losses on the very first day of operations exposed another weakness of the undertaking: the choice of Achmer and Hesepe as front-line airfields. Both lay directly beneath the main approach lane used by the bomber streams, thus exposing the jets to an increased danger of attack from escorting fighters. Nowotny had drawn attention to this unfavorable situation before the move, but his arguments had not won through. On the other hand his request for fighter cover for the extremely vulnerable jets during takeoff and landing was granted. III./JG 54, which was in northwestern Germany for rest and refitting following the costly defensive battles in northern France, was assigned to "airfield defence for special fighters." The *Gruppe* was commanded by Hptm. Weiss, with *Staffelkapitäne* Oblt. Heilmann, Lt. Crumpp, Hptm. Bottländer and Oblt. Dortenmann. So effective were its efforts during the weeks that followed that the Allies never again achieved a success like that of October 7 in spite of determined efforts.

If the successes of October 10 and 12 (two Mustangs shot down by Oblt. Bley and Ofw. Lennartz without loss) gave Nowotny hope that the initial difficulties had been overcome, the events of the very next day (October 13) were to shake his confidence badly. Following a training sortie, the undercarriage of Obfhr. Russel's aircraft broke away on landing at Hesepe. The Me 262 flipped over and suffered 75% damage. Russel was pulled from the wreck without a scratch. At about the same time *Oberingenieur* Leuthner took off on a demonstration flight. *Major* Eder, who had been transferred to *Kommando Nowotny* a few days earlier, witnessed what happened:

> "Leuthner had explained every detail of the machine to me and wanted to complete the exercise by demonstrating a textbook takeoff. He took off across the field with a strong tail wind and pulled the machine off the ground too soon. The aircraft stalled, struck a hangar, smashed through the roof and crashed onto the hangar floor. Leuthner was killed in the crash."

The alarming increase in flying accidents – a total of ten Me 262s was destroyed or damaged between October 4 and 13 – led Messerschmitt to dispatch a technical commission under the direction of Fritz Wendel. Beginning October 21, the commission held discussions at Achmer with *Major* Nowotny, the *Gruppe* Technical Officer, Hptm. Streicher, and the pilots in an effort to discover the causes behind the catastrophic losses. As far as Nowotny and Streicher were concerned, design flaws in the undercarriage and engines as the main causes for the losses (Preusker suggested that leaking fuel caused the radio equipment to oil up, resulting in a fire and loss of contact with ground control. Without guidance from the ground, the pilot was subsequently forced to land away from base or make a forced landing after losing orientation or running short of fuel, which often resulted in considerable damage to the aircraft). Wendel, on the other hand, reached a different conclusion:

"*Kommando Nowotny* has been in action since 3.10.44. Up until 24. 10. sorties had been flown on a total of three days. The Inspector of Day Fighters, Oberst Trautloft, was at the base during the first days and had made great personal efforts to ensure the success of the first fighter sorties with the Me 262.

He saw to it that several successful fighter pilots were taken from other units to form the core of this unit. The commander Nowotny is a successful Eastern Front pilot but is unfamiliar with the present situation in the west, and at 23 is not the superior leader personality necessary to guarantee the success of this vital operation. For example the following points:

1. The first day of operations by the Kommando went as follows: a large number of enemy fighters were over the airfield. Four of the Kommando's aircraft took off from Achmer and two more from the unit's second airfield, Hesepe, located six kilometers away. Of the aircraft which took off from Achmer two were shot down on takeoff, one during landing. One of the other two was also shot down, probably on landing as well. Own losses 3 or 4 (not known with certainty).

Like any other aircraft, the Me 262 is vulnerable during takeoff and landing. It must be possible and is possible that takeoffs occur when there are no enemy aircraft over the field.

2. There is a variety of opinions among the pilots and Staffel leaders as to the most suitable tactical employment of the Me 262, indeed there are even contradictory views. Clear tactical objectives and corresponding instruction of the pilots is lacking.

3. The majority of the pilots have received far too little instruction on the Me 262. No sorties were flown during the past ten days due to poor weather. This time should have been used for training, but nothing was done. Major Nowotny himself once landed with a less than fully extended nosewheel. The aircraft was heavily damaged in the incident.

4. This first fighter operations should provide the experience necessary to overcome the shortcomings and mistakes present in any new design. The pilots must therefore be trained to recognize the real shortcomings. Failing completely to appreciate this state of affairs, Major Nowotny has selected the following point, among others, as important: he feels that the electric starter, which until now has been a handle located on the right side console, should be replaced by a button on the instrument panel.

The starter is employed once for each engine before a flight. It is totally unimportant whether it is installed on the right or at the front.

Points 3 and 4 are especially significant as they illustrate the greatest weakness of our air force. This arm, which employs the most modern and complicated machines, in which a single man is often responsible for a machine requiring many thousands of hours to construct, is not even conscious of this fact. Pilots lack the necessary technical training. Intensive theoretical instruction is also missing during conversion to new aircraft types. As well as many aircraft, this would also save a great deal of fuel. As proof the following example:

Our twin-engined aircraft can be flown and, with some caution, landed following the loss of one engine. There continue to be many losses (of late with the Me 262 as well), simply because the rudder inputs by the pilots are completely wrong and have been learned wrong.

Instruction on type is particularly bad in Kommando Nowotny. The importance given to the technical side may be illustrated by the fact that the Gruppe Technical Officer at Achmer, Hptm. Streicher, is not a technician. The Staffel Technical Officer at Hesepe, the roughly 19-year-old Oberfähnrich Russel, is also a complete layman, who has himself recently destroyed two aircraft as a result of carelessness or inadequate training."

Wendel's harsh criticism corresponds precisely with the weaknesses in conceptual planning that are so difficult to understand now, but which characterized the *Kommando* from its formation to its disbandment. It is amazing that any success at all was achieved given such bad omens.

Arguments have arisen over the assessment of Nowotny. It's true that there might have been more technically capable fighter pilots for this special role of detachment leader. It is also undeniable, however, that Nowotny brought energy and willingness to his attempts to make the best of a situation where others would certainly have failed.

Following an enforced pause of about 14 days, on October 28 the *Kommando* resumed operations. The balance at the end of the day was two victories – a Mustang (Lt. Schall) and a Lightning (Lt. Schreiber) – and one total loss. While taking off from Achmer Oblt. Bley lifted off late and struck a steam pile-driver. His aircraft crashed and exploded, killing the pilot.

Four victories were scored the following day. Fw. Büttner and Ofw. Göbel each shot down a Thunderbolt, while Lt. Schreiber destroyed a Lightning with his guns and a Spitfire by ramming. Schreiber's Me 262 sustained severe damage and the *Leutnant* was forced to abandon the aircraft and take to his parachute.

Following several inconclusive actions on October 30, on November 1 Obfhr. Banzhaff shot down a P-51 over Holland. Banzhaff was himself shot down soon afterward, but managed to escape by parachute.

On November 2 a Mustang and a Thunderbolt were shot down by Fw. Büttner, while another P-47 fell to the guns of Fw. Baudach. The *Kommando* suffered one total loss: Uffz. Söllner crashed near Achmer following an engine failure. Another Me 262, that of Ofw. Göbel, sustained 30% damage in a taxiing accident. The victory-loss ration on November 4 was 1:3. After shooting down a Mustang, Ofw. Göbel was forced to crash-land his aircraft, which had been damaged in combat. The Me 262 sustained 95% damage. *Oberfähnrich* Banzhaff was killed near Lüneburg, probably as a result of enemy action. Ofw. Zander crashed near Hesepe while attempting to land with one engine out. The aircraft was totally destroyed. Zander was thrown clear, but miraculously he escaped unhurt.

Results were similar on November 6. Lt. Schall was the sole successful pilot, destroying a P-47. Lt. Spangenberg ran out of fuel and made a forced-landing near Lahnwerder, his aircraft suffered 50% damage. Ofw. Kreutzberg and Ofw. Lennartz were likewise forced to crash-land after running out of fuel. Both aircraft sustained 30% damage. Ofw. Baudach was involved in an accident while taxiing which resulted in 25% damage to his aircraft.

Generals Galland and Keller had scheduled an inspection at Achmer for the afternoon of November 7. Galland had already visited the *Kommando* several times and was deeply concerned over the high loss rate and disappointed at the meager success achieved by the new weapon, of which so much had been promised by, among others, himself.

After inspecting the two airfields at Achmer and Hesepe the two generals stayed in the Penterknapp barracks camp until late into the night, discussing with the pilots the problems which had arisen during the past few weeks of operations. Several pilots openly expressed their doubts as to the readiness of the Me 262 for combat operations and all referred to the many technical shortcomings which, in their opinion, had prevented the unit from achieving greater success.

Late on the morning of November 8 Galland, Keller, Nowotny, his adjutant Oblt. Wegmann and several other officers assembled in the command post following a report that heavy bomber units were forming up over southern England. Tensely the men followed the path of the bomber stream. Air situation reports soon revealed that the bombers' flight path would once again take them close by the jet bases. When the leading bombers were 150 km away four pilots prepared to take off: Lt. Schall and Fw. Büttner at Hesepe and *Major* Nowotny and Oblt. Wegmann at Achmer. While Wegmann's engines started easily, those of *Major* Nowotny's "White 8" refused to start. In spite of feverish efforts by the ground crew the cause could not be found and corrected. Oblt. Wegmann took off alone. At Hesepe, too, only one aircraft managed to get airborne. Fw. Büttner's Me 262 blew a tire while taxying. The undercarriage leg sheared off and the aircraft tipped to one side. Thus only two aircraft were able to set out against the vastly-superior enemy force. Both German pilots made contact with the enemy fighter screen at about 3,000 meters. Schall was once again successful, scoring lethal hits on a Mustang. Wegmann, too, scored a victory. Fired from a range of 200 meters, the explosive rounds from the four MK 108s blew a Thunderbolt to pieces.

The return flight by the American bombers and their fighter escort took place during the early afternoon. Once again their flight path led them close by the bases of *Kommando* Nowotny. Although four machines had been serviceable late that morning, by afternoon only the jet fighters of *Major* Nowotny and Lt. Schall were battle-ready. And so the two pilots took off alone against a numerically far-superior enemy. After climbing through a cloud deck, Nowotny and Schall reported contact with the enemy at an altitude of about 10,000 meters. Schall shot down two Mustangs in rapid succession. Then, according to the damage report, both engines flamed out without any change in throttle settings. Schall attempted to reach his base at Hesepe in gliding flight. But Lieutenant Kenney of the 357th Fighter Group was not about to allow this unique opportunity to escape him. He set out after Schall and showered the jet with a veritable hail of bullets. Schall realized he had no chance of getting home and bailed out. Seconds later the Me 262's fuel tanks exploded in a ball of fire.

Major Nowotny scored two kills during the course of his first combat sortie in the Me 262, a Liberator and probably a Mustang.

There are numerous versions of the subsequent events which led to the *Major*'s fatal crash. They range from, ". . . succumbed to the enemy's superior numbers . . ." to having been shot down by German anti-aircraft fire. The true sequence of events will probably remained shrouded in mystery forever. It is known with certainty that no one on the German side saw what took place above or in the clouds. Phony descriptions of what happened are probably attributable to "poetic licence." Let us then restrict ourselves to verifiable facts. Helmut Lennartz recalled:

> "I remember Nowotny's crash very well. Fw. Gossler, a radio operator with our unit, had set up a radio on the airfield. Over this set I and many others listened to the radio communications with Nowotny's aircraft. His last words were "I'm on fire" or "it's on fire." The words were slightly garbled."

The following are observations by two civilians who witnessed the last phase of the flight separately:

> "We saw one of the new aircraft come out of the clouds at a rather steep angle. There were no enemy aircraft to be seen or heard. The aircraft exploded at an altitude of about 300-400 meters. Wreckage, and body parts too, later lay strewn about a field over a wide radius."

The death of the *Kommandeur* was the tragic finale to operations by *Kommando Nowotny*. In view of the catastrophic losses the *General der Jagdflieger* could no longer avoid the conclusion that the initial attempt to employ the new weapon in a larger unit had failed. The results achieved had in no way corresponded to expectations and losses had become unbearable. The *Kommando* had scored 18 confirmed and 4 probable victories, while suffering 26 losses, although only eight of these had been due to enemy action.

The pilots of *Kommando Nowotny* were transferred to Lechfeld for "retraining." There they met about 25-30 other pilots who had in the meantime been transferred from various units to III./EJG 2, as *Erprobungskommando* Lechfeld had been retitled on October 27, 1944.

Oblt. Wörner, who was in charge of conversion training, did the best he could with the means available to prepare close-support, transport, bomber, reconnaissance, and even seaplane pilots, in addition to fighter and *Zerstörer* pilots, for action in the *Reichsverteidigung*. That the training received by the future jet pilots was restricted to a limited introduction to the type was due, on the one hand, to the inadequate number of Me 262 training aircraft and, on the other, to operational conversion training guidelines founded on incorrect principles. Several former Me 262 pilots agree: "The time at Lechfeld was largely wasted, not enough time was devoted to technical instruction. Not nearly enough emphasis was placed on this."

Little is known of the unit's operational activities during the first half of November and only one victory is known for sure. It was scored by Hptm. Eder, one of the experienced Reich Defense pilots with 53 confirmed kills. Vectored onto a high-flying reconnaissance aircraft by ground control, Eder attacked the Lightning in a dive from out of the sun. He took one last look at the weapons indicators and engine instruments. This took only seconds but almost cost him his life. When he looked up again the tail surfaces of the Lightning filled his windscreen. Eder had completely underestimated his jet's rate of closure. There was no time to turn away. A frightful jolt shook the Messerschmitt. Eder had rammed the enemy aircraft. He waited for his aircraft to come apart but nothing happened. The Me 262 flew on quite normally. Eder cautiously initiated a turn to look for the enemy, but the Lightning had disappeared. The fate of the enemy aircraft was explained hours after his landing. It had crashed and burnt out near Schleissheim.

Over the next few weeks the abortive dress rehearsal was followed by a series of victories which took place without incident. According to an RLM document Eder's victory total was raised by eleven in the period October 1, 1944 to January 1, 1945, bringing it to 64. Unfortunately, the exact dates of his victories can not be determined.

On November 22 a powerful force of American bombers attacked Munich. Helmut Lennartz recalled:

> "The next morning the damage assessment reconnaissance aircraft turned up, right on time. A Mustang. It was shot down by Lt. Weber. The next day a Lightning tried its luck. It fell to the guns of Fw. Büttner. Then the Amis sent a Mustang escorted by four Lightnings, but that didn't stop 'Siggi' Göbel from getting the reconnaissance machine. The opposition was determined to have its photos, and sent more reconnaissance aircraft. But these too were lost. On November 26 a Mustang was shot down by Major Sinner and a Lightning by Ofw. Buchner. On November 27 another reconnaissance machine was reported. Ofw. Kreutzberg and I took off at 1110. Lt. Preusker guided us cleanly toward the enemy machine from out

The Messerschmitt 262, Germany's last trump card in the skies.

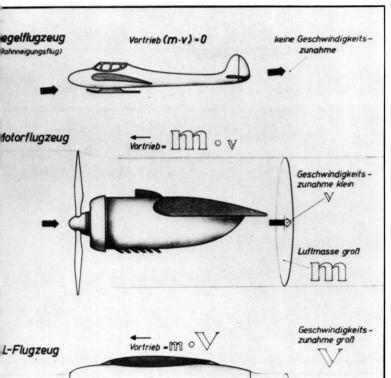

Segelflugzeug
(Rahnneigungsflug)

Vortrieb (m·v) = 0

keine Geschwindigkeitszunahme

Motorflugzeug

Vortrieb = $\mathbb{m} \circ v$

Geschwindigkeitszunahme klein

v

Luftmasse groß

$\mathbb{m}$

L-Flugzeug

Vortrieb = $m \circ V$

Geschwindigkeitszunahme groß

V

Luftmasse klein

m

$\frac{kg \, sec}{m}$ sekundlich erfaßte Luftmasse, $v \frac{m}{sec}$ Geschwindigkeitszunahme der erfaßten Luft

Vortriebserzeugung

Vergleichsbild

JFM
5453

Comparison of the propulsive efforts of various types of aircraft (glider, propeller-driven, jet powered).

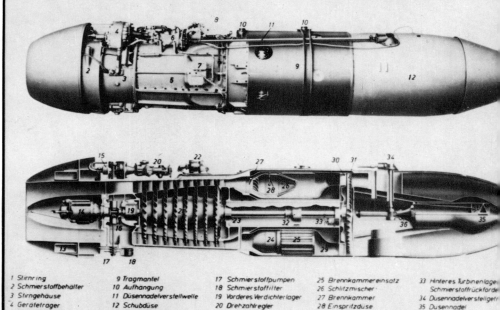

1 Stirnring	9 Tragmantel	17 Schmierstoffpumpen	25 Brennkammereinsatz	33 Hinteres Turbinenlager
2 Schmierstoffbehälter	10 Aufhängung	18 Schmierstoffilter	26 Schlitzmischer	Schmierstoffrückförder
3 Stirngehäuse	11 Düsennadelverstellwelle	19 Vorderes Verdichterlager	27 Brennkammer	34 Düsennadelverstellgetr
4 Gerätetrager	12 Schubdüse	20 Drehzahlregler	28 Einspritzdüse	35 Düsennadel
5 Verdichtergehäuse	13 Kraftstoffringbehälter	21 Verdichterlaufer	29 Sammler	36 Düsennadellagerung
6 Olmotor	14 Riedelanlasser	22 Kraftstoffilter	30 Leitkranz	
7 Zundgerate	15 Einspritzpumpe	23 Hinteres Verdichterlager	31 Turbinenläufer	
8 Bediengestangehebel	16 Abzweiggetriebe	24 Muffel	32 Vorderes Turbinenlager	Stand

Sondertriebwerk
Ansicht u. Schnitt

JFM
5450

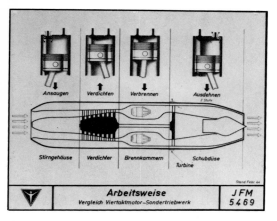

Arbeitsweise
Vergleich Viertaktmotor-Sondertriebwerk

JFM
5469

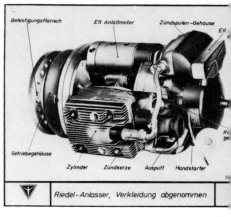

Riedel-Anlasser, Verkleidung abgenommen

Exterior and sectional views of the Junkers 004 jet engine. 1. Nose ring 2. Oil tank 3. Entry duct 4. Engine accessory housing 5. Compressor casing 6. Servo motor 7. Ignition coil 8. Control lever 9. Outer casing 10. Mounting bracket 11. Nozzle control shaft 12. Jet nozzle 13. Annular fuel tank 14. Riedel starter 15. Injection pump 16. Auxiliary drive 17. Oil pump 18. Oil filter 19. Forward compressor bearing 20. Speed governor 21. Compressor rotor assembly 22. Fuel filter 23. Rear compressor bearing 24. Flame tube 25. Combustion chamber liner 26. Slot mixer 27. Combustion chamber 28. Fuel injector 29. Exhaust gas collector 30. Stator ring 31. Turbine disc 32. Forward turbine bearing 33. Rear turbine bearing with oil recirculating pump 34. Nozzle control gear 35. Exhaust cone 36. Nozzle mounting

Bottom left: A Junkers drawing comparing modes of operation of piston and jet engines.
Bottom right: A view of the Riedel starter with outer housing removed.

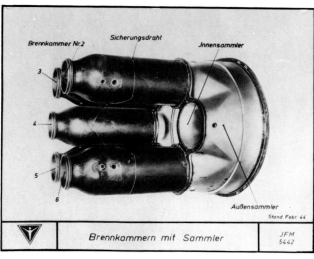

Leitkränze

Läufer

Stand Febr 44

Verdichter, geöffnet | JFM 5430

Brennkammer Nr.2 | Sicherungsdraht | Jnnensammler

3

4

5

6

Außensammler

Stand Febr 44

Brennkammern mit Sammler | JFM 5442

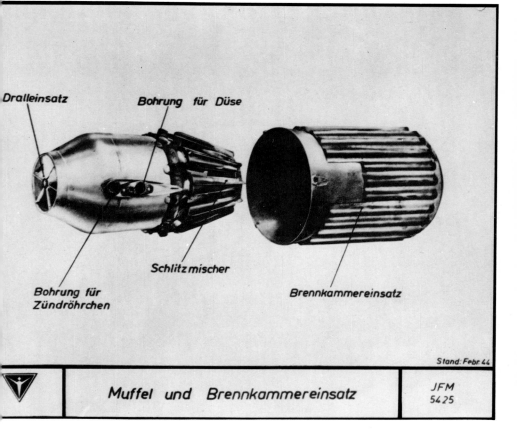

Dralleinsatz

Bohrung für Düse

Bohrung für Zündröhrchen

Schlitz mischer

Brennkammereinsatz

Stand: Febr 44

Muffel und Brennkammereinsatz | JFM 5425

Top left: A view of the compressor section showing the guide-vane rings and compressor rotors. Top right: Combustion chambers and collector. Bottom: Flame tube (left) and combustion chamber liner.

Project P 65 wind tunnel model used to determine the most aerodynamically-favorable location for the engines. Top: Engine pods on underside of wing. Bottom: Engine pods on upper surface of wing.

Artist's drawing of Project P 65 based on Project Specification II.

Three-view drawing of the Me 262, circa November 1940.

Three views of the
*BMW P 3302,
forerunner of the BMW
003.*

Gerät P 3302   0324

Gerät P 3302   0325

Gerät P 3302   0326

Me 262 V1 with Jumo 210 G engine mounted in the fuselage nose. Photographed at Lechfeld late 1940, early 1941.

Preparations for the historic first flight of an Me 262 on pure jet power on July 18, 1942.

Final checks and adjustments to the Jumo 004 jet engines V9 and V10.

*Leipheim, July 18, 1942,
0840 hours. Me 262 V3 is
ready to take off with
Messerschmitt
Flugkapitän Fritz Wendel
at the controls.*

*There is a huge buildup of
smoke as the aircraft
begins to roll . . .*

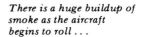

. . . lifts off

. . . and climbs away.

Heinkel's parallel development, the He 280. It was cancelled in favor of the Me 262 on March 27, 1943.

On October 1, 1942 the Me 262 V2 began flight testing as the second jet-powered test aircraft. It crashed on April 18, 1943 during its 48th flight as the result of a spontaneous change of tailplane incidence while being flown by Ostertag.

Me 262 airframe beneath the wing of an Me 323 Gigant prior to being dropped over the Chiemsee in an attempt to determine the aircraft's maximum speed.

Placed in service on June 6, 1943, the V5 was the first prototype with a (fixed) nosewheel undercarriage. The aircraft was damaged on August 4, 1943 during braking trials at Lechfeld, when it blew a tire and overran boundary lighting and a narrow-gauge railway track.

Belly landing by Me 262 V7, Werknummer 130 002, registration VI+AB, on February 21, 1944. Following repairs the aircraft crashed for unexplained reasons while on a test flight on May 19, 1944.

The Me 262 V9 with streamlined cockpit canopy and swept-back horizontal stabilizer. This was one of the first attempts, begun in February 1944, to raise the Me 262's critical mach number.

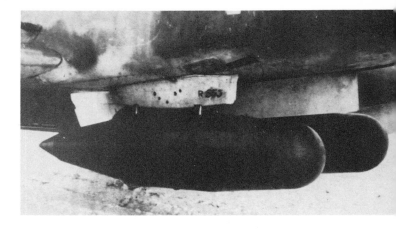

Test installation of two jettisonable, wooden-exterior, 300 liter long-range fuel tanks. Lechfeld, February 1945.

Two versions of a cut-back fin and rudder aimed at improving the aircraft's directional stability at high speeds.

Production version of the Me 262 A-1 fighter

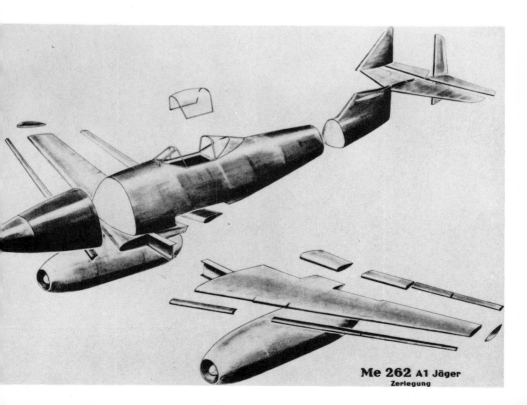

Me 262 A1 Jäger
Zerlegung

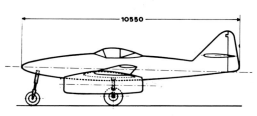

10550

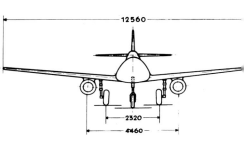

12560

2320

4460

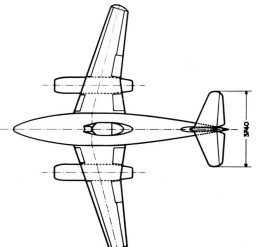

3740

The Me 262's weapons installation: four MK 108 cannon.

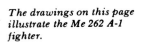

The drawings on this page illustrate the Me 262 A-1 fighter.

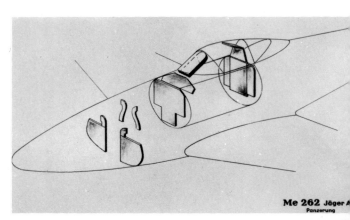

Me 262 Jäger A
Panzerung

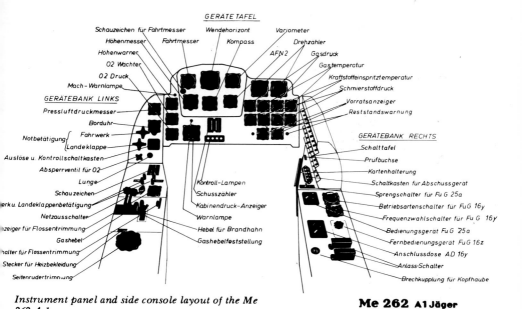

GERATE TAFEL

Schauzeichen für Fahrtmesser
Höhenmesser
Höhenwarner
O2 Wächter
O2 Druck
Mach-Warnlampe

Fahrtmesser
Wendehorizont
Kompass
Variometer
Drehzahler
AFN 2
Gasdruck
Gastemperatur
Kraftstoffeinspritztemperatur
Schmierstoffdruck
Vorratsanzeiger
Reststandswarnung

GERÄTEBANK LINKS

Pressluftdruckmesser
Borduhr
Notbetätigung
Fahrwerk
Landeklappe
Auslose u. Kontrollschaltkasten
Absperrventil für O2
Lunge
Schauzeichen
erk u. Landeklappenbetätigung
Netzausschalter
nzeiger für Flossentrimmung
Gashebel
halter für Flossentrimmung
Stecker für Heizbekleidung
Seitenrudertrimmung

Kontroll-Lampen
Schusszähler
Kabinendruck-Anzeiger
Warnlampe
Hebel für Brandhahn
Gashebelfeststellung

GERÄTEBANK RECHTS

Schalttafel
Prüfbuchse
Kartenhalterung
Schaltkasten für Abschussgerat
Sprengschalter für Fu G 25a
Betriebsartenschalter für FuG 16y
Frequenzwahlschalter für FuG 16y
Bedienungsgerat FuG 25a
Fernbedienungsgerat FuG 16z
Anschlussdose AD 16y
Anlass-Schalter
Brechkupplung für Kopfhaube

Instrument panel and side console layout of the Me 262 A-1

Me 262 A1 Jäger
Jnstrumenten-Aufteilung

Cockpit instrument panel.

Drawing of Me 262 cockpit layout.

Me 262 A1 Jäger
Führerraum

Supplementary
instrument panel
with TSA 2
controls as installed
in the high-speed
bomber version.

Right side console.

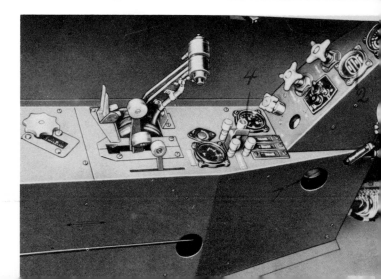

Left side console.

of the sun. It was still about 500 meters above me. I was leaving a heavy contrail and the pilot must have seen me. Suddenly he began to emit smoke. He had probably engaged emergency boost and was trying to climb away. It seemed to me to have been the right thing to do, because I only closed with him slowly. Had a fighter pilot been sitting in the cockpit who could have turned with me at this point, I don't know if I could have shot him down. However he flew straight ahead. During my attack from behind I saw three or four flashes on the enemy machine, then I roared past him. I did not see the Spitfire again, my windscreen was so heavily iced-up that it looked like frosted glass. My wingman also lost sight of him. On the flight home I saw a wall of fog creeping over Lechfeld as if someone was pulling a huge handkerchief over the airfield. Three-quarters of the airfield had already disappeared. I called my wingman and advised him that we had to land quickly or we'd never make it. He was unable to land and came down at Neubiberg instead. I entered the dense fog as soon as I landed. As I rolled out I used the edge of the concrete runway and the turf to orientate myself. When I reported back I at first received an angry dressing-down from the Kommandeur. First I had not brought my wingman back with me and second I had not brought down the enemy aircraft. He had been at the command post and the machine had flown away over Saarbrücken. I simply couldn't believe it. The devastating effect of the ammunition should have torn the machine apart. We sat down to lunch feeling rather low. The Kommandeur used the opportunity to make several more deprecatory remarks. Until now the Americans had not been able to get their damage assessment photos, but now they had them. Suddenly the telephone rang; it was for the Kommandeur. His face brightened. After he had hung up he said to me: 'Lennartz, after lunch go get a bottle of champagne. The Stuttgart flak called and has confirmed your victory.' The fuselage and engine had fallen five kilometers apart, and the pilot was later captured near Waldenbuch. After the war I learned that his name was Pilot-Officer L. Courtney of 683 Squadron and that he had taken off from San Servo, Italy."

On November 26 a Mosquito from San Servo belonging to 60 South African Squadron had an uncomfortable encounter with an Me 262 from Lechfeld. Lt. Fritz R.G. ("Contrail") Müller of JG 53 was vectored into the Salzburg area by the "*Sturmvogel*" ground control center. Müller reported:

"Flying at 9,000 meters I was able to make out the enemy machine from a great distance as it was leaving behind heavy condensation trails.

So as not to give myself away I climbed to the condensation altitude before turning in behind the Mosquito. That my attack miscarried was due to my unexpectedly high rate of closure. I fired anyway, even though it was half aiming and half guesswork, because I wouldn't have a chance for another surprise attack. In addition I had to cease firing sooner than usual for safety reasons. The Mosquito immediately dove away steeply and finally plunged into a cloud deck. I didn't know whether the dive was controlled or would result in a crash."

Although a flak unit stationed in the area had observed a Mosquito in a vertical dive and "confirmed" the victory, years after the war it turned out that, although badly damaged, the Mosquito had managed to reach its base where it made a crash-landing.

In the past five days the Me 262s had achieved a considerable success. However this was overshadowed by two flying accidents on November 26 in which the pilots were killed. Ofw. Rudolf Alf crashed near Buchenau while on a test flight, and Lt. Schreiber, who had scored the first victory in the Me 262 in July 1944, crashed while landing at Lechfeld. Once again Helmut Lennartz:

"Schreiber and I were scrambled at 1020. We had been on course for about 10 minutes when Schreiber turned back. One of his engines had flamed out. When he lowered the undercarriage on short final the machine dropped sharply. There was a strong head wind and Schreiber was unable to reach the airfield. Slit trenches had been dug right on the approach to the runway and these were Lt. Schreiber's undoing. I watched the landing from the air and saw the aircraft turn over short of the runway. When I went up to the machine soon afterward I realized that Schreiber had been crushed to death beneath his aircraft."

Three weeks prior to these events, on November 14, 1944, Hitler had authorized the entire output of Me 262s to be employed in the fighter role, ". . . under the express condition that each aircraft must be capable of carrying at least one 250kg bomb if required . . ." This allowed Galland to take the first steps toward the formation of a jet fighter *Geschwader*.

Even if Hitler himself now stressed, ". . . the extraordinary importance attached to increasing production of the Me 262 . . ." and demanded the adoption of every measure, ". . . to achieve the highest possible output of this high-performance fighter . . .", the hopes of many responsible persons of being able to bring about a turn in the air war by employing large numbers of superior Me 262 fighters was illusory. Since early 1944 conditions had become so unfavorable and the enemy's military superiority so overwhelming in the East and West that it could not have been balanced by any single weapon, no matter how outstanding.

Virtually every publication on the topic has referred to the "missed opportunities" and devoted much space to the "tragedy of the Me 262 jet fighter." Missed opportunities? Tragedy? Was it really? Proponents of a "stab in the back legend" all too readily overlook the fact that, in spite of the intensive efforts of all involved authorities, technical development of the airframe, engines and equipment did not reach a minimum level of maturity consistent with large-scale production until the winter of 1944/45. Fundamentally new technologies had to be developed, improved and perfected in areas such as aerodynamics, statics, metallurgy, thermodynamics, production and weapons before this revolutionary new warplane was ready for front-line service.

The development and production of such a completely new weapons system could not be conjured up overnight. A schedule was drawn up in 1940 which covered the entire project from the design and mock-up stage through the delivery of drawings, construction of production facilities, procurement of domestically-produced equipment such as instruments, radio equipment and weapons, the manufacture of individual components, final assembly, manufacturer's testing and finally service trials, which were scheduled for early 1943. This schedule could have been adhered to only if all the interrelated and time-synchronized plans could have been carried out on time.

But the timetable soon came to a standstill through factors which were no one's fault. Industry's predictions regarding estimated development times of individual sectors of the new technologies, especially in the field of jet propulsion, proved to be overly optimistic. Work on the combustion chamber, in which compressed air from the compressor was heated to the turbine entry temperature through the injection and burning of atomized fuel, was begun in 1939 and was supposed to have been completed in early 1942. In fact development of the combustion chamber was not completed until autumn 1943. As nothing was known of such devices in advance, it took years before the configuration was found which satisfied the demands placed on the combustion chamber:

– secure, continuous combustion within the entire operating range,
– completest possible conversion of fuel energy into heat,
– conversion with minimum pressure loss,

– even temperature distribution at the end of combustion chamber without peak exotherms.

The development of the compressor and the turbine, a decisive factor in the overall effectiveness of the engine, was also very time-consuming and was brought to a preliminary conclusion only after many setbacks. One especially severe handicap was the growing shortage of chromium and nickel, alloying elements which greatly increased the durability and heat resistance of steel.

The first engines were constructed without regard to the amount of "rationed materials." For example, each Jumo 004 initially used 88 kg of nickel. These amounts were drastically lowered by the RLM as development progressed – by late 1943 only 24.4 kg was authorized for each engine – and the choice of materials became ever more limited.

Systematically improving the new propulsion units, in spite of all these handicaps, to the point where they could enter large-scale production during the later stages of the war was one of the miracles of the German aero-engine industry. The extent of this achievement by the German technicians and engineers becomes clear when compared with jet engine development in Great Britain and the USA. In spite of ongoing work on jet propulsion under far more favorable conditions, it was some years after the war, and following the evaluation of the German experience, before the Allied nations were able to produce engines which equalled the performance of the Jumo 004, BMW 003 or Heinkel HeS 011. Neither the responsible designers, bureaucratic confusion nor even the delays caused by senseless demands from the RLM can be blamed for the fact that the jet engine was not truly ready for front-line service until the winter of 1944/45. The sole cause, as can be proved from available documents, was delays in development. The "belated" testing and operational debut of the jet aircraft can only be viewed in front of this background.

The developmental process of the entire Me 262 project, which would have been time-consuming even in peacetime conditions, was slowed by shortages of equipment and semi-finished materials, insufficient preparations in the areas of energy, transport and materials, shortages of skilled personnel and the ever more aggravating effects of the Allied bomber offensive. Front-line testing, which was also the first broadly-based flight testing of jet engines, resulted in further demands on the manufacturers, as it brought to light many of the propulsion system's teething troubles. The pilots made justifiable requests for improvements, especially in regard to reliability, but these simply could not be met in the short term by the hopelessly overburdened engineers and technicians.

Once the final design hurdles had been cleared, the way was finally clear for an unconditional expansion of Me 262 production. However the increasing devastation of the transport system and the aviation industry, which in September 1944 had set an absolute production record of 5,178 machines of all types but within a few weeks suffered the loss through bomb damage of about 40% of its production capability, prevented implementation of this ambitious delivery program.

A further negative factor in the failure to meet all objectives, meaning the reequipping, especially of the Bf 109 units, with high-performance fighters and regaining air superiority, was the shortage of experienced pilots and unit leaders. Even though Göring had ordered on November 17, 1944, that: "A special pilot corps must be raised for the Me 262, which will give us a special advantage," the fearful bloodletting which the Luftwaffe had suffered during the air battles of the previous year could not be made up qualitatively by the increased output of new pilots or by the retraining of pilots from disbanded bomber units.

Notes:
[1] *Erprobungsstelle Tarnewitz* was the Luftwaffe testing station responsible for aircraft cannon and machine guns.

Chapter III
Formation of Jagdgeschwader 7

Geschwaderstab and III. Gruppe are Formed – First Successes, First Losses in December – Transfer to the Berlin Area – The Formation Process is Halted – Priority to the Engagement of Fighters or Bombers? – Changes in the Geschwader and Gruppe Commands – Formation Progresses rapidly in Spite of all Difficulties – More Crashes than Successes in January – The Waiting is over, III Gruppe Operational – I Gruppe Hobbles along behind – Problems with the Engines – Deficiencies in Conversion Training – Fuel Shortages – Bomber Pilots Become Fighter Pilots – Shortage of Two-seat Trainers – Development of the Two-seater – The Ergänzungsgruppe – Operations by the two Gruppen in February

Authorization for production of the fighter variant raised hopes among the High Command and many other desperate optimists that Germany might once again be able to strike back at the enemy in the air through "massed operations" with the Me 262. In the face of the bitter reality, however, these hopes remained nothing more than a pipe-dream. Nevertheless, *General der Jagdflieger* Galland did not hesitate to exploit the opportunity which had been offered him. By transferring II./JG 3, the *Stabsstaffel* of III./JG 6 and especially capable pilots from other units to Lechfeld for conversion to the Me 262, Galland created a pool of personnel for the creation of a jet fighter unit. An agreement was reached with the Messerschmitt and Junkers Firms to place the training of the necessary technical personnel on a broader base. The former *Kommando Nowotny* served as the foundation on which the new unit was built. On November 19, 1944, in the course of the setting-up of the first Me 262 *Geschwader*, it was redesignated III./JG 7.

Jagdgeschwader 7 had been formed in August 1944. However, due to the acute shortage of pilots and replacement aircraft at that time, plans to equip two *Gruppen* with the Fw 190 at Königsberg could not be realized. The OKL issued a new directive in October 1944, changing the unit's equipment to the Bf 109 G-14 and specifying that II. *Gruppe* was to be formed at Ziegenhain, Czechoslovakia. However, *Luftflotten-Kommando Reich* was unable to carry out the new orders for the same reasons as before. Finally, on November 12, 1944, plans to equip JG 7 with piston-engined fighters were dropped. Increased in size to three *Gruppen*, the *Geschwader* was converted to the Me 262. *Oberst* Johannes Steinhoff, wearer of the Oak Leaves with Swords and former *Kommodore* of JG 77, was named to command the unit. In continuous action since 1939, he had experienced the highs and lows of the German fighter arm with JG 52 and JG 77. Steinhoff had 170 victories to his credit, obtained over England, the Eastern Front and the Mediterranean.

In pursuing his goal of making the jet unit ready for action as quickly as possible, Steinhoff found himself facing nearly insurmountable difficulties. The training capacity of III./EJG 2 was inadequate, and deliveries of new aircraft were slow. Under these conditions equipping all three *Gruppen* at the same time appeared to be out of the question. Therefore it was decided to form III. *Gruppe* first, utilizing elements of the disbanded KG 1 *Hindenburg*, and to commit it to defensive operations in late December in the Berlin area against USAAF daylight raids against the Reich capital. The second *Jagdgruppe*, I./JG 7, was to be formed in late January 1945. Formerly II./JG 3, the *Gruppe* was renamed I./JG 7 on November 27, 1944. II./JG 7 was to be the last *Gruppe* to be formed.

While the machines and personnel of III. *Gruppe* were being assembled at Lechfeld, work was under way on the jet ground organization at the planned "Silver Bases" at Brandenburg-Briest, Oranienburg and Parchim. Work proceeded under the direction of the commander of III. *Gruppe*, *Major* Hohagen, with the capable support of the *Geschwader* Technical Officer, Hptm. Streicher, the *Gruppe* Technical Officer, *Oberinspektor* Grote, and the Signals Officer and future director of the unit's command post, Lt. Preusker.

Within a few days of completing the timetable, expectations of an accelerated completion of the formation of III./JG 7 had to be revised considerably. By late November deliveries of aircraft were already hopelessly behind schedule. Forty machines should have been delivered by November 30, however the unit's actual strength was 11 Me 262s. Moreover the following weeks saw only an insignificant increase in the number of available aircraft. Deliveries of new aircraft remained completely inadequate, while losses through bomb damage, technical failures during flight or pilot error – 10 aircraft were written off and another five suffered varying degrees of damage during December – further delayed the achieving of operational status. Far worse than the material losses were the losses of unit personnel: at least four pilots of III./JG 7 lost their lives during December 1944. On the 6th Uffz. Renner crashed near Osnabrück while on a transfer flight, and on the 15th Uffz. Wilhelm Schneller was killed near Schwabstadl while on a training sortie. Fw. Helmut Wilkenloh lost his life on December 23 near Landsberg/Lech, also during a training sortie. On the 29th a veteran pilot, Fw. Erwin Eichhorn, was killed when his aircraft stalled on approach to Lechfeld following an engine failure. The aircraft crashed on the concrete runway in full view of his horrified comrades.

There are only a few known successes to offset these losses. On December 2 Lt. Weber shot down a Lightning. Weber was awarded the Iron Cross, First Class after shooting down three Mosquitoes. At the time *Reichsmarschall* Göring remarked: "A fantastic feat with a ship whose engines stop above 6,000 meters and fall apart over 750 kph." On December 3 Ofw. Lübking destroyed a B-17 of the US 15th Air Force.

The onset of winter weather at the end of the first week of December not only reduced sharply the number of combat sorties, but also had a direct effect on the unit's conversion training. Even though the program was already unable to keep up with demands it had to be almost completely shut down for two weeks. This set back the planned completion date even further.

Training resumed on December 20 following an improvement in the weather. As well, the operational restrictions which had been placed on III./ JG 7 so as not to threaten the build-up of the *Gruppe* were eased. *Hauptdienstleiter* Saur had pushed hard for the lifting of restrictions and complained bitterly to Speer: "After we possess a certain number of superior Me 262 aircraft, enemy reconnaissance machines will no longer be able to fly over Germany unmolested and go on providing the enemy with worthwhile targets for precision bombing. If protection of production sites and airfields by regular forces cannot be organized, at least the factory test pilots, almost all of whom are experienced combat pilots, can be authorized to fly armed machines and thus keep enemy aircraft clear of the immediate area." Whether test pilots actually took off to defend Lechfeld and Leipheim as demanded by Saur is not known. What is known is that pilots of III./JG 7 took to the air and were successful. An enemy reconnaissance patrol was almost completely wiped out on December 23. Within a matter of minutes the photo-reconnaissance aircraft, a P-38 of the 7th Pursuit Group, and an escorting Mustang were destroyed by Ofw. Büttner, while another Mustang was shot down by Fw. Böckel. Ofw. Büttner was again successful on December 29, downing a Mosquito. This kill raised his victory total on the Me 262 to seven enemy aircraft. On the last day of the year Fw. Baudach, who had previously been active as an instructor, scored his fourth victory by shooting down a Mustang over Lechfeld.

The first phase in the formation of III./JG 7 was concluded in the first days of the seventh year of the war when the unit reached its authorized strength of 40 pilots. The first pilots were ordered to their new bases as the advance guard: 9. *Staffel* under Hptm. Eder to Parchim, 10. *Staffel* under Oblt. Schall to Oranienburg and 11. *Staffel* and the *Gruppestab* to Brandenburg-Briest.

The High Command hoped that by the beginning of the new year it would be able to introduce into the Reich air defense, if not an entire *Geschwader*, at least a powerful *Jagdgruppe* equipped with the most modern fighters. But this hope proved illusory. For one thing, the unit's equipment strength increased only slowly during the first half of January – not until January 19 did it reach 19 Me 262s – and for another, training of pilots in flight procedures and tactics remained far below requirements. Due to the absence of criteria, the training provided pilots by the former Lechfeld Jet Test Detachment, which had been disbanded by the chain of command on October 27, 1944, and attached to *Ergänzungsgeschwader* 2 as III. *Gruppe* (as IV. *Gruppe* until mid-February), was generally limited to a pure type conversion.

The limited number of combat sorties flown by the *Gruppe* during the early days of 1945 continued to be directed against reconnaissance aircraft and escort fighters due to a mistaken assignment of target priorities and inadequate evaluation of previous experience in jet fighter operations. This changed on January 5, 1945. That day Hitler, on advice from Speer, ordered the Me 262 used primarily against bombers. But the directive was met by vigorous opposition from some commanders and pilots, who felt that this was not the best role for the Me 262.

Some officers argued that tying down the Allied fighter escort would once again give the conventional fighters an opportunity to attack the heavy bombers en masse, instead of being scattered long before reaching the bomber stream and becoming involved in costly air battles. Several times in the past the mere appearance of jet fighters had been enough to draw the Allied fighters away from the Fw 190s and Bf 109s. Finally, after forcing the enemy to jettison their long-range tanks, the jets could utilize their superior speed to disengage and likewise attack the bombers.

The argument sounded plausible, but in face of the enemy's over-whelming superiority at this stage of the war the necessary conditions were just not there. While the Germans possessed only a few jet fighters, the Allies could dramatically increase the number of escort fighters if need be. The hoped-for result could have become a disadvantage by further exacerbating the already unfavorable numerical ratio. In the end the direct engagement of Allied fighters was ruled out on technical grounds. Since the days of Thierfelder it had been recognized that the high wing loading and rudder forces of the jet fighter made it impossible for it to stay with Allied fighters in tight turns, and that victories over enemy fighters occurred only when the Mustangs or Thunderbolts were taken by surprise or reacted incorrectly when attacked. A combat report submitted by a pilot of the Lechfeld Test Detachment in September 1944 reveals the powerlessness he felt when unable to shoot down an enemy fighter in the course of a ten-minute combat:

> "While flying at high altitude I was vectored toward a Mustang flying at 1,500 meters. As I was about to open fire from a range of 400 meters the enemy dove away steeply to the right. A tight right turn placed the enemy in front of me again, but the Mustang evaded to the right. I made a new approach, but the enemy turned toward me. I also failed to reach firing position on my fourth pass. I therefore broke of the engagement."

Based on statements by prisoners, German authorities were aware that the Allies had prepared an entire bag of defensive measures in the event of attack by jet fighters.

Instructions for crews of four-engined bombers offered little in the way of suggestions: "On spotting jet fighters, gunners are to immediately call out direction of attack, altitude and range. The pilot will either climb or descend." The notes given pilots of single-engined fighters, however, were extremely detailed, as shown by this example:

> "Two fighters being pursued by a jet fighter: If the left aircraft is attacked, both aircraft should fly a parallel left turn on the element leader's command. The jet will be unable to follow due to the Mustang's tighter turning radius. The right aircraft will be in a favorable position to fire on the jet. If the right aircraft is attacked, the same maneuver should be made to the right. If the jet fighter attempts to follow the evading aircraft, the aircraft under attack must immediately turn back through 180 degrees so as to have the jet in a favorable firing position as it passes. If the pair is

attacked from the side, it should turn toward the jet. In this way neither is in a favorable firing position."

Provided the Allied fighter pilots followed these instructions, even large formations could survive attacks by several jet fighters without loss if well led. On February 21, 1945, for example, 32 Mustangs of the US 479th Fighter Group encountered 15 jets of III./JG 7 over Potsdam at an altitude of 5,000 meters. Although described by the Americans as being "very experienced, aggressive and disciplined," the Germans were unable to reach firing position in spite of employing every tactical maneuver in the book. After twenty minutes their dwindling fuel supplies forced them to break off the battle.

Ignoring the experience gained to date, theorizing Luftwaffe commanders continued to regard the destruction of reconnaissance aircraft and fighters as the primary role of the Me 262. So strictly speaking, *Kommando Nowotny*, whose combat orders stated: "The *Sturmjäger* are to clear the way to the bombers by tying up the Allied fighter escort," was doomed to fail from the start.

The author has a report from early 1944 which analyzes the combat experiences of *Erprobungskommando Nowotny* and JG 7. Discernable between the lines are the opinion-forming process and the "use against fighters or against bombers" controversy. It must have been created by the JG 7 command at that time, but also by someone who wanted to see the Me 262 employed exclusively against enemy fighters and at the same time take a swipe at the *Blitzbombers*:

"A Assessment of the Me 262 in Air Combat:
Speed superiority over all enemy fighters. Element of surprise always assured. Employed in formation, the Me 262 is also capable of shooting down an enemy who has spotted his attacker or who accepts combat. (Note victories against slow, maneuverable aircraft in Russia, I-16, I-153.)

B Conditions for Success in Air Combat:
(a) High level of training in fighter tactics
(b) High level of gunnery training or experience
(c) Mastery of machine in all flight attitudes
Aircraft is vulnerable during takeoff and landing, but the same applies to the Blitzbomber.

C Which Should be the Jet Fighters's Primary Targets?

Me 262 fighter operations to be directed primarily against enemy fighter-bombers and fighters as well as escort fighters. These may be carried out with success for the reasons described in A. Only by approaching head-on can successful attacks be made on four-engined bombers without heavy losses. However, attacks from in front demand outstanding accuracy and experience and a high degree of skill as a fighter pilot. (Closing speeds of 1100 – 1400 kph.) Attacks from behind are more costly than with conventional day fighter units, because the same defensive fire has to be flown through, the enemy gunners are presented with a larger target, our aircraft are more vulnerable and the present armament requires the closest possible approach so as to ensure a kill.

D Alleged Bombing Accuracy of the Blitzbomber can only be attributed to self-deception or intentional exaggeration.

E Employment of the Me 262 in the Defense of the Reich
Employment against escort fighters is promising and will increase the success of conventional propeller-driven fighters against four-engined bombers. Skilled employment of conventional fighter units and Me 262s in same area will guarantee the greatest success."

This report, instructive as it is, gives some indication of the battle which was going on behind the scenes and is so one-sided that it can scarcely have earned its author much credit from Hitler and Göring. In essence it said that the Me 262 could be flown successfully only by the most skilled pilots, that its greatest potential lay in combatting enemy fighters and that engaging heavy bombers was basically a hopeless undertaking. These were certainly not the expectations placed on the Me 262 fighter, namely the stopping of the American daylight raids.

In early 1944 the Luftwaffe Operations Staff prepared a report on previous operational use of the Me 262. Results of the investigation were damning:

"Initial operations with the Me 262 in the fighter role have brought negligible success as a result of incorrect tactical employment. Losses exceed victories. New tactics must be developed."

The arguments died away unheard. Nothing changed. It was not until Hitler intervened that the unsuccessful attack concept was revised. Some unit leaders opposed the order on the previously-mentioned grounds, but following Hitler's decision Göring was unwilling to listen to any arguments. He demanded that sorties be flown "as the Führer intended," and ordered that enemy fighters "were to be attacked only in passing."

Bypassing *Oberst* Steinhoff, Göring instructed *Major* Weissenberger, *Kommandeur* of I./JG 7, which was then in the formation process, to develop new operational guidelines as quickly as possible. Weissenberger also held the view that the long-range goal should be a cooperative effort between jet, piston-engined and even rocket-powered fighters, however he felt that as an immediate measure the Me 262 could fulfill the task set for it, as the jet fighter's speed would allow it to penetrate the enemy fighter screen with little danger to itself and attack the heavy bombers with a high probability of success.

Steinhoff and Hohagen had thus been neutralized. Involved like many other senior line officers in the disputes between the *General der Jagdflieger* and the Commander-in-Chief of the Luftwaffe, they were relieved of their posts in late December. Steinhoff was accused of inactivity, because he had failed to hasten the formation of the *Geschwader* during his approximately six weeks as *Kommodore*.

With the naming of *Major* Weissenberger as *Kommodore* and *Major* Sinner[1] as *Kommandeur* of III. *Gruppe* on January 21, the jet fighter *Geschwader* finally received the impulse which was to determine the subsequent history of JG 7.

The hastily-formulated proposals for the accelerated completion of III. *Gruppe* and the *Geschwader*'s future operations submitted by Weissenberger to the Commander-in-Chief of the Luftwaffe met with Göring's unconditional approval. According to Weissenberger's and Sinner's projections, the organization of personnel in most areas, the retraining of pilots and the expansion of the ground organization could be concluded within 20 days provided certain conditions were met.

By devising a sensible division of work free of jurisdictional rivalries the two unit leaders systematically eliminated most of the existing shortcomings within the 15 days allowed by Göring. Luftwaffe signals personnel were involved, answering special requests in the fields of navigation and ground control by installing additional radio beacons in the operating area. Through intensive training within the *Gruppe*, concentrating on formation flying and cooperation with ground controllers (use of the FuG 25a and FuG 16 zy[2], pilot familiarity with the aircraft was greatly improved. Problems relating to fighter control were soon overcome thanks to the outstanding work of the *Geschwader* Signals Officer, Lt. Viktor Preusker, who organized a system suited to the demands of this new type of unit and brought in the equipment necessary to make it work.

Thanks to excellent cooperation between the *Geschwader* and *Gruppe* headquarters and the *Staffeln*, and with the selfless support of authorities who were never organizationally responsible, III. *Gruppe* was soon making good progress towards becoming fully operational.

Outside help was provided at Oranienburg, where *Oberst* Knemayer, the base commander, effectively supported the Schall *Staffel*, and at Parchim, where the *Gauleiter* of Mecklenburg aided the Eder *Staffel*. Only at Brandenburg-Briest was there any tension in dealings with the local commander, made worse by the commanding general encroaching on Sinner's jurisdiction as *Kommandeur* of III. *Gruppe*. This finally led to Sinner moving his headquarters to Parchim and commanding the *Gruppe* from there.

The unit also received very welcome support from the commander of 1. *Jagddivision*, *Oberst* Heiner Wittmer, who used the full authority of his office to protect the *Gruppe* from outside interference. "The specified completion period did not pass without crises," recalled Sinner:

> "One day an incoming raid was reported. The flying weather was excellent. For hours endless bomber streams passed over Brandenburg airfield on their way to Berlin. Although we were protected by Göring's directive, personages senior and most senior, qualified and unqualified, imploring and frantic, demanded incessantly that we send at least part of the *Gruppe* into action. There was no way we could do it. Assembling the dispersed aircraft beneath the enemy fighter screen and the bomber stream was out of the question. In view of our own plans and Göring's protective decree no preparations had been made. In any case, as things stood our participation would have added little to the defensive effort. On the contrary, it would have provoked premature countermeasures by the American air force and thereby considerable losses, and would thus have prevented us from achieving our primary objective – the quickest possible completion and sudden employment to achieve a high degree of effect."

Thanks to the personal intervention of *Hauptdienstleiter* Saur the allocation of aircraft from the new assembly facility at Briest and the factories in southern Germany ran considerably more smoothly than before. However the supply of engines and replacement parts from the inadequately stocked Jüterbog distribution point continued to be unsatisfactory. This situation did not improve until March 1945, when two motorized distribution points were assigned.

The chronic shortage of replacement parts, which at times temporarily lowered the *Gruppe*'s operational readiness to 65%, technical problems which seriously compromised the Me 262's usefulness as a front-line aircraft, and the generally poor level of workmanship of the aircraft, which often required time-consuming corrective work by the ground elements of III./JG 7, led *Generalmajor* Diesing, Head of the Department for Air Armament, to outline these shortcomings in a stinging letter to the responsible authorities:

". . . The 8-262 type aircraft exhibits a number of shortcomings, most of which have been known to the Messerschmitt Firm for a long time, but which have so far not been corrected. In numerous cases it has been demonstrated that a tire defect or hard landing during flight operations results in the undercarriage leg being torn from the wing, rendering the entire wing unusable. The damage cannot be repaired at the unit level. Supplies of new wings either cannot be obtained or come at the cost of new production aircraft, as the building of wings is the biggest bottleneck in series production. Aircraft so damaged are thus not available for operations for some time. Following the first verbal complaints it was determined on May 5, 1944 that: the definitive solution must provide for structural reinforcements within the wing and go out to the factory by May 13, 1944.

"To this date, however, a satisfactory solution is still not in sight and the deadline of April 1, 1945 mentioned by Messerschmitt for definitive series introduction is unacceptable.

"The situation is the same regarding other as yet unanswered complaints. It must therefore be demanded emphatically that any measure which will lead to the final elimination of these long-standing complaints be adopted, before thousands of new aircraft are delivered whose operational potential is limited due to the shortcomings which still exist.

"Likewise, new requirements demanded for operational reasons are to be worked in significantly faster than before if they are to fulfil their purpose. The . . . proposed deadline . . . contradicts the assessment of the armaments staff . . . and is unacceptable."

Diesing's harsh criticism was borne out by events. III./JG 7 alone reported nine total and seven partial write-offs as a result of technical defects during January 1945. The often dramatic moments experienced by a pilot after the appearance of a technical defect are reflected in a III./JG 7 fault report:

"I took off at 1133 on 1.1.45. After takeoff I climbed to 10,000 meters. Both of my engines failed after a brief flight at this altitude. I immediately switched off both fuel pumps and closed both fuel cocks. I pulled both fuel cock levers back to the stop position while pressing the ignition buttons. Soon afterward three Mustangs appeared. I put the aircraft into a dive from 6,000 meters all the while attempting to make radio contact, but I received no response. On reaching 4,000 meters I attempted to restart the engines, opening the left fuel cock and switching on the fuel pump for the forward tank. While in the stop position I pressed the ignition button on the left throttle lever several times, but the engine failed to start. Afterward I tried the same procedure with the right engine, which likewise failed to start. Further attempts to start the engines at lower altitudes and airspeeds down to 350 kph were unsuccessful. I therefore decided to make a forced landing in the Uelzen area. The landing was made in a field with the undercarriage down. The nosewheel leg and main undercarriage broke off in a furrow. The engines contacted the ground and were likewise ripped away. The left engine struck the fuselage, which broke off aft of the auxiliary fuel tank."

Other pilots were less fortunate in dealing with technical malfunctions. On January 14 Me 262 "Red 12," flown by Ofhr. Hans-Joachim Ast of 10./JG 7, plunged vertically into the ground near Crivitz from an altitude of 4,500 meters. Ofhr. Schnurr of 9./JG 7 was killed on January 23. According to the damage report he was conducting a test flight in Me 262 Werk-Nr. 110 564 following a double engine and generator change. According to civilian eyewitnesses, the aircraft was in level flight at about 600 meters when it suddenly pitched forward into a vertical dive and crashed near Lübz.

As well as the losses attributable to technical faults, the *Gruppe* also suffered casualties as a result of enemy action. Lt. Heinrich Lönnecker was killed on the first day of the new year. He and three other members of the *Staffel* were sent to support the piston-engined fighters of JG 300 and JG 301 which were engaged with about 1,200 bombers and 1,400 long-range fighters of the 8th Air Force. It was midday and the American formations were flying in an arc around Berlin in the direction of Kassel. The *Schwarm* was jumped by Mustangs of the 336th Fighter Squadron. Lt. Franklin Young scored hits on Lönnecker's aircraft, which went down west of Fassburg. III./ JG 7 lost another aircraft through enemy action the next day. An incomplete and partly illegible *Gruppe* document states: "2.1.1945. Werk-Nr. 500 ..4, shot down and crashed, 99% write-off."

The author has been unable to uncover any details of combat operations during the following two weeks. The next confirmed action against the USAAF took place on January 14, when the Eder *Staffel* was ordered to join an air battle raging between the Bf 109s and Fw 190s of JG 300 and JG 301 and the fighter escort accompanying approximately 600 heavy bombers which were moving irresistibly toward their targets in central Germany. Parchim was reporting only two combat-ready aircraft at this time. They were nevertheless ordered to take off. Two aircraft. Two aircraft against hundreds.

The result was inevitable. Fw. Heinz Wurm ran into Mustangs of the 357th FS over Wittstock and following a brief engagement was shot down and killed by Lt.Col. Roland R. Wright. Wurm's wingman also found himself in a hopeless situation. His name is unknown, but his combat report has survived:

> "At 1242 on 14.1.1945, I took off as part of a Maple *Rotte* to intercept Anglo-American bomber and fighter formations. While climbing through 6,000 meters I suddenly noticed the right engine temperature climbing sharply. I immediately eased back the throttle and looked at the right engine. I saw that my aircraft was losing a great deal of fuel between the fuselage and right engine near the landing flap. I then shut down the engine. A few minutes later I tried to restart it, during the course of which the engine began to smoke heavily. Over the radio I heard that enemy fighter-bombers were attacking Parchim. I called the JG 7 command post and asked for permission to land at Brandenburg-Briest, but was ordered to land at Neuruppin. There were several enemy fighter units in this area. I saw Mustangs flying on a reciprocal course about 1,000 meters above me, three to my left and four to my right. They immediately dove and attacked. I dove away at a 15 degree angle in an effort to evade the attack, but my aircraft was still hit in the left wing, engine, fuselage and cockpit. I sustained a grazing wound and was injured by splinters. I hauled my aircraft around to the right and bailed out. The aircraft struck the ground near Lögow, in the Neuruppin district."

The events of this day once again demonstrated the futility of employing very small formations of Me 262s against the enemy.

But Hitler and Göring expected results, and this led repeatedly to unjustifiable actions which resulted in bitter losses that could have been avoided.

A third loss from enemy action is known from January 1945. On the 19th Uffz. Heinz Kühn, at Lechfeld for conversion training, was shot down and killed by enemy fighter-bombers near Ingolstadt while on a training flight.

In general it can be stated that III. *Gruppe*'s activities during January/February 1945 were severely limited in favor of pilot training within the unit. Surviving log books reveal that the majority of sorties during this period were training flights, air-firing missions, high-altitude flights, formation flights and radio flights.

It seems unlikely that III./JG 7 suffered any further losses during the final days of January 1945; nevertheless the balance for the month was shocking. Personnel losses: 5; aircraft written off: 13; up to 65% damage: 10. And the successes? Only two air victories are known; both were B-17s, shot down by *Hauptmann* Eder. The dates are not known for certain, possibly January 14 and 17, 1945.

February 1 saw the first success by a young *Leutnant* who by the end of hostilities was to become the top scorer on the Me 262 with 23 confirmed kills: Lt. Rudi Rademacher. Rademacher had already achieved 98 victories with I./JG 54 in the East and five more with *Ergänzungsgruppe Nord* at Sagan. Transferred directly to JG 7 on January 30, 1945, he carried out six training flights the same day totalling 150 minutes in the air. The next morning he took off on his first combat sortie in the Me 262.

Vectored by a fighter controller toward a reconnaissance aircraft in the Hildesheim area, Rademacher sighted the enemy aircraft over Braunschweig at about 11,000 meters. Taking advantage of the cover offered by the enemy aircraft's condensation trail, he attacked from a slightly higher altitude. The Spitfire pilot was taken completely by surprise and went down following a brief burst of fire.

Two days later, on February 3, Rademacher took off with several machines of 11. *Staffel* to intercept a small formation of heavy bombers with fighter escort approaching Magdeburg. Dozens of Mustangs and Thunderbolts forced the *Schwarm* to veer away before it could reach a favorable firing position. The jet fighters made repeated attempts to shake off the fighter screen. Rademacher finally managed to get through and destroyed a Flying Fortress near Halle, the only member of the *Schwarm* to do so.

Several other pilots were successful on February 3. Uffz. Schöppler shot down a P-51, while Lt. Weber, Lt. Schnörrer and Oblt. Wegmann each destroyed a four-engined bomber. Unfortunately the log books of these pilots have not survived, so the author has been unable to confirm the dates.

Over the next few days the weather deteriorated, with low cloud over III./JG 7's bases preventing the pilots, most of whom were not trained in instrument flying, from taking off to engage the ongoing American incursions. Not until February 9 did the jets again see combat, and once again it was Rademacher who emerged victorious, destroying two B-17s in the Berlin area. It is also quite probable that Hptm. Eder and Oblt. Wegmann each shot down a B-17 and Lt. Schnörrer a P-51. In addition to attacks by conventional fighters, 8th Air Force reports for the first time mention encounters with larger numbers of jet fighters in the Berlin area, "the jet fighters made repeated attempts to reach firing position, but were turned away by our fighter escort and lost two aircraft."

It is known with certainty that only aircraft of III./JG 7 were in action in the Berlin area that day. The unit's loss reports, which are complete well into March 1945, do not list any losses on February 9.

February 12, 1945 was the deadline set by Göring for III./JG 7 to achieve operational status. In spite of the many obstacles encountered in the past weeks, Weissenberger and Sinner were able to report to the Commander-in-Chief of the Luftwaffe that the unit was operational. The level of pilot training had reached an acceptable level under the prevailing circumstances; construction of the ground organization was largely complete and, with 50 machines, the aircraft complement had even exceeded the authorized level by ten. Approximately seven weeks after its formation, III./JG 7 had become the first fully-operational jet fighter unit.

But what was the status of the second Me 262 *Jagdgruppe*, I./JG 7, which according to OKL planning should have been operational at the end of January 1945? On returning from an inspection trip to the front-line units, *Flugkapitän* Fritz Wendel reported:

> ". . . The pilots of I. *Gruppe* have for the most part completed their conversion training. All that is missing is training in close formation flying and cooperation with ground control. As of February 9 this *Gruppe* had 12 aircraft. With normal output from the Briest assembly facility the *Gruppe* should likewise be operational by the end of the month . . ."

But Wendel's prognosis was too optimistic; it was not until early April 1945 that the *Gruppe* reached its full operational strength. Formed from elements of II./JG 3 and bolstered by pilots from other units, I. *Gruppe* was initially to have been brought to operational readiness at Alperstadt, near Weimar. Conversion training for the three *Staffeln* under Oblt. Grünberg, Oblt. Stehle and Oblt. Waldmann was to take place at Lechfeld.

General der Jagdflieger Galland named one of the Luftwaffe's most capable and successful unit leaders to command the *Gruppe*: *Major* Theodor Weissenberger. His meteoric rise had begun two years earlier, in autumn 1942, with 6./JG 5 in Norway. On November 13, 1942, after scoring 38 kills as a *Zerstörer* pilot, Weissenberger was awarded the Knight's Cross. Following the pause in operations during the winter his score began to climb rapidly – in March 1943 alone he scored 33 victories – and when he took over

7. *Staffel* in mid-June 1943 his score stood at 91. Seven kills on July 4, 1943 took him over the hundred mark. Barely four weeks later he became the 266th member of the *Wehrmacht* to receive the Oak Leaves. By the time he was named *Kommandeur* of II./JG 5 in mid-April 1944, Weissenberger's tally had risen to 175. Many of his kills were achieved under extremely difficult conditions. The air war in the far north placed extreme demands on the flying personnel. In summer the sun never fell below the horizon, which meant 24 hours of readiness for pilots and technical personnel. During the winter months daylight was restricted to a few hours of twilight. Loneliness, freezing cold, snowstorms and the often very primitive conditions at front-line airfields made conditions profoundly more difficult. Furthermore, the pilots knew all too well that if they were shot down or forced to crash-land during operations over the Polar Sea or the vastness of Russia they stood little chance of returning home. This was a burden which only the most strong-willed could endure.

Transferred to the Western Front, Weissenberger experienced the inferno of the invasion and convinced the last of the skeptics who smiled at the "easy" victories of the aces from the Northern and Eastern Fronts. By the end of July 1944, in only nine days of operational flying, he scored another 25 victories over Anglo-American fighters, thus raising his total to 200.

Galland had made an outstanding selection in naming Weissenberger to command I./JG 7. His understanding of difficult technical matters, his leadership qualities and his indisputable talent for organization made him extremely well qualified to take over the second Me 262 *Jagdgruppe*.

Weissenberger's intensive efforts to accelerate the completion of I./JG 7 proved ineffective, however. The decentralization of jet training, ordered by the OKL at the end of November on account of the standing patrols maintained by the Allies over Lechfeld, resulted in delays in training pilots for the new unit. I./JG 7 transferred to Unterschlauersbach, near Nuremburg, and began training under less than favorable conditions using the few available Me 262s. The training program ran into frequent delays resulting from the loss of training aircraft; five aircraft were written off in the period December 1 – 22, 1945 alone. Initially I./JG 7 had no aircraft of its own. For weeks the operational readiness reports recorded pointedly: pilots available, aircraft assigned. Such reports were submitted on November 30, on December 10 and December 27.

On December 10, 1944 the OKL decided to abandon Alperstedt in favor of a new base: Kaltenkirchen in Holstein. It was hoped that this choice would not only allow the jets to cover the Hamburg – Bremen – Lübeck area, but at the same time form an initial defensive front against American incursions against Berlin. However, the selection of Kaltenkirchen was to prove a mistake. Not only did it lie directly beneath the main approach lane for the bomber streams, thus rendering it vulnerable to attack from fighters sweeping ahead of the bombers, but the flat plains of northern Germany favored the formation of extended fog belts, which often halted all flying for days at a time.

Like the training of pilots, the expansion of Kaltenkirchen within the "Silver Construction Program" lagged far behind the plans. *Oberstingenieur* Franz Frodl, assigned by Galland to I./JG 7 as technical officer, recalled:

> ". . . When I arrived at Kaltenkirchen on January 8, 1945 as the advance detachment of the technical section, conditions were catastrophic. The only member of the flying personnel there was 'Specker' Grünberg. Three non-flyable jets sat in a corner of the airfield, there were no replacement parts to be found and no jet engine workshop. Workers from a concentration camp were busy extending the runway, and if that wasn't enough the fog was so thick that you couldn't see the hand in front of your face. We needed weeks before the field was halfway in shape for conducting flight operations."

When the retrained pilots finally arrived at Kaltenkirchen in mid-January 1945 a lack of aircraft meant that they could not receive the required instruction in tactics and formation flying or carry out orientation and air firing flights. So *Major* Rudorffer, like Weissenberger a very successful fighter pilot with 212 victories, who had assumed command of the *Gruppe* following Weissenberger's appointment to the post of *Geschwaderkommodore*, found himself with a unit which was a long way from being ready for operations. The number of Me 262 fighters on strength grew slowly during February, reaching 12 aircraft on February 12, the day III. *Gruppe* became operational, allowing the pace of operational training to increase.

Little is known of flying accidents during I./JG 7's working-up phase. A 99% write-off was recorded on January 15, 1945, and the first total loss occurred on February 15. Uffz. Werner took off in Me 262 Werk-Nr. 130 171 on a maintenance test flight. After being airborne for 25 minutes the Me 262 developed an engine fire and crashed near Alveslohe. Werner was killed.

At the end of November the alarming rise in the number of engine failures experienced by every Me 262 unit during the past weeks led to a thorough checking of new and damaged production engines by the *E-Stelle* at Rechlin. Concluded in late January 1945, the action discovered an aggravating number of material, assembly and design problems and fully confirmed complaints from the units that "no engine lasts more than eight to ten hours." Compressor damage, elongation of compressor blades due to excessive temperatures, fractures due to increased brittleness, labyrinth scoring, separation of the nozzle pintle, "on average the Riedel starter was changed at least once per engine due to inadequate performance," excessive oil consumption, "in a number of engines the turbines were improperly balanced. The vibration caused by the out-of-balance turbines led to the loosening of engine components (conduits, partition lines) and subsequently to engine fires." These were only some of the *E-Stelle*'s findings. Not all of the damage could be laid at the door of the manufacturers, however. Many of the damaged power plants showed typical signs of improper handling by the pilot. As a result the Head of the Department for Air Armament, Diesing, felt obliged to direct a letter to the commander of the Rechlin Testing Establishment:

> "It appears to me advisable to convert several front-line jet engine test stands for demonstration purposes in training pilots destined for jet-powered aircraft. The idea is to install on the test stand control and monitoring systems similar to those presently in use in jet aircraft. This will give the pilot an opportunity to become familiar with the operation of the power plant on the test stand before commencing training on the jet aircraft and thus avoid damaging engines already installed in the airframe through operating errors.
>
> "Chief TLR/Fl. E requests that *E-Stelle* Rechlin collaborate on this assignment within the framework of the development of the front-line test stand."

Implementation of this proposal would undoubtedly have led to a reduction in flying accidents due to improper handling. The war situation did not allow it, however, and also kept Junkers from overcoming the engine's material and design shortcomings.

The high loss rate due to technical breakdowns, discovered as a result of careful research and published here for the first time, may at first cause the reader to shake his head in disbelief. Such numbers do not fit the image of the Me 262 presented in previous publications. They mention nothing of turbine fires, of a tendency for the aircraft to trim nose-down, of landing gear legs being torn out on landing; nothing of dozens of crashes which cost the lives of so many pilots. And why? Because it would call into question the carefully-fostered myths which had grown up around the Me 262.

It is the responsibility of every chronicler to present frankly both the bright and the dark sides. This does not mean treading further down the well-trodden paths of eternal optimists and irresponsible illusionists, depicting only glowing successes while shamelessly sweeping the high losses of the jet *Gruppe* under the table. Annoying as it may be to have to take leave of the fondly-held notion of jet pilots cheerfully flying the belated wonder weapon after the motto "we're riding through the bomber stream," the truth is always preferable to mere wishful thinking.

Inadequate technical skills at the unit level, poor construction and workmanship and failure to comply with appropriate servicing and operations manuals all had an effect on jet units' flying and operational activities and operational readiness, as illustrated by an extract from a report by Messerschmitt's field technical office written on February 5, 1945 following a visit to KG(J) 54 at Giebelstadt:

> Formation flight on 23. 1. 45, 1000 hours.
> Scheduled to take off: 16 aircraft.
> 4 aircraft could not taxi, as:
> 1st aircraft: Right Riedel failed;
> 2nd aircraft: Tailplane adjustment at V 30. Circuits not adequately secured. (Tailplane trim could not be operated);
> 3rd aircraft:Tailplane adjustment not functional, loose connection due to engine vibration;
> 4th aircraft: Leak in emergency compressed air line.
> Commenced takeoff: 12 aircraft.
> 2 aircraft had to abort takeoff, as:
> 1st aircraft: Improperly loaded (fuel tanks were full, but no ammunition loaded);
> 2nd aircraft: Differential pressure gauge not indicating correctly.
> Achieved flight: 10 aircraft.
> Still combat-ready after landing: 4 aircraft.
> 1st aircraft: Windscreen iced up (windscreen rendered totally opaque by snow thrown up by aircraft taking off ahead. Pilot unable to see and crashed);
> 2nd aircraft: Pump installation out of order (after the pilot was in the air he selected the rear tanks for both engines. Fuel continued to be drawn from forward tanks which emptied rapidly, resulting in an off-field landing. Inspection revealed that the two fuel pipes, which are connected by the system of fuel valves, had in fact been

mixed up.);

3rd aircraft: No 'gear down' indication (pilot tried emergency lowering of undercarriage, likewise no indication. Impact of landing restored operation of indicator.);

4th aircraft: same as 2nd aircraft.

5th aircraft: (a) according to pilot aileron linkage jammed (inspec tion revealed rubbing of push rods in guides.)
(b) oscillations around lateral axis.
(c) airspeed indicator giving faulty readings (line was leaking).

6th aircraft: damage to Riedel starter.

Loss figures from III./EJG 2, KG 51 and JG 7 were comparable. A comprehensive technical report by the technical officer of III. *Gruppe*, *Oberinspektor* Grote, compiled on March 3, 1945, listed the following causes for 42 aircraft losses:

pilot error	13
technical faults	19
enemy action	10

Evaluation of surviving damage reports shows that in many cases the technical faults and resulting flying accidents must be seen as direct results of improper handling by the pilot. The following is a typical example:

> "Aircraft's right engine flamed out. Because of the dangerous situation the pilot did not allow sufficient time before landing when extending the undercarriage and did not pay attention to the gear indicator; as well he failed to lower the landing flaps. The nosewheel was not locked in position when the aircraft touched down and therefore collapsed. The fuselage nose struck the ground and at the same time the aircraft swung to the side."

A debriefing report by the Messerschmitt field technical service said:

> "In hearing many of the details reported to me I got the impression that some of our pilots approach every machine very breezily with the catchphrase 'little fish, little fish,' but that fundamentally they understand very little about this design."

The wording is undoubtedly exaggerated, however criticism of the travelling staff, which was aimed at the way the Luftwaffe was training pilots, was, as the report shows, thoroughly justified.

It must be conceded, however, that a clear line cannot always be drawn between losses through "pilot error," or improper handling, and "technical failures" so many years after the events took place.

Here is an example. The following entry appears in III./JG 7's loss lists under 31. 12. 1944: "Werk-Nr. 500 039. Crash landing following failure of both engines. Pilot error."

What lies hidden behind these dry words is recounted by Hellmut Detjens. His memory of that crash landing more than 36 years ago is as vivid as if he had put the machine down on its belly only yesterday:

"On 31. 12. 1944 I took off with Lt. Weber after Lightnings over Seeland. Although I was flying with the throttles wide open I could not keep up. (Several days earlier, following a sortie, Weber had made an intermediate landing at Lärz with Arnold, Giefing and me. Arnold's and Giefing's machines were shot, and the hydraulic brake line of Meyer's aircraft had ruptured. After that he flew my machine, which was serviceable and flew well but displayed varying engine temperatures, pressures and revolutions, back to Brandenburg. He alerted the mechanic to the problem and had the engines 'switched.') Weber did not throttle back, but instead flew on alone. Finally I saw him disappear as a dot in the sky. Just then an engine failed. Below me was a solid cloud deck. I informed Weber that I was heading back and turned onto a reciprocal course of 077 degrees, all the while calling Brandenburg. There was no reply even though I broadcast that 'my horse was lame.' I was also unable to get a response from any other ground station. Not until my other engine failed did Brandenburg call in. I transmitted 'Tuba' (message for ground-based DF homing) and descended toward the clouds. They informed me that they could not locate me and that I must be very near the base. When I broke out and gained sight of the ground I informed the ground station that I was not over Brandenburg, there were no lakes – only forest! I saw a flat area with no trees ahead, rather yellow – like sand. I put the nose down to gain speed and then levelled off, below me nothing but trees. But then . . . my landing field, undulating and consisting of craters. I didn't have sufficient speed to pull up and climb, so I banked slightly and set down gently on a slope. One engine caught in a crater and was torn off. The machine slid a short distance and stopped. I jumped clear and ducked into a crater to wait and see if anything was going to explode. After tearing off my helmet I heard a whistling sound – but not the droning of bombers – and an impact. I had force-landed on the Jüterbog firing range where they tested new ammunition."

Was this accident due to the "inexperience of Uffz. Detjens," as Lt. Weber wrote in the damage report he submitted as element leader, "as D. failed to recognize the base and made a forced-landing due to lack of fuel, and as he also mistakenly used a fuel gauge installed contrary to normal practice," or were technical faults to blame. After all this time who can say for sure?

In this context a very experienced and successful Me 262 pilot drew an appropriate comparison:

> "Someone used to driving a VW who takes part in a road rally in the midst of winter under the worst road conditions in a Mercedes 600 could not be expected to master the technically-demanding vehicle right away and at the same time handle all the sharp turns perfectly."

A number of pilots were undoubtedly overtaxed by the extreme demands placed on them by conversion training, which was often squeezed into a few days. In the end insufficient preparation caused them to come to grief with this fast machine. Lt. Günther von Rettburg of 10./JG 7 might serve as an example. For years he had flown nothing but the Me 323 *Gigant*. In February 1945 he was retrained on the jet fighter and was killed near Parchim on his first combat sortie.

In general, pilots who had received peacetime training on single-or twin-engined fighters had little difficulty converting to the Me 262. Their sound training and great experience allowed them to quickly recognize the machine's weaknesses and act prudently in the event of an in-flight technical failure, greatly reducing the risk of an accident.

Highly-skilled pilots like Lennartz, Müller, Grünberg, Stehle and Wegmann, to name but a few, soon came to possess unbounded confidence in the new type. Many former Me 262 pilots share Fritz Stehle's view: "Actually I have good memories of the bird. I flew it for more than half a year and had problems on only one occasion."

Thus the factors which enabled experienced pilots to achieve such impressive success during the final months of the war were technical understanding, mastery of the machine in all flight attitudes, good fighter and gunnery training, experience and the ability to exploit the aircraft's advantages after assessing the tactical possibilities. Nevertheless, some young, inexperienced pilots also scored an astonishing number of victories flying the aircraft.

The ceaseless Anglo-American bombing of the German fuel industry had devastating consequences, not only for the activities of the flying units, but also for the training plans of the various branches of the Luftwaffe. As a result of the reduction in allocations to flying schools and replacement training *Gruppen* – in February 1945 about 80% less than the previous month – training of replacement personnel for long-range reconnaissance, single-engined night fighter and Me 163 units was halted completely, training for KG 26 and KG 53 deferred and plans to convert several units to the close-support role – apart from an anti-tank *Staffel* – had to be shelved.

Although the fuel shortage was sorely felt by the reconnaissance, bomber and training units, its greatest impact was on the fighter force, where the present situation must lead to the unavoidable collapse of the air defence of the Reich in the near future. The 150 day-fighter pilots, 30 bad-weather pilots and 50 pilots for the Me 262 which were to be trained with the fuel assigned to the training organization by an OKL order of February 1, 1945 could never hope to replace the disastrous losses of the previous two months: 719 killed, captured and missing and 274 wounded in December 1944; 639 killed, missing and captured and 148 wounded in January 1945. 1,779 casualties in two months! The German fighter arm was being wiped out in a hopeless battle against an all-powerful enemy.

The growing weight of the Allied attacks on hydrogenation plants and the transportation system in February 1945 made the training of even 230 fighter pilots questionable. The Training Department of the OKL had made a study of the fuel requirements for the training of jet pilots.[3] In view of the apparently impressive savings in time and fuel involved in converting bomber pilots to fly the Me 262, a decision was made which was understandable given the precarious fuel situation and the fighter arm's terrible pilot losses, but one which, if carried out as planned, would have meant the final end of the air defence of Germany: the planned reequipping of disbanded bomber units with the Me 262 and their use as "bomber units in the fighter role" within the Defense of the Reich.

In Sinner's view:

> "The notion of exploiting the potential in instrument-experienced bomber pilots for fighter operations was sound in principle. It should have succeeded had it been implemented much earlier and above all if systematic attention had been paid to the completely different piloting and tactical requirements of the fighter arm without impediments of prestige regarding training and command. This was possible, as proved by several bomber officers who voluntarily fought in our unit with growing success without

making any claim to command positions. In addition to the pilots, the bomber observers, radio operators and flight engineers, most of whom possessed years of experience and specialized knowledge, would have constituted a valuable pool of personnel for training as fighter pilots.

"The attempt to create effective fighter units from existing bomber units through largely in-house retraining failed, largely because the use of irrelevant standards resulted in an overestimation of the suitability of bomber pilots for the fighter role.

"The bomber arm was considered the elite of the air force by leading Luftwaffe commanders from Wever to Koller, and they thus felt themselves superior in worth to fighter pilots. In contrast to the latter, all bomber pilots possessed a "C" rating[4] and were instrument trained. They flew their heavy aircraft deep into enemy territory in all kinds of weather on missions lasting hours and were almost helpless when exposed to the enemy's defenses. Careful and extensive preparations were vital to the success of their missions. They overlooked or played down the fact that fighter pilots flew sophisticated, demanding single-seaters without observers, radio operators or gunners and with limited instrumentation, and were thus confronted with problems in navigation and combat which bomber pilots did not meet in their carefully-planned missions. It had been their bitter experience that they usually came out second best in combat with fighters, in spite of all their bravado. As a result many bomber pilots concluded that they could be successful as fighter pilots with little risk and without special training. As well, many officers who had risen to command positions as a result of outstanding success in action were simply not prepared 'to start from the bottom' in the bloodied fighter arm under hopeless combat conditions."

Sinner had undoubtedly addressed the central points of the problem. To those responsible, however, they seemed unimportant. KG 6, KG 27, KG 30, KG 40 and KG 55 all handed in their aircraft, and their technical personnel were incorporated by Messerschmitt and Junkers into the production process. The majority of the pilots began retraining as fighter pilots at various fields in southern Germany. In mid-March, however, almost all the training plans were stopped. Only elements of KG(J) 6 and KG(J) 30 were equipped with the Me 262 and committed to action in the Prague area during the final days of the war.[5]

Like many other unit commanders, *Major* Weissenberger vainly opposed this conversion order and spoke correctly of its psychological impact on the *Jagdwaffe*. As he feared a frittering away of the already inadequate training resources, which had to have a negative impact on the supply of pilots to JG 7, he solicited pilots from other fighter units, ignoring the usual channels, and retrained them in the front-line *Gruppen*.

Weissenberger sent some pilots to III./EJG 2 in southern Germany for more thorough conversion training; however, from February 1945 these, too, were hurried through the training program.

The training process began at Landsberg with a briefing on the Siebel 204 or Bf 110 and two, perhaps three circuits with one engine shut down to familiarize the fighter pilots with the flight characteristics of twin-engined aircraft following an engine failure. This initial phase of the training program lasted three or four days. The second, theoretical phase, which was carried out at Lechfeld, consisted of lectures on the design, principles of operation and prescribed handling of jet engines, fuel management, general behavior of the Me 262 at various speeds and run-throughs of takeoff and landing procedures. The final training phase, practical conversion to the jet fighter, also took place at Lechfeld and began with three flights in an aircraft with a 50% fuel load to allow the pilot to become familiar with the jet. This was followed by a high-altitude flight at 8,000 meters, another at 10,000 meters, a cross-country orientation flight, two gunnery flights and finally a practice sortie in *Rotte* or *Kette* formation. Total flying time for conversion to the new type was approximately 6 hours, to be completed within 2 to 3 days. For young, inexperienced pilots this was scarcely the solid foundation needed for action against an enemy who was well-trained, experienced and far superior numerically. As important as it was to the interests of all concerned, an improvement in training was not possible given the prevailing circumstances, although there were those, especially *Major* Bär, who had taken over III./EJG 2 from Hptm. Geyer in early January 1945, who endeavoured to gear the training of Me 262 pilots to operational requirements. But it was too late for a realization of his proposals for the reorganization of the jet pilot replacement program. The omissions of the past could not be made good. Whoever was in charge of the Luftwaffe's training program was also responsible for the jet pilots, and the result was highly unsatisfactory.

Similar statements by former Me 262 pilots run through the final weeks of the war like a scarlet thread – Georg Peter-Eder in October 1944, "Training? We had to teach ourselves everything!" Fritz Neppach in December 1944: "Pocket reference cards? Operating instructions? Pilot's notes? I never saw them! I arrived at ten-thirty in the morning, received a brief lecture on how the engines worked, then it was out to the airfield. I walked around the machine once, climbed into the cockpit and by eleven I was already in the air." Friederich Wilhelm Schenk in March 1945:

"On 15. 3. 1945 Lt. Stahlberg, Ofw. Pritzl and I came to JG 7. There I had about a week to come to terms with the technology of the Me 262. Then I made three training flights in one day. As there were no two-seaters these were made solo, the only assistance being by radio. My fourth takeoff in the 'thing' the next day was my first combat sortie. The conversion training of the others was at about the same pace, only Stahlberg had two days training and thus a few more flights before his first combat sortie."

Messerschmitt *Flugkapitän* Fritz Wendel, probably the most qualified man on the subject, declared in this regard: "Modern aircraft present a relatively complex picture. If a completely new type of aircraft is involved, it is even more imperative that the pilots receive an intensive theoretical background as part of their conversion to the new type. They must be completely familiar with the components of the aircraft and its engines and how they function. An appropriate number of good instructors could have been trained in cooperation with industry. Such a program would have prevented a large percentage of the accidents." There is probably nothing more to add to Wendel's argument.

The quality of training suffered further as the result of the lack of a sufficient number of two-seat trainers. Mastering the specific problems related to high-speed flight, like control and navigation, would certainly have been easier, especially for young pilots, under the expert guidance of an experienced instructor. Moreover, by simulating engine failures during these training flights it would have been possible to train the new pilots to react calmly, quickly and correctly in the event of the real thing happening. There was much to be concerned about when an engine flamed out: equalizing the gyroscopic moment around the yaw axis, switching of tanks as fuel was used up, increasing the rudder area by engaging the auxiliary tab while on approach and making immediate trim corrections on opening or closing the throttles.

Two-seaters remained a scarce commodity, however. A small number of machines began reaching the training units after the turn of the year (1944/45). Shortages of personnel and materials as well as the growing destruction being wreaked on the aircraft industry kept the program from being realized as planned. In the case of the Me 262 trainer as well, the efforts of those responsible were increasingly limited to merely coping with external events.

Development of the two-seat version was initiated on June 23, 1943 at the behest of the RLM. At a conference on the Me 262 representatives of the ministry submitted a proposal to have a number of production aircraft converted to dual-control training aircraft at a repair facility. Such aircraft, they argued, would ease the process of training future Me 262 pilots. The written concretization of this proposal appeared in Augsburg a mere 14 days later: "The Messerschmitt firm is charged with the design of a dual-control version of the Me 262, to include a full-scale mock-up and a prototype." Specifications for the trainer were finalized by the project bureau at the beginning of August and proposed the following significant changes from the single-seat fighter version on which it was based:

1. Extension of fuselage center-section to accommodate the larger cockpit.
2. Cockpit to consist of two pressurized compartments, equipped with dual controls as well as control levers and equipment required by the instructor.
3. Lengthened canopy.
4. Aft 900-liter tank to be replaced by an unprotected 400-liter tank beneath the instructor's seat.

So as to limit tire loads the aircraft's fuel capacity was restricted to 1,600 liters. Initially it had been feared that the greater weight of the two-seat version would require the strengthening or redesign of the undercarriage. However reducing the aircraft's fuel capacity resulted in a considerable reduction in its endurance as well. At full thrust at low level the Me 262 trainer's endurance was only 23 minutes, at 3,000 meters 38 minutes and at 9,000 meters 53 minutes. The maximum speeds calculated for the trainer, which was to be powered by Jumo 004 B-2 engines, were also about 35 kph less than those of the fighter, or 770 kph at zero altitude, 805 kph at 3,000 meters and 840 kph at 6,000 meters.

On September 7, 1943, only four weeks after the tender had been issued, Hptm. Behrens, the Me 262 project officer, Staff Engineer Beauvais and Oblt. Brüning of the *E-Stelle* Rechlin were able to inspect the mock-up constructed by Messerschmitt.

A thorough examination of the cockpit and the arrangement of instruments and equipment produced no complaints, and as the requested changes (FuG 16ZY and FuG 25a instead of FuG 14, the addition of an intercom and AFN indicators on the instructor's instrument panel, installation of a further 400-liter fuel tank for use with larger tires) could be implemented quickly, Messerschmitt began drawing up the definitive design documents on September 9.

From mid-October work on the trainer, including production of the prototype, had to be severely cut back in favor of intensified efforts to overcome the fighter version's problems in preparation for series production, in spite of objections on the part of the *Technische Amt*. Not until

January 1944, following the completion of some revisions to the airframe, did work resume fully on the two-seater. Design work was completed at the end of February with the delivery of the last design documents. Work on the prototype had also begun again, but progressed slowly on account of limited production capacity. The RLM stepped in on February 9, 1944 and proposed to Messerschmitt that, ". . . due to the approaching deadline it should allow the prototype to be built by Siebel at Halle." This plan was not realized, however, for reasons which are unexplained. It was not until about four weeks later, on March 2, 1944, that a company was found to carry out the test conversion and produce the trainer in quantity: the firm of Blohm und Voss. Following several preparatory conferences the department's official order for the quickest possible construction of, initially, two prototypes was issued on March 18, 1944. Two days later, on March 20, Hptm. Thierfelder, the commander of *Erprobungskommando* 262, which was then being formed, declared himself willing to release the fifth series aircraft, S-5, which had been allocated to the testing detachment. In early April the aircraft was broken down into its major components and shipped by rail to the Blohm und Voss Company's Wenzendorfer works.

The first machine was supposed to be ready to fly by June 15, 1944, but Blohm und Voss was unable to meet the deadline as several time-consuming changes to the Messerschmitt drawings proved necessary. Not until July 16 was "flight clearance for the Me 262 B-1 trainer for the purpose of flight testing" given.

The specification from August of the previous year had been updated to bring the new variant of the Me 262 up to the latest state of development in construction and equipment. The fighter version's armament of four MK 108 cannon in the nose was retained for gunnery training, and the fuel system comprised four tanks with a capacity of 1,700 liters. Takeoff weight, which in August 1943 had been calculated at 5,380 kg, had increased to 6,250 kg as a result of all the additions, which was about at the limit of what the undercarriage could support. Maximum speed was only slightly lower than that of the single-seater, however the aircraft was limited to 800 kph at all altitudes and 500 kph in bad weather as a stress analysis had not yet been made of the larger cockpit of the two-seater.

Initial test flights were carried out at Lechfeld and in early August the first two-seater (coded VI-AJ, Werk-Nr. 130 010) was handed over to the *E-Stelle* Rechlin). Type testing was carried out at the *E-Stelle* during the following weeks. The aircraft was also used for training and as a flying test-bed for a throttle lever brake, automatic pilot and a new version of the Jumo engine. On October 8, while landing after a test flight, the fuselage nose broke off, probably as the result of poor spot welding. The aircraft turned over and was totally destroyed.

In the meantime, following advance notice by the department on April 26, 1944, a contract was placed with Blohm und Voss for the production of 100 trainers (according to RLM Study 1036 from July 1944 it was considered necessary that 3-5% of all Me 262s be produced as training aircraft). Beginning with six machines in August and ten in September, and climbing to 15 per month from October 1944, the RLM hoped to be able to meet the Luftwaffe's needs.

Delays in production by Messerschmitt soon placed the RLM's planning in disarray, however. Deliveries of major components to Blohm und Voss for production of the two-seater were limited in number and late by weeks: only two sets of components were delivered to Blohm und Voss in May 1944, and three more in early June. Hitler's May 25, 1944 decree that all Me 262s were to be built as high-speed bombers also had a direct effect on the planned trainer series. Referring to Hitler's order, *Hauptdienstleiter* Saur, who had been assigned by Speer to watch over and guarantee production of the Me 262 "as the *Führer* intended," refused to allow even a few machines to be used for other purposes. "It must be emphasized," he stated at a fighter staff conference on June 22, 1944, "that in the future not a single machine may be released for any purpose except testing or delivery to the *General der Kampfflieger*. Everything else is out." And Galland: "Why bother at all with the trainer series when production is just beginning, as it will not be needed until later when production increases? We could certainly handle the first 100 production aircraft without dual controls. It has been shown that there are no difficulties in flight training. It's actually a great pity for this aircraft." At this point the project officer, Hptm. Behrens, became involved in the discussion: "I know that the General in charge of flying training continues to place great importance on the trainer. Based on previous experience I must emphasize: we need Me 262 training aircraft." *Major* Petersen, commander of the *E-Stelle*, reached the same conclusion: "I would like to underline the fact that we need several aircraft. We will have dozens of crashes." To this Saur, his hands tied by Hitler's directive, replied: "I can't make that decision. I ask that you leave me out of such things and seek the *Reichsmarschall*'s approval."

It is not known who made the *Reichsmarschall* aware of this affair, however Göring must have recognized the necessity of the fighter-trainer construction program because assembly work at Blohm und Voss continued, even though there were some delays due to the limited deliveries of components.

In July 1944 the RLM stepped in and involved another firm in the Me 262 trainer program, "in order to free up the Blohm und Voss company's production capacity for larger, more comprehensive projects at a later date." The new player was *Deutsche Lufthansa*. According to the RLM's plan, DLH was to join in production in November 1944 and assume total responsibility for production in April 1945, on condition that all documents relating to the modifications, such as design and production drawings, were supplied straight away and the necessary major components delivered within eight weeks.

This program also failed to come to fruition. The probable cause was the catastrophic situation in the transport sector. Parts manufactured at decentralized facilities – wings at Leonburg, fuselages at Regensburg, engines at Muldenstein, fuselage forward sections at Lauingen and tail assemblies at Wenzendorf – often arrived at Lufthansa's Berlin assembly plant weeks late.

When production finally began in mid-December 1944, the quota was lowered to accommodate the production of Me 262 night-fighters, which had been established at a rate of 3 aircraft per month.

Verifiable figures as to DLH's total production are not available, however realistic estimates place the total at between six and ten machines. Production at Wenzendorf was also far below what had been planned. In January 1945 a heavy bombing raid smashed the assembly line and 15 aircraft in the final assembly stage. It was a blow from which the factory never recovered. Only a few more machines left the assembly hall in the following months. In total, by war's end no more than 15 machines had been converted to two-seaters by Blohm und Voss and collected by BAL.

The first of the dual-control trainers were probably handed over to the training units in mid-November 1944; III./EJG 2's strength report for November 27 shows twelve Me 262 A-1s and an A-2, and for the first time a single Me 262 B-1. By the end of January 1945 the unit had three of the B-Version, the most it would ever have on strength. As the result of several crashes during delivery flights and the low production rate, the *Ergänzungsgruppe* received no further aircraft of this type.

In December 1944 the number of pilots transferred to Lechfeld climbed sharply. III./EJG 2's strength reports show only twelve instructors and 69 trainee pilots at the end of November; only four weeks later 28 instructors at Landsberg and Lechfeld were preparing 135 future Me 262 pilots for operations in the jet fighter. In spite of this conversion training continued at a slow pace; allocations of aircraft to the *Ergänzungsgruppe* remained far below requirements. On December 27 the unit had on strength 19 Me 262s, 10 Bf 109s and 10 Fw 190s, an improvement over the total of 12 jet and piston-engined fighters on hand on November 7, 1944, but far below the planned strength of 122 single-seat and two-seat Me 262s. According to Leo Schumacher, longtime wingman of *Major* Bär:

> "The technical condition of many machines was positively miserable, however. The majority of our aircraft came from the days of *Kommando Nowotny*, with all their production and design problems. They were always in need of repairs and their flight characteristics were at the limit of what was acceptable. In spite of the efforts of the ground services the aircraft could not be trimmed. They tended to drop one wing, and as a result of overly-thick rudder tabs many aircraft swung strongly about the yaw axis. The results of air firing were correspondingly poor, radio communications were usually impossible due to frequent equipment malfunctions, and poor manufacturing standards or rough upper wing surfaces reduced the aircraft's speed by as much as 50 kph. Our biggest problem, however, was the engines. Either we had none – once in February '45 10 of 14 aircraft sat useless for lack of engines – or they were on their last legs."

Inadequately prepared pilots training on trouble-prone aircraft under time constraints: the result had to be flying accidents. The inquiry into an accident involving Uffz. Helmut Schmidt, who crashed from an altitude of 60 meters while on approach to Lechfeld on January 7, 1945, concluded that the causes were technical deficiencies and incorrect handling. Schmidt survived the crash, but his aircraft, "White 1," was totally destroyed when it struck the concrete runway. A practice flight ended fatally for Gefr. Ferdinand Sagmeister. He crashed near Kleinaitingen on January 12, 1945 while flying "White 9." An investigation determined that technical problems and incorrect handling were also the cause of this crash. On January 20 Uffz. Hartung was in the air in Me 262 "White 10." While in horizontal flight at 2,000 meters the aircraft suddenly pitched forward into a vertical dive. The aircraft crashed with its pilot still aboard.

Between January 30 and February 6, 1945 four of the desperately needed two-seat trainers were lost while on delivery flights to the *Ergänzungsgruppe*: On January 30 Uffz. Stark of *Überführergeschwader* 1 lost his way while flying Werk-Nr. 111 471 and subsequently made a belly landing in a field when his fuel ran out. The aircraft sustained 70% damage. On February 2 Werk-Nr. 110 410's undercarriage collapsed following a hard landing; it slid along the runway, sustaining damage to the underside of the aircraft. On February 4 the left engine of Werk-Nr. 110 473 caught fire in flight and forced Ofw. Rettler to make an emergency landing. The aircraft sustained 60% damage. On February 6 a fourth Me 262 trainer was lost in the vicinity of Landshut, also as a result of an in-flight engine fire.

Engine failure was the cause of Uffz. Heinz Speck's fatal crash near Zusamaltheim on February 9, 1945. On February 11 Hptm. Grözinger crashed near Lager Lechfeld following an engine failure. His aircraft, Werk-Nr. 110 440, was a total write-off, but Grözinger miraculously survived with only minor injuries. On February 20 an engine failure claimed another victim: Fw. Germar Nolte crashed in "White 14" south of Lamerdingen and was killed. The next day Werk-Nr. 111 616 crashed near Lager Lechfeld and was written off. The fate of the pilot is unknown. Finally, on February 25 Oblt. Böhm failed to return from a training flight. His body was found in the wreckage of his aircraft near Deberndorf.

So far it has not been possible to verify any kills by pilots of III./EJG 2 during January and February 1945. Although defense of the training center was not the unit's responsibility, it may be assumed that experienced pilots were at least sent up to intercept the numerous reconnaissance machines which flew over Lechfeld day after day. In spite of diligent efforts by the author no precise dates have been uncovered (for example, Uffz. Köster shot down a Spitfire while undergoing conversion training at Lechfeld, before being posted to 11. *Staffel*, but the date is uncertain).

In the Berlin area, a unit operation planned by Weissenberger and Sinner involving every aircraft of III. *Gruppe* had so far been frustrated by unfavorable weather conditions. For days low cloud over the bases at Oranienburg, Brandenburg-Briest and Parchim had made a synchronized takeoff by all the jets and the assembly of the *Staffeln* into battle order above the clouds impossible.

The resulting actions by small formations of Me 262s against the many hundreds of bombers and just as many fighters could scarcely have succeeded. The small formations of jet fighters were usually split up long before they reached the bomber stream. Pursued by dozens of Mustangs and Thunderbolts, only rarely did the jet fighters get an opportunity to engage the heavy bombers. On February 14, 1945, for example, six machines of 11. *Staffel* and several aircraft of I. *Gruppe* attacked bombers of the US 8th Air Force in the Lübeck–Neumünster area as they were returning to England. The American fighter screen repeatedly forced the jets to turn away, but the Me 262s kept trying. Over Kiel they finally penetrated the fighter screen and destroyed three B-17 F bombers. The kills were credited to Lt. Rademacher, Uffz. Schöppler and Uffz. Engler.

But the Americans scored as well. One of the jet fighters was hit in the fuselage and tail. Using his superior speed the Me 262 pilot disengaged. The damaged machine failed to reach its base, however. Bothe engines failed and the pilot bailed out near Wittenberge.

Rademacher destroyed his sixth enemy aircraft, a P-51, while on an intercept mission against high-flying reconnaissance aircraft in the Hannover area on February 16. The next day aircraft from Parchim were in action. Georg Peter Eder, then *Kapitän* of 9. *Staffel*, recalled:

> "I took off with Ofw. Zander and Ofw. Buchner to intercept a bomber formation reported over northern Germany. We came upon the enemy formation south of Bremen. We were met by defensive fire from hundreds of guns from a great distance as we prepared to attack from the rear. My machine was hit and in an instant the left engine and wing were on fire. The aircraft was beyond saving. Bailing out after being hit was nothing new for me. I had already gone through the exercise sixteen times. I jettisoned the canopy, pulled the nose up to lose speed, disconnected my helmet lead and stood up in my seat. The slipstream took care of the rest. I may have struck either the fuselage or the tail surfaces, in any case I suddenly felt a terrible pain in my leg and head. I let myself fall to perhaps 2,500 meters then pulled the parachute release handle."

This was to be Eder's last action of the war. He was picked up with a broken left leg and head injuries and taken to hospital.

At about midday Ofw. Hans Clausen took off from Brandenburg-Briest on a maintenance test flight. About ten minutes after takeoff he reported to ground control that he was having trouble with both engines and was returning to Briest. Clausen's comrades saw the Me 262 turn onto final trailing flames behind both engines. The aircraft did not reach the airfield, however. At an altitude of about 150 meters the left wing separated and the aircraft spun down in flames. Clausen was killed in the crash.

The *Gruppe* lost another aircraft on February 18, the ninth so far that month. The *Kommodore* of JG 7, Theodor Weissenberger, who had been promoted to *Major* on February 10, described the incident in a letter to his wife:

> "At about 1620 on February 18, for amusement, but mostly so that I could get a good night's sleep, I once again took to my parachute.
> The day before I was in the air with Stehle on a training flight, and a terrific thing happened to us. Without intending to, we dove at such a speed that we were nearly unable to recover from the dive. In any case everything

turned out well and the lessons learned from this experience proved a tremendous help to our comrades.

And then on the 18th there was a crash and my left engine caught fire at an altitude of 8,000 meters. My first thought was to glide down. However, when I saw the fire eating its way through the wing, which was at the point of breaking off, I decided to bail out. I left my brave bird at 6,500 meters and let myself fall to 3,000 – 2,500 meters. It was extremely odd as I fell, because I was spinning, all the while trying to make out the ground, which I did only with difficulty. Then I reached back again to see if my parachute was really there. I pulled the release and a very hard jolt told me my parachute had deployed. Now I stayed quite still in my parachute, as I had the feeling that my harness might tear. Still hanging in my chute I saw my lovely bird crash and burn. I myself was being blown over a wooded area and towards some high trees. By pulling on the parachute lines and other measures I managed to land, still very hard, in a clearing. Now I'm lying in bed with either a minor concussion or a bruised brain. I am listening to the doctor's instructions and hope that I'll be well again in two days."

The next day I. *Gruppe* at Kaltenkirchen lost an aircraft. Fw. Alois Biermeier of 2. *Staffel* made a forced landing not far from Stubben, near Bad Segeberg. The incident report cited the cause as "technical problems." The aircraft was 80% destroyed and the pilot suffered considerable injuries.

During the morning hours of February 22, 1945, 1,400 bombers of the American 8th Air Force and 1,500 twin- and four-engined bombers of the 9th and 15th Air Forces, the 1st Tactical Air Force and the British 2nd Tactical Air Force took off to attack rail targets in Germany. The Allies concentrated their efforts on southern Bavaria, the Salzwedel-Lüneburg-Ludwigslust area and the Halberstadt-Hildesheim area. There was a powerful fighter escort and the Anglo-Americans attacked targets even in small towns, with the bombers of the 8th Air Force alone striking 33 transportation junctions.

According to OKW records the Germans had only a few fighter *Gruppen* to throw against this vast armada of enemy aircraft, as well as 34 Me 262 jet fighters. It may have been the first joint action by all combat-ready aircraft of JG 7. 9. *Staffel* took off from Parchim. The unit was now under the command of Oblt. Wegmann, who had taken over following Hptm. Eder's accident and *Major* Grötzinger's unfortunate death following a sudden illness. 10. *Staffel* under Oblt. Schall took off from Oranienburg and 11. *Staffel* under Lt. Weber from Brandenburg-Briest. This first large-scale mission was not to result in the expected number of enemy aircraft destroyed, however. Only two pilots of III./JG 7 returned to base with kills: Gefr. Notter destroyed two Flying Fortresses and Ofw. Buchner shot down a Mustang near Stendal.

I. *Gruppe* at Kaltenkirchen also received the order to scramble, but the unit was still in the formation process and only two machines were combat-ready that day. Oblt. Waldmann, *Kapitän* of 3. *Staffel*, and his wingman, Ofhr. Schrey, took off. West of Berlin the *Rotte* ran into the Allied fighter screen. At 1202 Waldmann shot down a Mustang and destroyed another moments later, at 1217, near Oschersleben.

These five victories were gained at a high cost. Three machines of III./JG 7 were lost in air combat. Near Schönwald Ofw. Baudach's machine (10./JG 7) was badly damaged by enemy fire. As he abandoned his aircraft Baudach, who had already been wounded, struck the aircraft's tail surfaces and suffered severe head injuries, from which he died several days later. Ofw. Mattuschka of 9./JG 7 bailed out of his burning aircraft near Hagenow. A third pilot, who has so far not been identified, was shot down near Döberitz.

American sources claim three victories over Me 262s in the area in which JG 7 was operating: Lt. Charles D. Price of the 352nd Fighter Group shot down a jet near Leipzig; Major Blickenstaff and Capt. Gordon Compton of the 353rd Fighter Group were each credited with half a kill, as were Lt. Kirby and Capt. Stevens of the 355th Fighter Group.

After the war Col. William C. Clark, former commander of the American 339th Fighter Group, said of these shared victories over Me 262s:

> "In a man against man battle, or more precisely aircraft against aircraft, our pilots had not the least chance against an Me 262. I have reviewed every available victory claim and am firmly convinced that not one of our pilots can claim to have shot down an Me 262 without support. The aircraft was simply too fast. We countered its superior speed with our numerical superiority. By staggering our squadrons in a given airspace we could screen a large area. When they attacked or flew away our machines dived on them from various directions at high speed and cut off their flight paths. If they made a sweeping turn in preparation for an attack we were often able to trap them from several directions. We enjoyed good success with these tactics. In this way we were able to shoot down eight machines and damage six on March 20 and 30 and April 3, 1945. Since several pilots usually scored hits on the Me 262 during the pursuit which subsequently led to the aircraft being shot down, the kill was shared equally."

In addition to the direct losses in combat III./JG 7 lost a fourth aircraft as a result of battle damage. Gefr. Notter had to belly-land his shot-up Me 262 at Stade; the aircraft was 80% destroyed. A fifth loss appears in *Gruppe* records: "crashed following engine fire, 99% destroyed." Two further aircraft sustained brake or undercarriage damage on landing (20%), and an eighth aircraft is listed with 30% damage following engine failure.

10. and 11. *Staffeln* were in action on February 24. They became involved in a major battle between Lüneburg and Hamburg with the fighter escort guarding about 600 B-17s and B-24s. Once again the Mustangs and Thunderbolts screened the bombers against the few German fighters so well that only two pilots of 11./JG 7 were able to score: Lt. Rudi Rademacher shot down a Liberator east of Lüneburg and Lt. Weber downed a Mustang.

On February 26 the Americans continued their terror attacks on the Reich capital, sending three air divisions of the 8th Air Force and 750 long-range fighters to Berlin. Several minutes before the jets of III./JG 7 were to take off, enemy fighters appeared over every one of the jet bases. On this occasion the massed German anti-aircraft defenses prevented the fighter-bombers from making accurate attacks. The only direct effect of the attack was insignificant splinter damage to buildings and aircraft. However the Allied attacks achieved the desired secondary effect: the bombers were able to unload their deadly cargo over the center of Berlin, unmolested by German fighters.

On February 27 the Americans attacked Halle and Leipzig. Lt. Rademacher attacked a B-17 which was lagging behind the rest of the formation. He scored effective hits on the bomber, which fell behind the others and soon afterward spun toward the ground.

During the last few days of the month action was limited to attempts at intercepting high-flying reconnaissance aircraft. The German fighters came away empty handed. On the other side, two machines were damaged beyond repair in forced landings following engine flame-outs or fires.

It had been hoped that JG 7, which had been built up during those long weeks in February, would be able to demonstrate its striking power with impressive victory totals. However results so far had been disappointing. Although it had destroyed 23 enemy aircraft, the *Geschwader* lost 14 of its own aircraft destroyed, while another 11 sustained up to 60% damage.

It was not only JG 7 which suffered considerable losses during February 1945. The other jet units also sustained serious losses in personnel and materiel. In the period February 19 – 26 alone, III./EJG 2, KG(J) 54, JG 7, KG 51, I.(F)/33, KG 76 and 10./NJG 11 lost 64 aircraft. According to available information, at least 125 jet aircraft, Arado 234s and Messerschmitt

262s, were lost during the month of February 1945 through technical problems, handling errors, enemy action or from unexplained causes.

Notes:

[1] Sinner had spent the previous weeks in southern Germany on behalf of the General der Jagdflieger on orders of the Head of the Luftwaffe Operations Staff, trying to step up the pace of flight-testing and delivery to JG 7 of completed Me 262s, which were at a standstill.

[2] FuG 16ZY: VHF transceiver used for communications as well as fighter control and homing. Remotely controlled, the FuG 16ZY could select frequencies for Y-control, communications between aircraft in formation, air-ground communications and the "fighter waveband" running commentary. ------------------FuG 25a: IFF (Identification Friend or Foe) device which transmitted an identifying signal to German radars.

[3] 1.	(a) Basic flight training	115 hrs. =	50 to. Otto
	(b) Weapons training	65 hrs. =	30 to. Otto
	(c) Jet training	10 hrs. =	20 to. J2
		180 hrs. =	35 to. Otto
			20 to J2
2.	(a) Fighter and gunnery training for former bomber pilots	10 hrs. =	4.5 to. Otto
	(b) Jet training	10 hrs. =	20 to. J2
		20 hrs. =	4.5 to. Otto
			20 to. J2

(Otto = high-octane fuel for piston engines)

[4] C-Rating: Pilot qualified to fly land aircraft over 5,000 kg and seaplanes over 5,500 kg.

[5] KG 54 was the first *Kampfgeschwader* to convert to the Me 262 in the fighter role, handing over the last of its bombers in September 1944. The unit carried out its first, limited fighter operations in November 1944.

Chapter IV
March 1945 - The Crucial Test

The First Large-Scale Operations – Development of the R4M Air-to-Air Rocket – First Use of the R4M on 18.3.1945 – Oblt. Wegmann is Put Out of Action – Catastrophe at Kaltenkirchen – Formation of I. Gruppe Is Further Delayed – II. Gruppe Exists Only on Paper – Only the Me 262 Can Stand up to the Overpowering Enemy – First Encounters with the US 15th Air Force – Kommando Stamp – Hitler Is Pleased with the Success – Bloody 31st of March for the RAF – Balance for the Month of March – With III./EJG 2 – Heinz Bär, the Great Example

> "*West-Reich.*
> *The Kaiser-Wilhelm Canal had to be closed because of mining. No attacks from the south. From the west the three American divisions in two groups; one in the Magdeburg-Braunschweig-Peine-Hildesheim-Nienburg area; the 2nd group against Chemnitz-Schwarzheide-Plauen; intercepted by the Me 262s for the first time. 8 victories, 1 loss.*"

A matter-of-fact entry in the ledger of the OKW for March 3, 1945; however it marked the beginning of large-scale operations by JG 7. During the previous month the jet fighters had been committed in twos, threes or fours, but now for the first time all available aircraft of the *Geschwaderstab* and III. *Gruppe* of JG 7 were sent into action at the same time and in the same area.

Twenty-nine Me 262s took off that day from Parchim, Oranienburg and Brandenburg-Briest. A major air battle began at about 1015 between Braunschweig and Magdeburg. No fewer than six enemy aircraft fell to the Parchim *Staffel*. Which pilot scored the first kill is not known with certainty. It may have been Ofw. Lennartz, who shot down a B-17 near Braunschweig. Two further Flying Fortresses were downed in rapid succession by Hptm.

Gutmann and Lt. Schnörrer. Ofhr. Russel damaged a fourth B-17. The American bomber was unable to keep up with the others and dropped out of formation. Following a wide turn Russel prepared to administer the coup de grace to the stricken bomber. But the explosive rounds from his MK 108s did not strike the B-17. Just as Russel opened fire, a P-47 of the fighter escort flew right through the hail of cannon fire and exploded like a bursting shell. The *Kapitän* of 9. *Staffel*, Oblt. Wegmann, scored a double success: within the space of a few minutes he shot down a Liberator and a Mustang.

The battle was not entirely one-sided, however; the massed defensive fire from the bombers also took its toll on the German fighters: Knight's Cross wearer Hptm. Gutmann, a former bomber pilot with III./KG 53, was fatally hit over Braunschweig. His aircraft crashed 18 km south of Waggum.

At about the same time 10. and 11. *Staffeln* and the *Geschwaderstab* encountered the bomber stream between Magdeburg and Berlin. The American escort fighters gave the German jets little opportunity to set up for attacks on the bombers. Dozens of enemy fighters repeatedly forced the Me 262s to turn away from the bomber formations. The only German pilot to pierce the dense fighter screen was Ofw. Arnold. Near Genthin he shot down a Flying Fortress and a Thunderbolt. The *Gruppen-Schwarm* under *Major* Sinner carried out a frontal attack on a bomber formation when approximately over Rathenow but failed to score any decisive hits. Sinner carried out a second attack alone, this time from the rear. This attack, too, appeared to fail; all four of Sinner's guns failed immediately after he opened fire on a B-24. However the next day a flak unit in the combat area reported the crash of the target aircraft, a bomber of the 467th Bomber Group, and the number of victories on March 3 was raised to nine.

Happily the 1951 American chronicle entitled *Army Air Forces in World War Two*, which is usually reserved in its statements concerning losses to Me 262 fighters, agrees completely with German victory claims for March 3, 1945, "Six bombers and three fighters were shot down by Me 262s which appeared in larger numbers for the first time."

Nine victories, the first promising success for JG 7. There was one other German loss which did not appear in the OKW ledger, however. In addition to the loss of Hptm. Gutmann, III./JG 7 damage reports list the crash of another Me 262 as the result of enemy action and 98% damage to Werk-Nr. 500 222 following an independent change of trim. Unfortunately, the fate of the two pilots remains unknown.

The success of March 3 could not be repeated right away; bad weather hindered the combat activities of JG 7 for two weeks or more. Occasionally, when the cloud cover over the bases broke up, a few fighters were scrambled to intercept enemy fighter patrols, reconnaissance aircraft or small bomber formations. Results were correspondingly limited. Only a handful of victories were claimed during the period March 4-17.

Two enemy aircraft were downed on March 7. Ofw. Arnold destroyed a Mustang near Wittenberg, while a second P-51 was shot down southwest of Berlin. The following is *Major* Sinner's brief and precise combat report:

> "Scramble from Brest 1304. After a long search, with fuel getting low, Mustang squadron discovered and attacked over Jüterbog. A Mustang blew up in my fire. Slat damaged by pieces of enemy aircraft. Engines flamed out due to lack of fuel. Successful pinpoint landing at Brest with undercarriage down."

Two days later radar spotted an intruder, an enemy reconnaissance aircraft, over the Kiel Bight. Ofhr. Russel volunteered to take off. He was vectored onto the enemy aircraft west of the Danish island of Laaland. What happened high above the sea will probably never be explained. Walter Windisch, who was present in the command post when the incident took place, reported:

> "Radio contact between Russel and Preusker was broken. Suddenly the signal from his IFF set, the FuG 25a, was also lost. Whatever the cause, Russel must have crashed into the sea west of the island."

Lt. Weber, Lt. Ambs and Uffz. Giefing took off from Briest on March 14 with orders to intercept enemy reconnaissance aircraft. Ambs described the action in a discussion with the author:

> "After about 20 minutes flying time we sighted two Mustangs flying on a westerly course. Lt. Weber opened fire too early. The Mustangs were alerted to our presence and took evasive action. We broke away to calm the enemy fighters and then attacked the formation from ahead. With a closing speed of about 1,400 kph I fired my cannon from perhaps 300 meters. The Mustang flying in the lead position exploded into a thousand pieces."

On March 15 the 8th Air Force sent a powerful force to attack Zossen and Oranienburg. JG 7 was only able to get a few aircraft into the air. As a result only four kills were claimed, two B-24s by Lt. Erich Müller and a B-17 each by Ofhr. Pfeiffer and Fhr. Windisch.

On March 16 *Major* Weissenberger, the *Kommodore* of the

Jagdgeschwader, achieved his first victory flying the Me 262. He destroyed a Mustang northwest of Eberswalde at 1414 while leading a *Schwarm* against enemy fighter-bombers.

Due to poor weather conditions, JG 7 was only able to send up a few fighters to intercept a major American incursion against Ruhland, Böhlen and Cottbus on March 17. The Me 262s shot down four B-17s, two by Uffz. Köster and one each by Oblt. Wegmann and Ofw. Göbel.

JG 7's greatest test came with a change in the weather over northwestern and central Germany. Beginning on March 18 the jet fighter *Geschwader* fought a running battle with the Anglo-American air forces, the reconstruction of which forms the central point of this book. JG 7 was almost constantly in action until its transfer out of the Berlin area. On it rested the only hope of the German supreme command, which now clung desperately to the idea that the Me 262 might yet bring about a decisive turn in the air war.

Minutes of discussions at Führer Headquarters and in the RLM from those days are somber. Production of 1,000 Me 262s per month was demanded as quickly as possible:

> "... while once again emphasizing its decisive importance to the war, every measure is to be employed to increase output and production levels in the short term."

Specifications for ultra-modern successors to the Me 262, which could have been ready at best by mid-1947, were sent to the aircraft industry: "twin-engined jet fighter, blind landing, blind firing capabilities, rearward-firing defensive armament with blind firing, 2 hours endurance at full thrust at 10 km altitude, maximum speed of 1,000 kph."

Hitler decreed, he demanded, he ordered; but he forgot that the fronts were already deep in Reich territory, that a large part of the nation's production capacity had already been overrun, that the transportation system had been destroyed and that production of fuel was at a standstill.

The enemy gave Germany no pause for breath. Raids were launched by day and night on a scale never before imagined. The armaments industry and other installations vital to the war had long since ceased to be the target. The Allied strategy was now to break the will to resist and morale of the defenseless civilian population and accelerate the unavoidable conclusion to the war in Europe.

With the collapse of the conventional air defense the jets of JG 7 – perhaps 60 aircraft – carried the main weight of the defensive battle in northwestern and central Germany. In view of the ratio of opposing forces of approximately 50:1 it was an unequal struggle whose outcome could never have been in doubt. In spite of being vastly outnumbered, JG 7 was able to establish a limited tactical superiority on several occasions and achieve considerable success.

One such occasion was March 18, 1945, when 1,329 bombers of the US 8th Air Force, escorted by 733 long-range fighters, launched the heaviest terror raid of the war against the German capital.

The first wave of the bomber stream was approaching the outskirts of Berlin when the jet fighters of the *Stabschwarm* and III. *Gruppe* took off on a mission which was to be one of the high points in the history of JG 7. After assembling into cohesive battle groups (rarely possible due to the circumstances under which the jet fighters operated), the Me 262s which had taken off from Brandenburg-Briest and Oranienburg intercepted the enemy formations over the Nauen-Rathenow-Brandenburg-Potsdam area at about 1100.

The first B-17 went down at 1109, followed by the second at 1110. The victor: Theodor Weissenberger. At about 1114 three further Flying Fortresses were downed by Ofw. Lübking, Lt. Rademacher and Lt. Sturm followed moments later by a P-51 by Oblt. Schall. The Americans lost their sixth heavy bomber at 1117, shot down by Weissenberger. Seven victories within eight minutes!

But this was not the end. At about 1120 the Me 262s of 9. *Staffel* joined the battle, and they were armed with a new weapon whose density of fire, ballistics, spread and destructive power made it probably the ideal offensive armament for the Me 262: the R4M air-to-air rocket.

The starting point for the development of this weapon was a request made by the units in early 1944 for new and improved weapons with which to effectively counter incursions by American bombers.

The *Technische Amt* reacted immediately. Following careful examination of various submissions and proposals it decided to guarantee the future effectiveness of the fighter defense by selecting four different weapons systems:

- improvements of existing automatic weapons
- long-range weapons (large-caliber cannon and rockets)
- short-range weapons (vertically-situated weapons with optical sighting)
- special weapons with high density of fire

In particular the responsible authorities placed great hopes in high-density special weapons suggested by front-line units or proposed by industry. In theory these offered small formations of fighters or even individual machines a reasonable possibility of engaging a numerically far superior enemy.

The idea was for the fighters to fly through the bomber stream equipped with batteries of launchers for simultaneous firing. By firing a large number of projectiles simultaneously with a certain dispersion of the individual rounds, a "lane of fire" would be laid down through the tight bomber formations which, given sufficient explosive force of the warheads, should result in the destruction of several bombers at once. This method of firing after the "watering can" principle also guaranteed the success of pilots less well-trained in gunnery techniques. The *Technische Amt* sought to realize the so-called "shotgun theory" by pursuing two separate paths of development: multi-barrelled weapons and small-caliber rockets. The design of multi-barrelled weapons (50 mm *Jägerfaust*, 5 barrels; 30 mm MK 103 SG 116 *Zellendusche*, 7 barrels; 30 mm MK 108 SG 117 *Rohrbatterie*, nine barrels; 20 mm *Schlitter* (project), 32 barrels, 20 mm *Harfe*, 40 barrels and 20 mm *Bürste*, 70 barrels) produced little in the way of tangible results before the war ended. Development of small-caliber rockets, on the other hand, progressed very successfully. The corresponding technical specification was issued by the RLM's Department Fl.-E6 in June 1944:

> "An offensive armament (R) is to be developed whose warhead contains a sufficient quantity of explosives to destroy a large bomber with one hit. Technical guidelines: maximum velocity approx. 500 m/sec with thrust duration of approx. 1 second and contact fuse with self-destruct after 1,500 meters at the earliest. Stabilization through folding fins, which in the closed position are to be no larger than the diameter of the rocket body. Electrical firing. Lug mounting for use of the rocket in rails. Simple construction suitable for mass production while avoiding critical materials. Launching equipment with adjusting mechanism for attachment beneath the wings or fuselage of the aircraft:
>
> (a) for one rocket each = single shot device
> (b) for several rockets side by side = rack
> (c) for several rockets bundled concentrically = honeycomb
>
> Relay circuit for (b) and (c) so as to ripple fire rockets for the purpose of avoiding the disruptive effect of one rocket on another."

In mid-July 1944 the companies which had accepted the invitation to tender formed a working group which divided developmental responsibilities as follows: Fuse: Rheinmetall, Sömmerda and DWM Research Facility Lübeck; warhead: DWM Lübeck; combustion chamber and nozzle: Tönshoff GmbH, Horn-Lippe, Spreewerk Kratzau, Sudetenland, Brünn Weapons Factory, Prague; propulsive charge: WASAG, Reinsdorf; folding fins: C. Ruhnke and O. Wirth, Berlin.

Four weeks later a proposal was completed under the centralized administration of DWM and submitted to the RLM. The joint plan proposed a rocket with a length of 814 mm and a total weight of 3,500 g. It was planned that eight blade fins, opened automatically by aerodynamic drag immediately after launching, would stabilize the rocket's flight path. The warhead, with a caliber of 55 mm, was to contain 520-530 g of HTA explosive which would be detonated by an AZR 2 impact fuse. In the combustion chamber the 815 gram propulsive charge, with a burn duration of approximately 0.8 seconds, developed a gas pressure of approximately 240 atm, which gave the rocket a maximum acceleration of about 540 m/sec/sec.

As far as tactical use was concerned, the air-to-air rocket was intended primarily for use against aerial targets up to a maximum range of 800 meters, particularly by jet aircraft whose speed relative to the target was so great, even in an attack from the rear, that the time available to fire the standard automatic weapons was insufficient to achieve the necessary number of hits. Successful use of the new weapon demanded a relatively accurate estimation of distance to target; if fired too soon the entire salvo would miss the target. In order to eliminate this uncertainty factor it was planned to develop an automatic firing mechanism which would employ electrical range measuring to fire the rockets at the precise moment that the most favorable range was reached (Oberon firing method).

Evaluation of the new weapon, which had received the designation R4M (*R*akete, *4*kg, *M*inenkopf), by the RLM was extremely positive, and a development contract was issued at once to DWM.

Initial firing tests to determine spread and stability took place in late October 1944 at the Strelna weapons range near Brünn. Test results were extremely promising. While only 62% of the test shots could be evaluated – many rockets failed to ignite, while abbreviated flight paths of a further 16% pointed to uneven burn durations or insufficient gas pressure – the stability of all the test rounds was outstanding and the spread minimal, only 5/1000 of range.

In early November the first stationary firings from a honeycomb launcher were made by at Osterode by the Heber Firm, which had been given the task of developing the launching equipment (in connection with the planned installation of an R4M battery in the Bachem *Natter*). A report by

E-Stelle Tarnowitz described the results:

> "The rockets functioned inadequately. Between 15 and 320 ms delay between firings. The folding fins tore off or only partially deployed and the rockets affected each other in flight."

At the end of November Department E 6 began testing the R4M at Rechlin:

> "Manufacturing defects were discovered on delivery: out of true tubes with unequal wall thicknesses, nozzles installed incorrectly with poor interior finish. The poor ballistics of the rockets test fired from the ten-meter rail are traceable to these defects. Several of the rockets with folding fins demonstrated inadequate fin strength and some were lost on the rail due to faulty spot welding." The first air firings of rockets with fixed and folding fins were carried out in mid-December. The Rechlin report stated: "30% of the lug spring bands came off during loading. Restraint of the folding fins must be improved. Four hits on target (vertical spread 12 m, lateral spread 7.5 m), some of the rockets were lost in flight."

Meanwhile, burnout trials conducted by DWM to test the R4M's self-destruct capability were initially unsatisfactory. Burnout times varied by as much as three seconds. In many cases the igniter failed to go off or the self-destruct charge burned out.

By the end of January the manufacturer had overcome most of the technical problems. A reworking of the design drawings eliminated the problems with the folding fins, and dependable and uniform detonation of the explosive charge was assured through initiating ignition with Nitropenta mixed with a desensitizing material.

At first the causes of the uneven ignition and burning of the propellant charge remained largely unknown; dozens of test series produced little useful new information. Nevertheless in early February the *Kommandeur der Erprobungstellen* ordered the delivery of test rounds for initial service trials with JGr 10. Based at Redlin, near Parchim, this unit's role consisted of testing and developing special weapons, including launchers, proposed by the units or offered by industry. A DWM report dated February 19, 1945 stated:

> "During the firing trials which were begun immediately at Redlin it was discovered that a considerable number of combustion chambers burst and warheads broke off."

A thorough investigation by a specialist commission sent by DWM found that the powder had not been mixed homogeneously. The accumulation of fast-burning elements at the moment of ignition resulted in considerable surface expansion which led to bursting of combustion chambers. The technicians were also able to explain the breaking off of the warheads: the threads for installation of the warhead were cut very eccentrically; as well the threads and the chamber axis were more or less inclined towards one another. The remaining supporting cross-section in the propulsion chamber was so thin that even fairly low gas pressures resulted in the warhead breaking off.

Finally, the commission also discovered the cause of the uneven burning of the propulsive charge: the propellent rods delivered by WASAG had been produced to different standards.

In spite of the chaotic conditions during the final weeks of the war the involved companies succeeded in an extraordinary effort in correcting the problems which had been identified. From then on there were no significant complaints about the rockets delivered to the front-line units from mid-March 1945 and fired in action.

In addition to the previously-mentioned problems the test firings at Redlin demonstrated that the launcher developed by the Heber Firm was unsuitable for general service use. According to Georg Christl, commander of JG 10, and Karl Kiefer, his technical officer:

> "It was clear to us that the design and building of a really suitable launcher by the company would have meant the loss of two months. As we had been notified that the first live ammunition would be arriving in early March, there was nothing left to do but improvise with what we had. Acting largely on the concept that this weapon was supposed to achieve a large-caliber shotgun effect, we finally decided on a rack with 12 rockets side by side. We completed the necessary drawings and had the first example built in a small joinery in Schwerin, using simple curtain rods for the guiding mechanism. After wiring up a rack we mounted it beneath the wing of a Fw 190, took cover as a precaution and ignited the rockets electrically. As hoped, the rounds slid smoothly from their rails. Our improvisation had worked perfectly. But not the rockets.
>
> "So much for flat trajectory and limited spread! The things smoked in wild curves around the entire area. We thought at first that the guide rails had been installed incorrectly, but soon found that firing all the rockets simultaneously produced strong vortices during the firing phase which decisively changed the flight paths of the rockets. We temporarily installed

the train release switch from an He 177 and ignited the rockets at intervals. But that was not the ideal solution. We discovered this several days later after using two relays, which on making contact launched six rockets each at two intervals."

The first problem-free launchings on March 15, 1945, led *Major* Christl to propose the R4M as a supplementary armament for the Me 262, as had been requested by *Major* Sinner, among others. Agreement was reached and a rack was installed beneath each wing of the Me 262 belonging to the technical officer of 9. *Staffel*, Lt. Schnörrer, at nearby Parchim. Sinner recalled:

"As we had no one qualified to make an assessment in questions of aerodynamics, we were forced to turn to the Messerschmitt Firm for advice. A few hours after my call to Augsburg, *Flugkapitän* Wendel appeared in an Me 262 and without further ado flight tested the converted machine. No negative changes in flying qualities were discovered, perhaps a minor loss of airspeed in the climb. Shortly afterwards Lt. Schnörrer carried out the first air firing test. This did not go quite as planned, as several rockets failed to leave their rails and burned out on the rack, fortunately without detonating the warheads. A second attempt, likewise by Schnörrer, went so smoothly and satisfactorily that the *Staffel* immediately began converting the other aircraft, and the necessary steps were initiated to convert the other *Staffeln* as well as I. *Gruppe*."

The new weapon received its baptism of fire on March 18, 1945: six aircraft of 9. *Staffel*, each with twenty-four R4M rockets beneath the wings, attacked enemy aircraft over Rathenow. The pilots were Lt. Schnörrer, Oblt. Seeler, Ofhr. Windisch, Fhr. Ehrig and Ofhr. Ullrich. Leading the formation was Oblt. Wegmann.

The impact of the rockets, which were launched from about 400 meters, was devastating. "Shattered fuselages, broken-off wings, ripped out engines, shards of aluminum and fragments of every size whirled through the air," stated one of the participating pilots, "it looked as if someone had emptied out an ashtray."

Things had happened so quickly that later none of the pilots could say with certainty how many kills he had scored. It is still not certain how many bombers actually blew apart in the rocket salvoes. According to credible statements by German pilots who took part in the action the total was between six and eight. In view of the uncertainty surrounding the event the kills were later credited, not to individual pilots, but to III. *Gruppe* as "air victories for Germany."[1]

The memory of the events following this memorable attack are burned indelibly into the consciousness of Günther Wegmann:

> "We had already been in the air for some time and our fuel was slowly running out. As our aircraft were still fully armed, however, we decided to make a second attack with cannon. Roughly over Glöwen I got a B-17 in my sights and opened fire. I saw flashes as shells struck the left wing of the enemy bomber, but at the same moment my aircraft was hit by return fire. The windscreen shattered, the equipment and instrument panels were wrecked. At the same time I felt a heavy blow against my right leg. I immediately broke off the attack and flew at high speed out of range of the enemy guns. When I felt along my leg with my hand I discovered a hole almost big enough to shove my fist through. Oddly enough I felt no pain. As my machine was still flyable in spite of the damage I decided to try to land at Parchim. I descended slowly, but at 4,000 meters flames suddenly shot from my right engine. The aircraft was now beyond saving. I jettisoned the canopy and bailed out. I came down near Wittenberge. One of the first people on the scene was a Red Cross sister, who skillfully bandaged my injured leg and stopped the heavy flow of blood."

Help had come too late, however; several hours later Wegmann's leg had to be amputated in hospital.

Though badly wounded, Oblt. Wegmann had once again escaped with his life. Not so lucky was his wingman, Oblt. Seeler, who was killed during this second battle. Like Wegmann he was hit by return fire from the bombers and went down with his machine 5 km southwest of Perleberg.

Farther north, at Kaltenkirchen, a disaster was occurring at this hour. The ceiling over the base was far below the 800 meters considered by Weissenberger to be the minimum necessary for jet takeoffs. Under these conditions a mission by pilots who were, for the most part, untrained in blind flying had to entail a considerable risk. Hans Grünberg recalled:

> "Although I had warned the commanding 2nd Jagddivision at Stade of the likely consequences, a short time later I got a call from Major Richter, the Ia, who related to me Göring's outburst on hearing the situation report from Stade: 'Make those simpletons get a move on, or I'll go down there personally and give them a boot to get them going'."

And so the order to take off was given at Kaltenkirchen. A *Schwarm* under the command of Oblt. Grünberg took off first. The fighters climbed through the first layer of cloud without incident and began to orbit. Then followed the second formation under Oblt. Stehle. After reaching an altitude of about 1,000 meters they too began circling as agreed upon. Then the third *Schwarm* – Oblt. Waldmann, Lt. Weihs, Ofhr. Schrey and *Flieger* Reiher – began its takeoff roll. Waldmann, Schrey and Weihs took off into the low cloud and climbed away. Left behind was Reiher's jet. The cause: engine failure during takeoff. As the three jets climbed through the dense cloud disaster struck: Lt. Weihs' "Yellow 5" rammed the aircraft of Oblt. Waldmann, who was flying in front of him. Both aircraft were so badly damaged that seconds later the pilots jettisoned their canopies and bailed out. Weihs landed safely in a field moments later. However for unknown reasons Waldmann failed to pull his rip cord. He fell to the ground near Schwarzenbeck, his parachute pack unopened. "Yellow 2" with Oblt. Schrey on board also failed to return from this fateful flight. The circumstances of his death are still unclear. It seems likely that he was jumped by waiting enemy fighters as he climbed through the highest layer of cloud. His body was found that evening near Eggenbüttel.

The balance on March 18, 1945: of 37 machines committed 28 reported engaging bombers and escort fighters of the US 8th Air Force, in the course of which the pilots claimed 13 enemy aircraft destroyed as well as six damaged and forced to drop out of their formations. According to a report by the Wehrmacht Operations Staff the fighters scored 13 confirmed and two probable victories.

The *Geschwader* lost three pilots killed and one badly wounded. Five machines sustained 99% damage and had to be written off; two others were damaged as a result of enemy action.

The day's operations once again confirmed that even a relatively small number of experienced Me 262 pilots could take on far superior enemy forces with acceptable losses, provided they were employed correctly. The conditions necessary for success were first recognition of the course and altitude of the enemy by the fighter control center, and second proper employment of the unit by the unit leader for an attack from the most favorable position. Should the formation break up while approaching the enemy, attacks by lone aircraft were much more dangerous and chances of success much less. "Reforming was almost always impossible," explained F.W. Schenk"

"As a rule there were many enemy fighters in the air, our fuel capacity was too limited and with the enormous speed of the Me 262 one quickly lost sight of his fellows. As well we had no navigation aids with which to reassemble."

For these reasons the first pass had to be "on the mark."

Although the *Geschwader* had reason to be proud of its success, it must be stated that the losses inflicted on the 8th Air Force by JG 7 did not even amount to 1% of the aircraft committed. It was a pinprick which the Americans could easily endure. Nevertheless the Commander-in-Chief of the US 8th Air Force, General Doolittle, for the first time showed serious concern over the growing threat to his bombers posed by German jet fighters. Two days later, on March 20, following a conference with Air Marshall Tedder, he ordered his bomber fleets to switch their targets to jet fighter production and assembly sites. He also ordered stronger fighter escorts for incursions into central and northern Germany and constant surveillance of suspected jet bases by reconnaissance aircraft and long-range fighters.

In the end JG 7's success of March 18, 1945 was to trigger an avalanche which only three weeks later, on April 10, was to bury the *Geschwader* beneath it.

March 19, 1945

During the late morning the German fighter controllers tracked a bomber stream 100 km long and 20 km wide as it crossed the front, which already lay deep inside Reich territory, and headed towards central Germany. They were powerless to do anything about the massive incursion. In many places the flak had already been withdrawn to support the steadily-retreating army units. For a long time the Allies had had nothing to fear from German piston-engined fighters. Missions over Germany proper had become almost pleasure flights for the Anglo-Americans. Only within JG 7's area of operations, when the warning call "blow jobs, seven o'clock high!" rang out in their earphones, were the bomber crews shown evidence that even with only a few weeks left in the war the German fighter arm had not been completely eliminated. So it was on March 19 when the first wave of the three American bomber divisions came within range of the jet fighters stationed around Berlin. III./JG 7 received the order to take off at about 1350. The unit's fighters came upon the American bombers in the Zwickau-Jena-Plauen area. Four Flying Fortresses were shot down in rapid succession by Ofw. Lennartz, Oblt. Schall, Ofw. Arnold and Lt. Schnörrer, who had provisionally taken over command of 9. *Staffel* after Wegmann was injured. Lt. Rademacher also increased his already impressive total of victories in the Me 262 by shooting down a Mustang. In addition at least three bombers were so badly damaged that they had to drop out of formation, one by Ofw. Reinhold.

But not all of the jets returned to their bases when the air battles were over. Ofw. Mattuschka was shot down and killed by Mustangs of the fighter escort over Eilenburg. Information on the death of Harry Mayer is contradictory. Official documents note in relation to the loss of Werk-Nr. 111 545: crashed near Brandenburg following aerial combat. However a fellow *Staffel* member alleges that Mayer's aircraft crashed after takeoff from Briest, when the trim spindle broke and the aircraft pitched forward into a vertical dive.

Elements of I. *Gruppe* from Kaltenkirchen attacked the withdrawing armada at about 1500. Gefr. Heim reported the certain destruction of a B-17, while Uffz. König claimed to have probably destroyed another Flying Fortress.

American claims of three Me 262s shot down by their fighters are close to the losses reported in German documents, which show two pilots killed, two aircraft destroyed and two damaged.

March 20, 1945

Following a long period of waiting at cockpit readiness, the pilots of JG 7 in the Berlin area and at Kaltenkirchen had resigned themselves to an uneventful day, when at roughly 1530 strong American forces were reported approaching Hamburg. The takeoff order for the battle-ready machines of I. and III. *Gruppen* was issued shortly before 1600. Twenty-two jet fighters got airborne. They came upon approximately 400 B-17s and B-24s of the 8th Air Force northwest of Hamburg at an altitude of 8,000 meters. The bombers were on their way to attack the hydrogenation plant at Hemmingstedt. The Me 262s used their superior speed to break through the fighter screen in a shallow dive. One member of 9. *Staffel*, Fhr. Ehrig, distinguished himself in this action, shooting down two Flying Fortresses and a Liberator in a single pass. Other B-17s were claimed shot down by Oblt. Sturm, Fhr. Pfeiffer, Fj.Ofw. Heiser, Fhr. Christer and Fw. Pritzl.[2] Ofw. Buchner damaged another Fortress. These claims (9 heavy bombers destroyed) are considerably higher than the actual American losses (four B-17s, one B-24, two P-51s) in the area in question. In evaluating the German claims it must be remembered that it was not always possible to determine with certainty the damage inflicted during the high-speed attacks by the jets. In addition there may have been a number of double claims on this day.

The US 8th Air Force avenged these losses with the destruction of three Me 262s. Ofhr. Gehlker was shot down and killed by defensive fire from the bombers over Bad Segeburg. Uffz. Mehn was pursued into the Kaltenkirchen area by Mustangs after breaking off the engagement and was shot down as he approached to land. Ofw. Büttner escaped with only minor injuries after bailing out of his blazing Messerschmitt over Kiel-Holtenau after being shot up by Mustangs.

In the three days from March 18-20, 1945, JG 7 flew 111 sorties. In spite of initial fears on the part of the *Geschwader* command, the high operational ready rate which had been achieved by the unit, especially by III. *Gruppe*, was not adversely affected. The assembly operation at Briest was functioning relatively well and deliveries of new machines to the *Staffeln* were running smoothly.

The ground crews who serviced the aircraft and the men of the workshop platoons are deserving of the highest praise. In spite of the intermittent deliveries of replacement parts and engines, they repaired battle damage, fixed unserviceable engines and corrected general technical faults in aircraft and equipment amazingly quickly. Following a visit to Brandenburg-Briest on 20.3.1945, a commission of the Messerschmitt field technical service found that:

"Discussions with the Geschwader Technical Officer, Hptm. Streicher, and the Gruppen Technical Officer, Oberinspektor Grote, as well as inspection of the fault reports and daily serviceability reports of the 8-262, revealed the following condition:

45 machinesof these	80-85% combat ready
Unserviceable less than	48 hours:
Engine faults	34%
Undercarriage faults	35%
Control surface change	5%
Nosewheel change	5%
Wing change	4%
Ground and radio	3%
Test flights	10%

Aircraft losses or partial losses:
The last 14 aircraft losses or partial losses reveal the following picture:

Engine trouble	40%

Incorrect handling, loss of orientation	20%
Undercarriage faults	20%
Obstructions on takeoff and landing	15%
Tire problems	5%

> The pilots must definitely receive more training and instruction on the type, especially in the cockpit of the aircraft."

Given the existing circumstances this recommendation, which in many cases was a reasonable one, could simply not be carried out on the necessary scale. The pilots, especially those who had been sent directly from a piston-engined fighter unit to JG 7 without spending any time with the *Ergänzungsgruppe*, were faced with an almost impossible task: their leaders expected them to achieve impressive and decisive results flying the fastest, most heavily-armed fighter of the Second World War, but failed to provide them with the basic requirements, namely thorough flight, weapons and tactical training. Therefore the results inevitably lagged far behind the potential in spite of the determination of the pilots.

F.W. Schenk, formerly of 10./JG 7, commented on these problems as follows:

> "In such a thrown-together group, as JG 7 was, the pilots truly faced nearly impossible tasks. They didn't know the aircraft, the enemy, his tactics, our own tactics or the very refined Reich Defense system – and what was more, they were almost all insufficiently trained, they couldn't fly on instruments or fly 'blind,' as bad weather approach and navigation was also called, and yet they had to be able to fly. Here lay the great calamity of JG 7 and that of the many 'missed' victories."

Since its formation in February III. *Gruppe* had largely been able to maintain its authorized personnel and equipment strength of 36 pilots and aircraft, plus the pilots and aircraft of the *Geschwaderstab*. On the other hand I. *Gruppe* at Kaltenkirchen, with a total of about 25 Me 262s on hand, was still not fully equipped.

The achieving of full operational status by the unit was held up primarily for three reasons:

– inadequate output by the Briest assembly facility,

– priority in deliveries to III. *Gruppe*,
– formation of JV 44 at the expense of I./JG 7.

Efforts by the *Geschwader* and *Gruppe* commands to achieve full operational readiness did not bear fruit until early April 1945. Following the delivery of several machines from southern Germany, the departure of JV 44 from Briest and the completion of the transfer of I. *Gruppe* into the Berlin area, the number of aircraft on strength with the *Gruppe* climbed to 33, nearly reaching the authorized strength of 36 Me 262s.

The formation of II./JG 7 was totally delayed. Orders for its formation were issued on January 12, 1945, but the *Gruppe* did not officially come into being until four weeks later, on February 12, 1945, "On authority of the *General der Jagdflieger* II./JG 7 (formerly IV./JG 54) is to reequip with the Me 262." The retraining of II. *Gruppe* under its new commander, *Major* Hermann Staiger, began at the end of February 1945 with theoretical instruction at Landsberg, which was followed on March 15 by the commencement of practical training at Lechfeld. The first group of pilots completed conversion training in early April 1945. They were transferred to Brandenburg-Briest, where II. *Gruppe* was to be equipped from the assembly facility located there. Formation of the *Gruppe* never got past the initial stages for well-known reasons. The few machines assigned to the new unit flew into the Protectorate as part of the withdrawal by the *Geschwader*, where they were finally incorporated into I. and III. *Gruppen* (2). Of the remaining pilots undergoing conversion training at Lechfeld, those whose level of training sufficed were likewise transferred to the Prague area from April 15/16 to reinforce JG 7. Those pilots whose training was not yet complete withdrew to Mühldorf when the Americans approached Lechfeld and subsequently went into captivity with the fragmented elements of JG 7 in southern Germany.

March 21, 1945

"From the south 600 bombers in two groups against Vienna, Bruck, Villach, Graz and the Bavarian-Swabian area, where airfields were hit hard . . . From the west 1,100 American bombers against the ground organization in northwestern Germany: five of 15 airfields knocked out. Some of the bombers against central Germany (Plauen, Chemnitz). Further 150 British bombers against Bremen harbor, others against Münster. In the west 500 twin-engine bombers and 1,900 fighters."

This extract from the OKW situation log clearly illustrates the hopeless situation in which the bloodied German fighter arm nevertheless continued to fight with the courage of desperation. Conventional fighters rarely got through to the bomber formations any more; the Bf 109s and Fw 190s usually suffered catastrophic losses before they got anywhere near the bombers.

Only the jet fighters of JG 7 could hold their own in spite of the extreme numerical superiority of the Allies, who on this day suffered their heaviest losses at the hands of the German jet fighters so far: no fewer than 13 four-engined bombers and a fighter were destroyed in a total of 25 contacts with the enemy.

Aircraft of the *Geschwaderstab*, of 11. *Staffel* from Briest and of 9. and 10. *Staffeln* participated in the air battle over the Leipzig-Dresden-Chemnitz area. The two latter units had moved to Parchim the day before following repeated fighter-bomber attacks on their base at Oranienburg.

At about 0915 the Me 262s, attacking in *Staffel* wedge formation, struck the bomber stream from out of a thin layer of mist. The sudden appearance of the jet fighters took the fighter escort completely by surprise. An original combat report kept by Fritz R. G. Müller illustrates how the experienced Me 262 pilots cleverly exploited any tactical advantage offered by the battle situation:

> "I saw the bomber stream northwest of Dresden flying on an easterly course at 7,500 meters, and about 10 km to the south a Boeing with four Mustangs as escort on the same course at the same altitude. I immediately attacked the Boeing from a slightly higher altitude from behind and to the left. I fired a short burst at a range of 300-150 meters and observed about ten hits in the fuselage and left wing. The left wing immediately broke off and the Boeing went into a steep spin. After diving vertically for 2,000 meters the burning bomber disintegrated. I was unable to observe the impact as I had to get away from the four pursuing Mustangs."

The escorting fighters tried desperately to screen their charges from the Me 262s, but they could not prevent bomber after bomber from being shot down by the determined attacks of the jets. *Major* Weissenberger, *Major* Ehrler, Fhr. Pfeiffer, Lt. Schnörrer and Ofw. Arnold each reported the destruction of a B-17 on their return, while Oblt. Schall claimed a P-51 destroyed. The *Schwarm* under the command of Lt. Weber had a very successful but at the same time tragic mission. Alfred Ambs and Ernst Giefing recreated the events of that day in the summer of 1981:

"There were four Me 262s in a *Kette* left formation, Lt. Weber, Lt. Ambs, Uffz. Giefing and a fourth pilot. We were directed onto the bombers from behind and to the left by Lt. Preusker at an altitude of about 6,000 meters. When Lt. Weber gave the order to open fire we were already taking a lot of defensive fire."

Alfred Ambs recalled:

"I had the last B-17 full in my sights when I loosed off a short burst. The B-17 exploded in a tremendous fireball and ripped apart two other Boeings flying in its immediate vicinity. I had never seen such an explosion. Lt. Weber was unable to take evasive action and flew straight into the fireball. Terrified, I pulled up and to the left. Giefing swept past beneath me and then pulled up as well. Then we flew a second attack. I watched as Giefing shot down two Boeings one right after the other. I myself took a hit in the fuel tank and my radio failed. Below me was a town where major roads converged, then an airfield on which stood Bf 109s and Fw 190s. However, as I approached I was met by heavy friendly anti-aircraft fire. I overshot, retracted the undercarriage and after reversing direction in a steep turn belly-landed at Cottbus with my last drops of fuel. During the attack Giefing was hit in the left foot and his electrical system and engines failed. He was forced to make an emergency landing in rough terrain near Grossenhain, in which the machine was totally written off.

"That evening, after receiving medical attention, we were flown back to Brandenburg in a Siebel 204. *Oberst* Rudel, who had witnessed some of the air battle from the ground and seen the crashing enemy machines, had already sent a wire congratulating us on a total of seven B-17 kills."

JG 7 suffered one other loss in addition to Lt. Weber. Uffz. Kolbe of 10./JG 7 was hit by return fire from the bombers and crashed near Tharandt. About two hours later aircraft of I. *Gruppe* attacked the withdrawing formations. Lt. Weihs and Gefr. Heim scored two further confirmed kills over B-17s, while Uffz. König claimed a P-47 probably shot down.

According to American sources the US 8th Air Force lost only eight B-17s and ten P-51s that day and the 9th Air Force a number of P-47s. At the same time they claim the destruction of nine Me 262s by the escort fighters. These claims are contradicted by an original III./JG 7 document from March 21, 1945: "Own aircraft destroyed: 2; damaged: 2; own personnel killed: 2; wounded: 2."

On many days the German victory claims and Allied loss figures were conspicuously disproportionate, which in the past has often led to unqualified statements from both camps. From the American view many losses were sudden and unheralded. A solitary diving attack at 900 kph in hazy weather or dense cloud often went unnoticed by the enemy, especially by fighters, and the resulting loss of an aircraft was attributed to ground fire, premature detonation of the aircraft's bombload, mid-air collision or unexplained causes. On the other hand, victory claims by German pilots were no longer subjected to the lengthy confirmation process through channels as had been the practice earlier in the war. This involved finding the wreck, obtaining statements from air or ground witnesses, meetings of the victory commission, etc. It can therefore be assumed with a high degree of probability that there were a number of double claims among the victory reports which were submitted in good faith. Sorting out who actually scored the kills, which would have been confirmed under normal circumstances, is no longer possible.

German fighter pilots have always tried to report their victories as accurately as possible. Discrepancies between claims made immediately after an action and the actual losses suffered by the enemy can no longer be explained and under the circumstances must be accepted as unavoidable.

For these reasons, in spite of careful research it will never be possible to determine the exact number of enemy aircraft shot down by the jet units.

March 22, 1945

Operations by the Allied air forces on March 22 were dedicated primarily to the tactical support of army units: attacking in waves, approximately 800 twin-engined bombers of the US 9th Air Force and about 900 fighter-bombers smashed the thin lines and the hastily-constructed defensive system which Army Group B had thrown up east of the Rhine against enemy forces advancing out of the Remagen bridgehead. 1,331 bombers of the 8th Air Force attacked transportation centers, military installations and airfields in the Rhein-Main area which bordered the combat zone. As per a directive issued by Doolittle, jet bases within the attack area were considered prime targets. The precision with which the bombardiers in the B-17s and B-24s carried out their assignment is revealed in the damage reports submitted by the base commanders at Giebelstadt and Kitzingen: "Attack Giebelstadt 1331-1338 hours. In the dispersals:

79 Silver (Me 262), 2 Ju 88, 4 Bf 109, 1 Arado 96, 2,500 450 kg bombs. Damage to aircraft: 1 Ju 88 95%, 1 Ju 88 90%, 1 Silver 90%, 1 Silver 80%, 1 Silver 60%, 2 Silver 15%, 3 Silver 5%, 3 Silver 3%, 1 Bf 109 10%, 1 Bf 109 5%. Other damage: 2 soldiers killed, 7 soldiers wounded. 1,000 craters in landing area, 200 craters in runway. Field lighting knocked out. Airfield unserviceable. Expected restoration of airfield: 30. 3. 45."

Kitzingen looked much the same:

"Attack 1334-1355 hours. Damage to aircraft: 1 Ju 88 100%, 1 Fw 58 100%, 3 Silver 70%, 1 Silver 50%, 1 He 111 35%, 1 Ju 88 25%, 2 Ju 88 15%, 4 Silver 7%. Other damage: 8 killed, 25 wounded, 1 missing. 1,194 craters in landing field, 150 craters in runway, 184 craters in taxiways. Heavy damage to buildings. Restoration of landing field and taxiways about 14 days. Restoration of runway about 8 days."

The day was in sight when JG 7's bases too would be blasted by a hail of bombs.

Industrial areas in Austria and central Germany were the targets for about 700 heavy bombers of the US 15th Air Force. Elements of the air fleet were directed against the Ruhland hydrogenation plant near Dresden. Conventional fighters as well as the Me 262s of III./JG 7 rose to defend the facility. The jets intercepted the bombers in the Cottbus-Bautzen-Dresden area as they flew in from the south at about 7,000 meters.

Luftwaffe Operations Staff documents show 27 jet fighters in action that day, which all found the bombers thanks to the excellent work of fighter controller Preusker. The Parchim *Staffel* played a leading role in the overall success. Six B-17s were shot down by Lt. Schnörrer, Knight's Cross wearer Ofhr. Petermann, who flew with an artificial arm, Fhr. Windisch, Fhr. Pfeiffer, Ofw. Lennartz and Ofw. Buchner. A P-51 was also destroyed by Oblt. Schall. Pilots of 11. *Staffel* and the *Stabsschwarm* also contributed to the impressive total: Lt. Ambs, Ofw. Arnold, Uffz. Köster, *Major* Ehrler and *Major* Weissenberger each claimed a B-17 destroyed, while Lt. Lehner claimed a P-51 as a probable.

The Germans lost three pilots killed in this action: Fw. Eichner near Altdöbern, the experienced former *Eismeerjäger*[3] Ofw. Lübking, and a third whose name is unknown. A member of the *Staffel* witnessed the loss of Lübking:

"Ofw. Lübking was in the first group of an Me 262 formation which made contact with a formation of Fortresses north of Leipzig. During the course of the battle he shot down a Boeing and pulled up over it at high speed. At that instant the B-17 exploded, taking Lübking down with it. Later they found the wreckage of the Boeing, the Me 262 and Lübking's paybook."

It is believed that Lt. Herbert Schlüter of 11./JG 7 also destroyed a B-17 that day. Schlüter had been transferred to JG 7 from I./JG 300 in November 1944. He converted to the jet fighter at Unterschlauersbach; however, on graduation he was not sent to an operational *Gruppe* but was detached for duty as an Me 262 acceptance test pilot. In early January 1945 he and three other pilots, Georg Seip, Eberhard Gzik and Hanns Gross, were ordered to report to *Major* Gerhard Stamp at Rechlin. Stamp formed an Me 262 test detachment there, which as far as personnel and supply was concerned was under the command of JG 7. The purpose of the detachment was to investigate the potential for attacking massed bomber formations with air-dropped weapons. In Stamp's opinion bomber formations could better be broken up by dropping large-caliber bombs, incendiary bombs, 50 mm mines, etc. than through attacks with cannon or small rockets. The *Major* was unable to prove the validity of his theory, however, as the realization of his plans foundered on the absence of usable acoustic or barometric fuses. As well, the GPV-1 sight (*Gegner-Pfeil-Visier* with manual lead predictor) intended for installation in the Me 262 existed only in prototype form. The detachment was disbanded in mid-March 1945 as a result and the pilots incorporated into the *Jagdgruppen* of JG 7.

The question must therefore remain open as to whether the "bombs against bombers" concept would ever have achieved the results expected by Stamp, namely the breaking up of bomber formations, even if all the technical requirements had been met.

Similar methods had been investigated in 1943 by JG 11 and *Erprobungskommando* 25; following a brief period of surprising success they were terminated on Milch's recommendation because of limited probability of success.

JG 7's success against enemy bombers – 50 four-engined bombers had been destroyed since March 18 – led Hitler to speak words of praise for the jet fighter unit's actions during the evening situation briefing at Führer Headquarters. According to a document from Speer's department:

"The Führer is extremely pleased over the success of the 262 against

Handover of the first production aircraft to the Luftwaffe in April 1944. On the left is trials officer Gerd Caroli.

Bottom left: Hptm. Werner Thierfelder, commander of the Me 262 Test Detachment at Lechfeld. August 1943.

Bottom right: Three founding members of Jagdgeschwader 7. Fw. Erwin Eichhorn (with fire extinguisher) and Fw. Helmut Lennartz (right) in front of the Me 262 V8, the first aircraft assigned to E-Kdo Lechfeld. April 1944.

Following Hitler's decision on May 25, 1945, to employ the Me 262 as a bomber, the Kommando was left with only a small number of aircraft with which to carry out its testing program.

Production of a special fuel for jet engines began in January 1944 at the Leuna plants in Merseburg. About 1,000 tons of an interim fuel, consisting of 97% unleaded B4 and 3% lubricating oil and designated J1, was produced from about mid-April 1944. This was replaced by the actual jet fuel, J2. From mid-March 1945 this was increasingly supplemented by lower-grade J3 fuel, which led to frequent in-flight engine failures.

Pilots of
Erprobungskommando
Lechfeld in the
summer of 1944. From
left: Fhr. Kaser, Fw.
Eichhorn, Fw.
Lennartz, Fw. Oppers
(ILO).

Ofhr. Neuhaus,
transferred from II./ZG
26 to E-Kdo. Lechfeld
(2nd from left), and
Hptm. Thierfelder (on
the shoulders of his
comrades). This photo
was taken at Kharkov
in the summer of 1942.

From left: unidentified,
Lt. Schreiber (on the
telephone), Lt. Weber,
Fw. Puttkammer (radio
operator).

From left: Lt. Schreiber, Ofw. Recker, Junkers mechanic Peter, unidentified, Fw. Lennartz.

Fw. Paul Ziesch (radio operator), Lt. H.G. Müller and Lt. Weber.

Lt. Alfred "Bubi" Schreiber. He scored the first victory in the Me 262, probably on July 26, 1944, shooting down a Mosquito over the foothills of the Alps.

Bottom right: Karl Kiefer, technical officer of Erprobungskommando Lechfeld and of JG 10. He was deeply involved in the development of the R4M air-to-air rocket.

The Royal Air Force's wonder bomber, the de Havilland Mosquito. Virtually invulnerable to attack by conventional German fighters, it was the preferred target for the jet fighters between July and September 1944.

The Flying Fortress — the Boeing B-17. On August 15, 1944 Helmut Lennartz shot down the first Flying Fortress to fall to the guns of an Me 262. On Hitler's order they became the Me 262's primary target from January 1945.

The aftermath of an American daylight raid on the Messerschmitt factories on July 21, 1944. Above: Regensburg. Below: Augsburg.

With the intensification of the Anglo-American bombing offensive against the German aircraft industry, the assembly of major components was increasingly transferred to well-camouflaged forest sites.

A truly gigantic project. All Me 262 production in southern Germany was to have take place in this bunker near Landsberg am Lech. Begun in March 1944, the project was still incomplete when the war ended. The facility was to have produced about 900 jet fighters per month.

*Above: An Me 262 of
Erprobungskommando Nowotny.
Taken at Achmer, this is the only
photograph of an aircraft of this unit
discovered so far by the author.*

*Center left: Major Walter Nowotny,
recipient of the highest decorations for
bravery and commander of the first
Me 262 fighter unit. This is probably
the last photo of the Major, taken only
days before his death.*

*Center right: Funeral ceremonies in
the Wiener Hofburg in honor of
Walter Nowotny, killed November 8,
1944.*

*Bottom: A memorial at the spot where
Nowotny's aircraft crashed, near
Bramsche.*

Most publications identify the aircraft in these photographs as belonging to
Kommando Nowotny. In fact the instructional film from which they are taken was
shot at Lechfeld, and the aircraft belong to III./EJG 2. According to Messerschmitt
documents, Werknummer 110 813 was completed at Leipheim in the first week of
December 1944.

Due to a shortage of two-seaters, III./EJG 2, the jet pilot replacement training unit,
employed standard single-seat fighters as training aircraft.

One of the Me 262 B-1a trainers captured and test flown by the Americans. Limited numbers of this variant were delivered to the training units beginning at the end of November 1944.

Two views of the rear cockpit of an Me 262 B.

Lechfeld, November 1944. From left: Major Georg-Peter Eder, Major Hohagen, first Kommandeur of III./JG 7, Major Andres, Kommandeur of III./EJG 2, Oberst Trautloft and Oberst Wörner, director of Me 262 conversion training with III./EJG 2.

Hptm. Theodor Weissenberger, Kommodore of JG 7 from January 1945.

bombers and envisages a version of this machine with strengthened armament (50 mm, two 37 mm and R4M) making a decisive contribution to the war effort. He has ordered that maximum output must be assured in the short term no matter what the consequences and in the armaments field he expects the new units to be totally equipped as soon as possible."

March 23, 1945

Heavy bombers of the American 15th Air Force once again attacked refineries at Ruhland, where production of fuel ceased completely following this double blow. The Luftwaffe had little with which to counter the American incursion. Nothing is known of operations by conventional fighters, but JG 7 put only a handful of machines into the air. A Luftwaffe Command Staff document reveals that only 14 jet fighters saw action, claiming two confirmed and one probable victories during the course of eleven combats over Chemnitz. *Major* Ehrler was credited with two B-24s destroyed and Ofw. Reinhold a B-17 probably destroyed.

American sources confirm these claims, revealing the loss of three bombers to attacking Me 262s in the area of operations in question.

March 24, 1945

The American air forces continued their bombing offensive against the ground organization of the Luftwaffe and jet aircraft assembly sites begun three days before, committing all available forces. During the morning 1,033 heavy bombers of the 8th Air Force laid waste to fourteen airfields in western Germany and five more in the northwestern part of the country. Approximately 400 Liberators and Flying Fortresses of the 15th Air Force attacked targets in Bavaria, including München-Riem and the jet bases at Neuberg, Plattling and Erding. Elements of this air fleet had separated from the main bomber stream over the Alpine foothills and set course for central Germany. Radar stations followed the path of the approximately 250 heavy bombers as they flew over Nuremburg, Bayreuth and Plauen. It became increasingly clear that their target was the Reich capital. 11. *Staffel* and the *Stabsschwarm* were ordered to take off shortly before 1100. Vectored onto the bomber formations approaching from the south by Lt. Preusker, the 16 jets met the enemy over the Dessau area. The Americans lost a number of aircraft (in total 9 B-17s, 1 B-24 and 1 P-51) but gained a measure of revenge by shooting down three Me 262s. All three pilots were wounded and saw no further action. The Americans could get over their losses with a regretful shrug of the shoulders, but not the Germans. Their personnel losses were gradually assuming threatening proportions. Jet fighters could be replaced – 248 machines were completed in March and even in April 1945 decentralized operations were able to assemble 101 Me 262s – but well-trained and experienced jet pilots could not.

Those wounded that day were Oblt. Külp, Oblt. Wörner and Lt. Ambs, pilots with dozens of flights in jet aircraft. For Ambs the action had begun very successfully. He made his approach from a favorable tactical position from below. He easily broke through the fighter screen of Mustangs and opened fire on the leading machine of the lowest formation from about 150 meters. The Boeing showed the effects of Amb's fire immediately and spun away on fire:

> "I climbed and opened fire on one of the machines of the nearest formation from below. I observed hits in the left wing, which broke off shortly afterward. Then I pushed forward on the stick and attacked a third Fortress from a condensation trail. At first I aimed at the rear gunner then at the left wing root. Seconds later the wing separated from the aircraft. As I flew away from the bomber stream phosphorous shells suddenly struck my cockpit. My oxygen mask was riddled and splinters struck my face. I jettisoned the canopy and pulled up the nose of my Me 262 to lose speed. I bailed out at approximately 350 kph at an altitude of about 6,000 meters. I came down in a wood near Wittenberg. Branches shattered my kneecap and as well I tore the ligaments in my knee."

During the air battle Ofw. Arnold and *Major* Ehrler each shot down a heavy bomber, while Lt. Lehner and Lt. Rademacher claimed probables.

At about 1200 9. and 10. *Staffeln* from Parchim joined the battle. South of Berlin about 15 Me 262s, most of them armed with R4M rockets, met the waves of bombers as they advanced on a broad front toward the Reich capital. Bombers were destroyed by Oblt. Külp, Lt. Sturm, Oblt. Schall, Ofw. Pritzl and Ofw. Buchner. Oblt. Külp's "Yellow 5" was attacked by Mustangs, sustaining severe damage. The wounded *Oberleutnant* bailed out. "Yellow 6," the Me 262 flown by Oblt. Wörner, was also hit by enemy fire and set ablaze. Wörner, who only moments earlier had damaged an enemy bomber forcing it to drop out of formation, had to abandon his aircraft.

There is some uncertainty as to the date of a success scored by Oblt. Schuck and his wingman, but it occurred on or near March 24. Near

Neumünster they spotted a trio of enemy aircraft on a reconnaissance mission, a P-38 escorted by two Mustangs. While his wingman was able to dispatch the Lightning quickly, Schuck was forced to call upon all his skill as a fighter pilot to get his sights on the two Mustangs. They twisted and turned wildly and repeatedly avoided his attacks. Finally the first Mustang flew in front of his guns. The explosive rounds literally blew the fighter to pieces. The second Mustang tried to escape by diving. Schuck's cannon shells blew off the aircraft's right wing and the Mustang went down vertically trailing a long banner of smoke.

March 25, 1945

"At 0946 I took off to intercept major incursions reported in the Uelzen-Hamburg area. West of Uelzen I spotted the bomber stream flying north in the direction of Lüneburg at an altitude of 7,000 meters. Approaching from the south, I attacked a formation of fourteen Liberators shortly before they dropped their bombs on Lüneburg. At 1025 I opened fire on the aircraft flying on the extreme right side of the formation from a range of 350 to 250 meters and observed several hits on the fuselage and wing center section. Large pieces flew away. The Liberator began to burn fiercely and went into a spin. I was unable to observe the crash or the crew bailing out as I was hit right away and my left engine caught fire. I was forced to withdraw from the bomber stream flying on one engine. I landed at Stendal where I collided with a Ju 88 in Hangar 5."

This combat report by Lt. Fritz R.G. Müller, who has retained the original, is representative of JG 7's sorties against approximately 250 bombers of the 8th Air Force which, guarded by five fighter groups, attacked fuel storage installations in the Braunschweig, Hamburg and Lauenburg area. The air battles on March 25 were unusually costly for JG 7; according to an entry in the OKW's situation log the *Jagdgeschwader* scored seven kills but lost five of its own fighters. The reason for the high losses was probably the fact that the fighters, which took off at intervals from Parchim and Briest, were unable to form up into a cohesive striking force. Their attacks were made singly or in pairs and were widely scattered. The element of surprise, which usually unsettled the enemy and caused considerable confusion, was thus lost and the jet fighters encountered a well-organized defense.

Official documents, entries in flight logs, private notes and personal recollections by German pilots, as well as operational reports from the other side allow us to reconstruct the course of events with few gaps:

0800 hours. First reports of large enemy formations assembling over southern England reach the command posts.

0840 hours. The bombers cross the English Channel and the North Sea.

0855 hours. Radar stations determine that the majority of the enemy aircraft have turned back.

0915 hours. Direction of flight of remaining formations points toward northern Germany. JG 7 ordered to readiness. Kaltenkirchen reports "qbi" (4) at the airfield.

0930 hours. Enemy fighters in Hildesheim, Hannover and Soltau areas.

0940 hours. Scramble from Briest and Parchim.

0955 hours. First total loss by JG 7. Lt. F.W. Schenk is an eyewitness: "I don't know what number Lt. von Rettburg was to take off. The takeoff appeared to be completely normal, but just before he lifted off a concentrated flame was visible right behind his starboard engine. The engine was on fire. Von Rettburg had reached an altitude of 50 meters when his aircraft tilted slowly to the right, almost into a vertical bank. He lost altitude and the aircraft crashed and burned."

1010 hours. Lt. Preusker notes the first victories. Oblt. Schall and Lt. Schnörrer each report the destruction of a Mustang.

1020 hours. Near Lauenburg Lt. Rademacher attacks a B-24 and forces it to leave formation.

1025 hours. Lt. Fritz R.G. Müller shoots down a B-24 near Lüneburg.

1030 hours. Next victory and second total loss. Fw. Taube lost contact with the rest of his *Schwarm* after takeoff and attacked a Liberator over Rheinsehlen alone. The bomber's left wing caught fire and separated from the aircraft. Taube survived the destruction of the enemy bomber by only a few minutes. About a dozen Mustangs had sighted the Me 262 as it approached. They fanned out and dived on the jet from a higher altitude.

There was no escape. The Me 262 was hit in the fuel tank and blew up in a tremendous explosion.

1045 hours. Ofw. Buchner shoots down a Liberator south of Hamburg at 6,500 meters.

1050 hours. Ogfr. Windisch and his wingman Ofhr. Ullrich shoot down two further heavy bombers, but have to fend off heavy attacks by enemy fighters which shower their aircraft with a veritable hail of bullets. Windisch recalled: "After landing my aircraft looked like a sieve. We counted over thirty hits." Using their superior speed the Me 262s disengaged from the enemy and set course for home. The Mustangs were not shaken off, however, and stayed within sight of the Germans. Their chance came when the jet fighters descended for a landing and were forced to reduce speed. Flying in the lead position, Windisch managed to reach the flak corridor ahead of the hotly-pursuing Mustangs and landed unmolested. But not Ullrich. He became a victim of the Allied tactic of 'rat catching,' intercepting the jet aircraft immediately after takeoff or prior to landing. The Me 262 was raked by machine-gun fire at an altitude of about 250 meters. Ullrich's leap from the burning machine led to his death, as the altitude was too low for his parachute to deploy.

1100 hours. Oblt. Schätzle and his unidentified wingman are probably the last pilots to join the air battles that morning. They encounter a well-prepared fighter defense, which holds them at bay far from the bomber stream. Their fuel running low, the *Rotte* is finally forced to break off the action. As fighter-bombers are reported in the vicinity of Parchim the pair heads for Rechlin-Lärz airfield, farther to the east. There the events at Parchim are repeated. Like Ullrich, Schätzle is jumped and shot down by enemy fighters while approaching to land.

Still unexplained are five further total losses mentioned in official documents. Also unknown is the identity of the pilot who, according to an English document, inflicted serious damage on a Mosquito near Peenemünde. The aircraft was then hit several times by ground fire and had to make a forced landing. The crew was allegedly later taken to Parchim and interrogated there.

The date of the destruction of a B-24 near Perleberg by Uffz. Schöppler is likewise uncertain; it may have taken place on March 15 rather than March 25.

March 26-29, 1945

A low-pressure area passing over central Europe brought extensive rain, seriously hampering operations by the American air fleets during the final days of March. The American 8th and 9th Air Forces sent only about 300 bombers on missions against targets in southern and central Germany.

On March 27 weather conditions forced the US bomber units to call off all tactical and strategic operations. There was no respite for the long-suffering German population, however. Hundreds of American fighter-bomber patrols made even the smallest corner of the unoccupied Reich unsafe. They fired at trains and vehicles and shot at refugee columns, cyclists, pedestrians and playing children. The last traces of any moral objections to this manner of conducting warfare had long ago been tossed overboard.

The British did not let the poor weather keep their bombers from attacking targets in Germany. Escorted by three American fighter groups, about 500 RAF bombers attacked Paderborn, where precision bombing inflicted heavy personnel losses and material damage.

A tank farm near Bremen was the target for about 180 British bombers. They were intercepted by several Me 262s of the Kaltenkirchen *Gruppe* under the command of *Major* Rudorffer as well as a *Schwarm* belonging to 10./JG 7 from Parchim. Results were so-so. Only one Lancaster was shot down, by Lt. Günther Heckmann.

The weather over England cleared briefly during the early morning hours of March 28, allowing about 900 heavy bombers of the 8th Air Force to take off. Under the protection of hundreds of long-range fighters, this huge force crossed Germany's western frontier between Emden and Enschede on a direct course for the German capital. But not all of the deadly cargoes were intended for Berlin. Bombs were dropped on Minden and then Hannover. Near Braunschweig several formations changed course and headed north. These were intercepted by several Me 262s of I./JG 7. The jets made contact in the Stendal area, but only managed to destroy three aircraft, a B-17 and a P-51 by Oblt. Stehle, the first kills in the Me 262 for the *Staffelkapitän* of 2./JG 7, and a P-51 by Oblt. Schuck.

This was to be JG 7's only success on March 28. Ceaseless fighter-bomber attacks on Parchim and Brandenburg-Briest prevented the aircraft of III./JG 7 from taking off to intercept the approximately 500 American bombers which, unmolested by German fighters, added to the devastation in the center of Berlin.

The next day, March 29, weather conditions over England again forced the 8th Air Force to suspend its aerial offensive. The British leapt into the breach with their night-bomber units, which were experienced in blind flying, attacking various targets in northwestern Germany. Among others, Paderborn again suffered extensive damage.

March 30, 1945

"With the departure of the bad weather front during the night of March 29/30, our air fleet resumed the strategic bomber offensive with all available forces for the first time in four days. More than 1,250 heavy bombers attacked U-boat yards, harbor installations, tank farms and residential areas in Hamburg, Wilhelmshaven and Bremen with good results. Thirty jet fighters took off from their airfields around Hamburg; they circled our formations, but did not attack. Five Me 262s were shot down by the fighter escort."

To a large degree such dubious presentations, in this case by an American author from 1953, were accepted unquestioningly by other journalists and came to be accepted in the English-speaking world as typical of operations by German jet fighters. Statements such as: ". . . they playfully circled our formations but did not attack . . ." or: ". . . our boys were ready for them and in the mad scramble that followed shot down five and damaged three without losing any of their own number . . ." give no indication of a will to fight, to say nothing of major successes by the Me 262s. It is no wonder, therefore, that the success of the jet fighters has frequently been doubted in the past.

With a total of 36 Me 262s, the operational ready rate of I. and III./JG 7 on March 30 was unusually low. But even this relatively small number of jets could not be brought to bear on the enemy when a scramble was ordered. Engine trouble forced three pilots to abort their takeoffs, while three further jets returned to base early after developing undercarriage problems or losing an engine. In addition, a group of about 12 Me 262s of I./JG 7 was given an incorrect heading to fly by the ground controller and ended up nowhere near the enemy. Finally, with fuel running low, the fighters were forced to break off the action and head back to base. As a result of these problems only 19 Me 262s made contact with the enemy.

9. and 10. *Staffeln* at Parchim were scrambled to intercept the incoming bombers at 1300. At about 1320 they encountered elements of the 8th Air Force north of Lüneburg at 8,000 meters. Two kills were scored on the first pass, both by Lt. Schnörrer. Schnörrer's wingman, Ofhr. Petermann, claimed

a probable victory over a B-17. The furious defensive fire took its toll, however. As Schnörrer pulled away from the formation his machine was damaged by return fire. The experienced fighter pilot broke off the action and set course for home. Four Mustangs set out in pursuit and finally caught up with the jet over Uelzen at 2,000 meters. With only one engine operating at full power, the *Leutnant* saw no chance of escape. He jettisoned his canopy, rolled the machine onto its back and dropped clear. In bailing out he struck the aircraft's tail surfaces and sustained a serious leg injury.

A second formation from Kaltenkirchen fared little better than III. *Gruppe*. Under the command of *Major* Rudorffer about eight Me 262s attacked a bomber formation over the Hamburg area as it flew in from over the North Sea. Rudorffer destroyed two fighters in the melee, while a B-17 was shot down by *Flieger* Reiher and a P-51 by Gefr. Heim.

I. *Gruppe* also lost one aircraft in its mission. The Me 262 of *Fahnenjunker-Feldwebel* Jannssen was hit by enemy fire and subsequently caught fire. The pilot bailed out before the flames reached the cockpit.

There was probably one more success to add to I. *Gruppe*'s score on this day. Uffz. Geisthövel was the last of his *Gruppe* to take off from Kaltenkirchen:

> "I had starting difficulties and took off behind the others. Visibility was good with 5/8 cloud cover. Over Hamburg I spotted a Mosquito to my left. It was dropping route markers. I flew somewhat to the right before positioning myself behind the Mosquito with a left turn. He seemed not to have noticed me, as he took no evasive action, and I was able to move into position unhindered and open fire. My speed was too great to observe what became of the aircraft. What I did see was three Mustangs coming toward me from a higher altitude. Using my speed, I dove my Me 262 toward the clouds on a northerly heading. I dove through a hole in the clouds and saw the Kaiser Wilhelm Canal in front of me. That was my salvation, as I had time to reverse course. I immediately lined up on Kaltenkirchen's runway over Neumünster. Throttles back, flaps down, I immediately swept in for a landing, not knowing whether I had shaken off the Mustangs. I hadn't stopped rolling when an *Oberfeldwebel* came racing up on a *Kettenkrad* to tow me from the runway. I already had the canopy open, the turbines wound down and I shouted to the *Oberfeldwebel* that he should take cover as I probably had fighters behind me. We dove into a one-man hole just as all hell broke loose. The Mustangs made three passes. A mechanic and an *Oberfeldwebel* who failed to reach cover in time were killed. Three Me 262s were damaged and our barracks were also hit."

When the danger had passed and the men crawled from their holes they saw a black column of smoke on the horizon. Their worst fears were soon confirmed. Near Hemdingen they found the smoldering wreck of an Me 262. It was the aircraft of 2. *Staffel*'s technical officer, Lt. Schulte, who had taken off with his wingman to protect his returning comrades. However he was shot down not far from the airfield by aircraft of the 339th Fighter Group while still climbing.

March 31, 1945

During the previous weeks JG 7 had been able to demonstrate its growing striking power through an impressive number of aerial victories, March 18 and 21 being especially successful days. But on the last day of the month the unit was to exceed by a wide margin the greatest one-day success so far.

Outstanding control from the ground, clever and determined exploitation of existing tactical advantages and not least the supplementary R4M armament resulted in the confirmed destruction of no less than 19 four-engined bombers and two fighters as well as the probable destruction of another bomber. In achieving this victory total, which is also recorded in the documents of the Luftwaffe Operations Staff, the jet fighter *Geschwader* had reached a level of success which was never to be exceeded.

The 21 kills were achieved in a total of four unit missions in which I. and III./JG 7 played an equal part.

About 20 Me 262s of I. *Gruppe* and seven machines of III. *Gruppe* took off during the early morning hours on the first mission of the day, to intercept British and Canadian bomber formations. After approaching from the west by night and making confusing course changes over Germany, the bombers were finally approaching their targets. They were the same ones which had been attacked the day before by the American 8th Air Force – Wilhelmshaven, Bremen and Hamburg.

The pilots of I./JG 7 were roused rather harshly from their sleep, "Their were no incursions reported that morning, and we were still in bed," recalls Gerhard Reiher:

> "Suddenly we were ordered to scramble. Everything happened so quickly that I jumped into my flying suit still wearing my pajamas and ran out onto the airfield." A first group of perhaps ten to twelve aircraft under the command of Oblt. Stehle took off between 0805 and 0810. Over Bremen they were vectored onto a formation of 40 Lancasters by the

fighter control center at Stade. Due to the powerful fighter escort the fighters scored only two kills, both by the *Staffelkapitän*. They are still marked in Stehle's log book as "probables," although the wrecks of both Lancasters were found. The chaotic conditions at the time prevented the kills from being officially confirmed, however.

At about 0815, several minutes after the departure of Stehle's *Staffel*, a second group of about eight Me 262s under Oblt. Grünberg took off. They were vectored onto a wave of bombers which had already reached the urban areas of Hamburg. "There was a very high, thin overcast," continues Gerhard Reiher's account. "We dove through the overcast in loose formation and were presented with a unique sight: about 1,000 meters below us, at an altitude of about 8,000 meters, we saw squadrons of Lancasters and Halifaxes. They were not in formation and had no fighter cover. The dark-painted bombers stood out fantastically from the white cloud deck. It looked like a horde of bedbugs crawling across a bed sheet. As we were not in tight battle formation Oblt. Grünberg called to me: 'After them everyone!' The English had probably not reckoned on German fighters and definitely not on us. After the first attacks they twisted and turned like crazy. But it did no good. It turned into a massacre. I caught a Lancaster with a full burst and it exploded like a ripe tomato. I shot at one or two Lancasters without bothering to notice whether they caught fire or went down. It didn't matter any more whether the kill was confirmed or not. The end of the war was in sight, and in my eyes it was just a self-confirmation."

Another of the participants described the battle, "they really fell like flies, I had never experienced anything like it. Some of the British crews bailed out without us firing a shot."

Eight aircraft of 9. and 10. *Staffeln* had meanwhile joined the battle. The desperately-turning night bombers had no chance whatsoever against the jets of I. and III. *Gruppen*. They dove on the enemy at speeds of 950 kph, fired their rockets from close range, pulled up and made further attacks with their cannon. The effects of the R4M salvoes and the MK 108 explosive ammunition were devastating. Everywhere one looked there were pieces of aluminum whirling through the air, severed wings with engines still running, shattered fuselages, exploding fuel tanks and dozens of parachutes. It was a day the British and Canadian crews of 419 (Moose), 429 (Bison), 431 (Iroquois), 434 (Bluenose), 408 (Goose), 415 (Swordfish) and 425 (Alouette) Squadrons will probably never forget.

When the Me 262s finally broke off the engagement, their ammunition expended, Oblt. Sturm, Oblt. Grünberg (2), Lt. Todt (2), Lt. F.W. Schenk (2), Oblt. Schall (2), Fhr. Ehrig (2), Lt. Weihs (1 probable) and Flieger Reiher had scored a total of 13 kills without loss.

The day's victory total was raised by at least six during the afternoon. At about 1600 Oblt. Stehle led a formation against one of the numerous Lancaster formations, which for lack of suitable night bombing targets were increasingly joining the American daylight offensive. The small band of jet fighters came upon the British bombers near Osnabrück. The *Staffelkapitän* of 2./JG 7 shot down a Lancaster. 11. *Staffel* and the *Stabsschwarm* also saw action at about this time. 8th Air Force records show air battles with propeller-driven and jet fighters in the Zeitz, Brandenburg and Braunschweig areas, as well as the loss of 3 B-17s, 2 B-24s and 4 P-51s, mostly to Me 262s. It is not clear who the successful German pilots were. It is believed that *Major* Weissenberger, Ofhr. Windisch and Ofw. Pritzl each destroyed a B-17. *Major* Ehrler and Lt. Rademacher probably accounted for a Mustang each.

There is some doubt as to the question of German losses. Even the official sources are contradictory. An entry by the Luftwaffe Operations Staff records "two of our own aircraft lost" during actions by the jets against US units, while the situation log of the OKW refers to four aircraft lost. Neither figure can be confirmed and, following intensive research by the author, there is some doubt whether JG 7 suffered any losses at all that day through enemy action.

JG 7's operations during the second half of March 1945, the most successful period in the history of the *Geschwader*, had provided impressive proof of the striking power of this new generation of fighter aircraft. Even if JG 7 – one full-strength and one half-formed *Gruppe*, a total of 65 jet fighters – was unable to halt or even restrict the Allied air terror, this handful of Me 262s accomplished a feat which, given the unequal ratio of forces and unfavorable circumstances, must be rated highly: in approximately 400 sorties during the month of March 1945 the jets of JG 7 destroyed 108 four-engined bombers, 1 Mosquito and 22 fighters, and probably destroyed or damaged 17 heavy bombers and 3 fighters.

The unit's own losses were 22 pilots killed and 5 wounded. JG 7's victory/loss ratio was thus lower than that of conventional fighter units. The losses weighed heavily, however, as proven and experienced pilots like Eder, Wegmann, Schnörrer, Lübking, Weber and Ambs, to name but a few, could not be replaced at this stage of the war. Being constantly in action, JG 7 had no time for the systematic training of new pilots. Losses exceeded the jet unit's regenerative capabilities within four weeks of commencing combat operations.

Although large numbers of relevant documents and the assistance of former members of JG 7, without whose help the history of the *Geschwader* could never have been written, enable us to create a precise reconstruction of JG 7's combat activities during March 1945, only fragmentary information is available concerning the jet training and replacement *Gruppe*, III./EJG 2, during the same period. However, the few relevant sources do allow us to conclude that the unit's job of training replacement pilots for JG 7 became increasingly difficult during the course of the month. Among the causes were inadequate numbers of fighter trainers and two-seaters and dwindling deliveries of spare parts and engines, but the main hindrance was the ceaseless aerial surveillance by the enemy. "We were always scared to death," recalls one of the pilots retraining on the Me 262 in March 1945, "we scarcely got into the air when we were called back again."

The dwindling number of aircraft (a strength report from the third week of March shows only eleven Me 262s) not only slowed training, it also prevented the Lechfeld jets from effectively supporting the conventional fighter units by intercepting enemy incursions. When a few machines were scrambled it was usually to combat a direct threat to the base by fighter-bombers or small formations of bombers. Attacks by experienced instructors or pilots who had completed their conversion training led to the *Ergänzungsgruppe*'s first confirmed victory during March 1945 (the date is believed to have been March 9): a Marauder shot down by Hptm. Engleder. Hptm. Steinmann destroyed a B-17 on March 12 and another on March 15. Steinmann was also successful on March 18, destroying two Mustangs during a *Rotte* sortie with Lt. Bell.

Other victories in March and April were scored by Fw. Rauchensteiner (a P-47 on March 27), Lt. Mischkot, Lt. Harbort, Ofw. Humburg, Ofw. Kaiser, Ofw. Hübl, Hptm. Meyer, Lt. Timmermann and Lt. Bell.

On March 19, 1945, one of the most outstanding fighter pilots produced by the Luftwaffe and undoubtedly one of its most capable and experienced unit leaders scored his first kill flying the Me 262: Major Heinz Bär.

If anyone had earned the honorary title of role model, it was Heinz Bär. Born in 1913, his path to becoming a pilot had not been an easy one. With unshakable determination he made the jump from fitter and flight engineer to pilot and finally fighter pilot. When war broke out he was an *Unteroffizier* with JG 51. Due to his success in the French Campaign and over England he was promoted to officer in 1940. "Where Bär is kept waiting no more grass grows!" These pithy words, which he himself once used on a senior flak commander, were confirmed by his success. The Knight's Cross and the Oak Leaves were awarded him in quick succession in 1941. In February 1942 he became the seventh German soldier to be awarded the Knight's Cross with Swords and Oak Leaves in recognition of his 90 victories.

"Pritzl" Bär was at the top. Following his 113th kill his unit, I./JG 77, was transferred into the Mediterranean area. Bär outdid himself over Malta and North Africa. His accomplishments in the face of the overwhelming twenty-fold superiority of the British and Americans on this front bordered on the superhuman. Shaken by malaria and tortured by gastric ulcers, he scored a further 65 kills. However when the totally exhausted, physically depleted man could simply do no more he was thought badly of. The circumstances which led to his removal as *Gruppenkommandeur* were certainly not a glorious page for his superiors. After a long period of recovery Bär, in spite of illness and setbacks, regained his inner equilibrium. And that was something which was desperately needed in the furnace of the defense of the Reich in 1944. Temporarily downgraded to a *Staffel* leader in JG 1 (It was from this period that his motto, "In my own crate I'm *Kommodore*," originated), he scored another 28 victories, including 17 four-engined bombers. From autumn 1944 he led *Jagdgeschwader Udet* (JG 3). Tales of his wit, charm and his manly courage in the face of authority are legion. He was undiplomatic enough to speak his mind to everyone, whether they wanted to hear it or not. One of his former *Staffelkapitäne* wrote of him: "... he was one of the very best, if not simply the best." And even if he hadn't achieved 220 victories, making him the most successful fighter pilot against the Anglo-Americans next to Marseille, his nearly 1,000 combat sorties with hundreds of air battles would have been a feat which exceeded anything imaginable.

Bär closed the propeller fighter chapter in his career with the Luftwaffe's New Year's attack on Allied airfields in Holland and Belgium. During this operation, which was so costly for the Germans, Bär shot down his 204th and 205th victims, downing two Tempests over Eindhoven between 0923 and 0925. A few days later Bär gave up his command and took over III./EJG 2. His new duties kept him out of action for several weeks. Not until March 2 did he log his next combat sortie; it was also his first scramble in an Me 262.

Bär had flown the Me 262 for the first time at Wenzendorf in September 1944. It was not until January 1945, however, that he converted to the jet aircraft under the expert guidance of Fritz Wendel.

Proof of Heinz Bär's ability to learn as a pilot is provided by the fact that so completely had he mastered the Me 262 after only a few flights, that Messerschmitt involved him in the ongoing technical testing being done by the Lechfeld test detachment. Confirmation of this appears in an entry in his logbook, "About 80-90 flights in the Me 262 not entered, as they were made with Messerschmitt. Among them 50 mm cannon, R4M, winged bombs, drop tank tests and similar flights." In the course of his activities as a test pilot Bär achieved two previously unknown performance marks in the Me 262 which were probably never exceeded by any other pilot: during a performance test flight he achieved a speed of 1,040 kph, and during a flight in the *Heimatschützer* I, a fast-climbing interceptor version with a supplementary rocket motor in the aft fuselage, he reached an altitude of 14,700 meters!

Bär's first combat sortie in the Me 262 on March 2, 1945 was followed in the next few days by several scrambles which did not result in contact with the enemy. It was not until March 19 that he downed his 206th enemy aircraft. The following is the report by III./EJG 2's weapons group:

> "Sortie by Me 262 aircraft, Werk-Nr. 110 559, coded Red 13, pilot *Major* Bär. Fired on a Mustang with effect. First burst from behind then gun stoppage. Cocked weapons and fired second burst in a descending right turn. Hits observed. Ammunition expended: left upper 12 rounds, left lower 10 rounds."

His 207th victim fell on March 21: a Liberator spun down in flames after taking hits in the fuel tanks. Three days later, while flying with his longtime wingman and friend, Leo Schumacher, he downed a Mustang and a Liberator over Stuttgart, his 208th and 209th kills. By the time advancing American troops forced III./EJG 2 to transfer to München-Riem from Lechfeld on April 23, his kill total in the Me 262 had risen to 13. He went on to score three more victories with JV 44, which he led from the time of *General* Galland's wounding until the end of the war. His last three kills, two Thunderbolts on April 27 and another over Bad Aibling on April 29, were scored while flying the prototype of a new Me 262 variant with a reinforced armament of 2 MK 103, 2 MG 151/20 and 2 MK 108 cannon. Bär took possession of the aircraft, which had been completed at Lechfeld in mid-April.

With 16 kills in the Me 262 in only five weeks Bär had risen to the top of the list of successful jet pilots.

Information on the losses suffered by III./EJG 2 is as sketchy as that concerning missions and victories. Only three losses are traceable from March 1945. On March 4, 1945, Werk-Nr. 110 472 crashed due to pilot error, and another machine was apparently a 95% write-off on March 31 after a crash-landing away from base following an engine fire. The only loss where the pilot's name is known occurred on March 22: *Fahnenjunker-Oberfeldwebel* Recker was shot down by Mustangs over the south end of Lechfeld while on approach to land.

Notes:

[1] The 8th Air Force lost twelve B-17s and a B-24 on March 18. A further fourteen B-17s and one B-24 crashed or made forced landings in Allied territory on the return flight, eleven of them in areas occupied by the Russians. The Americans state that eight B-17s were shot down by flak. It is possible that they did not recognize the rocket attacks as such and assumed that the explosions were direct hits by anti-aircraft fire.

[2] It was here that II. *Gruppe* suffered its only known loss. Fw. Arno Thimm was shot down by Thunderbolts during the flight to Prague, probably on April 14 or 15. Seriously wounded, he bailed out and was taken to a hospital.

[3] JG 5 *Eismeer* (Polar Sea), so called because the unit spent most of its operational career in the far north flying from bases in Norway and Finland.

143

Chapter V
Toward the End

I. Gruppe Evacuates Kaltenkirchen – Major Sinner Is Shot Down and Fired Upon in His Parachute – The Death of Major Heinrich Ehrler – "Kommando Elbe" – The Gyro Gunsight – The 8th Air Force Smashes the Jet Bases – The Great Me 262 Massacre – The Geschwader Is Ordered to Move to Bavaria – The Flying Unit Gets Stuck at Prague-Ruzyne – Scattered to the Four Winds – Close-Support Operations – The End in Prague – A Pilot of JG 7 Scores the Last Victory of the War

April 1945

During the first days of April 1945 a low-pressure area moving in from the Atlantic across England and France toward western and northern Germany foiled the plans of the Allied air commanders to continue their destructive work of the previous month. 9th Air Force sources reveal that the only operations by its fighters on April 1 were fighter-bomber sorties flown in support of the army in the Fulda area. Efforts by the 8th Air Force were also limited. About 100 of the air fleet's approximately 1,500 heavy bombers flew harassing sorties against individual targets in northern Germany. Several Me 262s of the Kaltenkirchen *Gruppe* were able to intercept a small group of some 20 Flying Fortresses escorted by about 50 fighters in the Stendal area, but the enemy's superior numbers prevented the jets from getting through to the bombers. In the end only one B-17 was shot down, by Oblt. Stehle. Uffz. Köster may also have downed a Spitfire reconnaissance aircraft that day.

On the afternoon of April 1 orders were issued for the complete evacuation of Kaltenkirchen airfield, a move which caught the pilots and technical personnel of I. *Gruppe* by surprise. Hans Grünberg recalls:

"As usual we had tuned in the Calais soldiers' transmitter on the radio. Sometime during the afternoon an announcer suddenly declared that an air attack on our base was to take place within the next few days. We therefore had to withdraw to another air base immediately. But we really didn't have many choices. In fact the only bases in question were those which would permit us to continue flying without interruption. The decision was made within a few hours. 1. *Staffel* was ordered to transfer to Brandenburg-Briest, 2. *Staffel* to Burg and 3. *Staffel* to Oranienburg."

Had the *Gruppe* command not reacted promptly to this threat, the Kaltenkirchen unit would probably not have escaped destruction and the bombers of the US 8th Air Force would have been able to carry out their assigned mission on the morning of April 2. However, a solid cloud deck over Denmark and Schleswig-Holstein prevented them from achieving the planned destruction of the Luftwaffe's ground organization in northern Germany, which included Kaltenkirchen. The 700 heavy bombers turned back over the target area and returned to their bases. As a result the transfer of I./JG 7 was able to begin without hindrance and was completed by April 4.

It was during these hectic days that the *Kommandeur* of I. *Gruppe*, Major Rudorffer, was called away on other duties. A new *Kommandeur* was not named before the war ended. From April 3 the individual *Staffeln* of I./JG 7 continued to operate as before under the leadership of their *Staffelkapitäne*, more or less as independent units. Finally, on April 25 the remaining elements of I. *Gruppe* were amalgamated into a single formation under the command of Oblt. Stehle.

April 4, 1945

The difficult operations of the previous weeks over northern and central Germany had considerably reduced the fighting strength of both *Gruppen* of JG 7. The actual equipment strength of III. Gruppe, which since mid-February of the year had been about 45 machines, had fallen to 27. Thanks to the tireless efforts of the ground personnel, on the evening of April 3 the *Gruppe* was able to report to 1. *Jagddivision* in Döberitz that 25 of its Me 262s were still combat ready. I. *Gruppe*'s operational ready rate was the same, and with an actual strength of 33 Me 262s it was almost at its authorized strength of 36 aircraft. On the evening of April 4, 1945, JG 7 had 56 combat-ready aircraft, including the six jets of the *Geschwaderstab*.

But what could these 56 jet fighters hope to achieve against the 1,431 heavy bombers and 850 escort fighters of the US 8th Air Force which streamed in during the early morning of April 4 to attack targets in northern Germany? The bomber stream's targets included the harbors and residential areas of Kiel and Hamburg and five airfields, among them Parchim, III./JG 7's base of operations.

Takeoff orders were issued to the jet units at Burg, Parchim, Brandenburg-Briest and Lärz, in use by elements of 9. and 10. *Staffeln* due to overcrowding at Parchim, when the bomber formations reached the Bremen-Hannover area. At Lärz, Burg and Briest the Me 262s took off unmolested and were able to assemble over Stendal into a formation of about 25 aircraft. They were guided onto the enemy formations south of Bremen. Attacking in groups of four, the jet fighters penetrated the American fighter screen in a shallow dive and loosed off their cannon and rockets at the B-17s and B-24s.

A combat report by one of the German pilots provides a vivid illustration of the odds they faced as well as the courage and flying skill of the jet pilots, who managed to shoot down bomber after bomber in spite of the massed defenses:

> "On 4. 4. 1945 I took off from Lärz at 0916 as *Staffel* leader to intercept a major incursion reported in the Bremen-Hannover area. In the Bremen area I passed a formation of about 50 Thunderbolts flying on a reciprocal course at 8,000 meters. Afterward I was forced to turn away by 10 Thunderbolts coming from a higher altitude. Approaching from the south, I attacked 24 Liberators flying on a southeasterly course from ahead and to the right at an angle of 45 degrees. I fired all my R4M rockets at the first Liberator from a range of about 600 meters, allowing about 50 meters lead, and scored hits on the fuselage and wing center-section of a Liberator flying in the middle of the formation. Large pieces fell off the aircraft, which immediately fell behind and began to lose altitude. After about two minutes the Liberator reversed course and I prepared to attack a second time. But before I reached firing range the Liberator dropped a wing and began to go down in a left-hand turn. I observed six men bail out. Afterward the Liberator stood on its nose and went into a vertical dive. It disappeared into a cloud deck in the Bremen area at an altitude of 2,000 meters."

By the time the Me 262s were forced to break off the engagement for lack of fuel seven bombers had been destroyed for certain. The successful pilots were Lt. Schenk, Lt. Fritz R. G. Müller, Maj. Weissenberger, Lt. Rademacher, Oblt. Stehle, Fw. Pritzl and Fhr. Pfeiffer. One B-17 was claimed as probably destroyed by Gefr. Greim, as well as two fighters confirmed destroyed, a P-51 and a P-47, by Oblt. Schall and Lt. Weihs.

For the elements of JG 7 operating from Burg, Lärz and Briest the operation had been a success in spite of the strong bomber and fighter defenses, which inflicted considerable damage on a number of Me 262s.

Orders for the jets at Parchim to scramble were not issued until enemy fighters were over the base. The result was a fiasco. A few moments after taking off at 0915 the approximately 15 jet fighters were surprised by enemy fighters while forming up at low altitude. The Me 262s dodged and turned desperately in an attempt to shake off the Mustangs and Thunderbolts, but the Americans exploited their favorable tactical position to the full. Robert C. Havighurst, formerly of the 504th Fighter Squadron, wrote:

"We were hanging around over Parchim at about 2,500 meters. At approximately 0915 we spotted three Me 262s climbing through a gap in the cloud. We let them come nearer, losing altitude all the while. When the first Me 262 was in range I opened fire from above and behind. The German tried to shake me off in a descending left turn. Thanks to my greater speed I was able to stay with him easily and scored hits on his left wing. Suddenly I came under heavy anti-aircraft fire. I released my drop tanks and began evasive maneuvers to escape the light flak. The Me 262 used this brief period to behin climbing again. However, I was able to quickly get behind him again and began to fire once more. I observed hits on his forward fuselage and left wing. At about 600 meters the Me 262 suddenly went into a dive. I saw no parachute. I suspect the pilot was killed by a hit on the cockpit."

The name of the downed German pilot will probably never be known. Perhaps it was Lt. Lehner or Uffz. Heckmann or Ofw. Reinhold or one of the two so far unidentified pilots killed in the Parchim area between 0920 and 0935. The other Me 262s which had taken off from Parchim barely escaped destruction. Six pilots were able to lose their pursuers in the dense, low cloud and land their badly-damaged machines at secondary airfields.

One other pilot failed to make it back. Rudi Sinner described those fateful moments:

"On 4.4.1945 I took off from Parchim on a mission against enemy bombers. Enemy fighters were reported over the airfield at an altitude of 8,000 meters before we took off. It was obvious from the sound of the aircraft that their altitude had been greatly overestimated. It seemed certain to me that these reported fighters were waiting over the cloud deck (8-9/10) at 400 meters.

"Circling the airfield one-and-a-half times, I assembled about seven aircraft, while others remained behind in visual contact. I climbed on top through a narrow gap in the clouds and immediately noticed four aircraft with lancet-shaped wings in the sun above me and to the left. I immediately turned steeply toward the aircraft, as I could not escape with my inferior speed. The Thunderbolts dove away steeply. As I was about to dive after them I noticed four Mustangs pursuing a lone Me 262. While trying to drive them away I suddenly saw four more Mustangs diving at me from above and to the right. I turned beneath them but came under heavy fire while in the turn. Vertical defensive maneuvers or a dive to gain speed were impossible due to my proximity to the ground. I was now under continuous attack by eight Mustangs. I was hit the first time while trying to dive for the clouds. I decided to fire off my rockets when I was between the clouds. There were two Mustangs behind me, but they were some distance back. My rockets would not fire. As I was working on the weapons switches the cockpit began to fill with smoke. I again came under fire and saw that the left wing was ablaze. The fire immediately spread to the cockpit. I decided to bail out following a brief evasive maneuver. I left the aircraft at about 700 kph, missing the tail surfaces. I immediately saw that my parachute was torn and that my right leg was tangled in my harness and lines. I was firmly convinced that the parachute pack had separated from the harness. I pulled the release handle anyway, as I was close to the ground. There was a sharp tug on my leg and I turned over three times, but to my astonishment I saw that my chute was opening. There was only one belt connecting me to my parachute, but the jolt as my chute deployed was minor. With only one leg and my left arm hanging in the harness, I landed in a plowed field."

Sinner's description of the battle matches the reports submitted by the two American pilots who scored the decisive hits and in the end shared the victory over the *Gruppenkommandeur* of III./JG 7.

The accounts by both sides match until the point of Sinner's landing by parachute; it is at this point that they diverge. The combat report submitted by Capt. Kirke B. Everson of the 504th Fighter Squadron stated: "We made a pass for photographs."

Sinner's account, which was verified by a witness on the ground was somewhat different:

"Although I had pulled the release handle and the buckle had opened, I remained hanging in the parachute harness and was dragged about 20 meters to a barbed-wire fence. In the process I was attacked and fired on by two Mustangs. The Mustangs circled, and I remained motionless as long as I was in their field of view. When they flew away to prepare for another pass I ran about 25 meters from my parachute and lay quietly in a furrow. They then strafed my parachute."

This kind of behavior by American fighter pilots was not an isolated incident. Experience had taught German fighter pilots shot down over Reich territory that they could expect to be shot at while hanging helplessly beneath their parachutes. German jet pilots found themselves facing this threat on an increasing scale as the end of the war approached. The number of known instances suggests an Allied order to employ such measures to defeat the growing threat posed by the German jet fighters. Fritz Stehle and Ernst Pfeiffer both witnessed such events. A powerless Helmut Lennartz could only clench his fists in rage:

"My wingman Siegfried Göbel was shot down during a mission from Achmer. His parachute had barely opened when the Mustangs dove on him. I was unable to provide effective cover as my turning radius was too great, and the P-51s turned away to the side each time I got into firing position. Finally he landed in a meadow and ran into a nearby wood. Even there he was fired on repeatedly. We later counted more than 30 holes in his parachute."

Günter Wegmann experienced something similar and it was only with great difficulty that he talked *Major* Nowotny out of having a force-landed American shot. The American pilot had earlier fired on a German pilot coming down by parachute. The death of Lt. Erich Schulte was directly attributable to such brutal behavior. Official German sources state that he was "shot to death in his parachute by enemy fighters after bailing out on 30.3.1945." Unconfirmed sources also suggest that Lt. Schrey was killed while hanging beneath his parachute on March 18, 1945.

It is a dark chapter for the Allies in the history of the air war which so far has received only passing mention. It is not the author's intention to dwell on the subject so many years after the end of the war, but these incidents are part of the factual record and should not be covered up. To members of the Luftwaffe the actions of the Allied pilots were totally incomprehensible and unforgivable. They can probably only be understood in the light of the prevailing atmosphere of hatred. Humanity and fairness were minor considerations in those days.

On the evening of April 4 the commanders of JG 7 were forced to acknowledge that conditions for a continuation of the so far successful battle had abruptly and decisively worsened. Five pilots had been killed or were missing and three had been wounded, including a *Gruppenkommandeur*. Eight machines had been completely destroyed and no less than 23 Me 262s were in need of repairs for battle damage or other defects. What was more, the late morning bombing had wrought considerable devastation on vital Parchim airfield, with its technical installations and spare parts dump. The first long-awaited blow by the US Air Force against JG 7's ground organization had shaken the jet fighter *Geschwader* to its foundations. No prophet was required to predict the imminent, final outcome.

The extent to which the events of April 4 had weakened JG 7's fighting strength is demonstrated by the number of missions flown the next day: only five uneventful combat sorties were recorded on April 5. The next day 641 heavy bombers of the 8th Air Force escorted by 600 P-47s and P-51s attacked Halle, Leipzig and Gera, while about 100 medium bombers of the 9th Air Force struck targets in northern Germany. JG 7 sent up only a few aircraft to engage the intruders. Two enemy aircraft were shot down, but these two victories came at a high cost: the life of *Major* Heinrich Ehrler.

One of the Luftwaffe's most successful fighter pilots with more than 200 confirmed victories, Ehrler had worked his way up to become *Kommodore* of JG 5. On November 12, 1944 he was in Bardufoss on an inspection trip. His *Geschwader*'s III. *Gruppe* had transferred there a few days earlier after reequipping with the Fw 190. Ehrler was somewhat concerned because airfield conditions were poor and would not allow the unit to get off the ground quickly if required.

At about noon that day a small specialist bomber formation of the RAF approached over the Baltic. It crossed the coast of Norway outside the range of III. *Gruppe* and overflew the Swedish border in flagrant violation of that country's neutrality. Over Swedish territory the formation altered course and flew north parallel to the border. Abeam Tromsö the British aircraft again altered course and headed across Norway toward the badly-damaged battleship *Tirpitz*, which was lying in open water. It was not until this point that III./JG 5 was informed of the danger by the aircraft warning system. Although every serviceable aircraft scrambled immediately and set out after the British raiders, the warning had come far too late to prevent a catastrophe. The bombers approached their target unhindered by German fighters; struck by heavy-caliber bombs the *Tirpitz* sank, taking more than 1,000 German seamen to their deaths. All those directly involved, including Ehrler, were ordered to Berlin to explain the circumstances which had led to this disaster. As a result of the findings charges were laid by a military court, and following the trials some severe sentences were handed out. Ehrler was sentenced to three years imprisonment, to be served after the "final victory." The argument was that he had gone along on the intercept mission, "for the purpose of satisfying his own ambition" and had handed over the job of directing the fighters to an inexperienced command post *Unteroffizier*.

It was probably due to Weissenberger's influence that Ehrle was sent to JG 7 to "prove himself" in action. He arrived at Brandenburg-Briest on February 27, 1945, and after receiving conversion training within the *Gruppe* flew a number of successful sorties with the *Geschwaderstab*. There are differing versions of what transpired during his last battle. According to one version Ehrler shot down two Fortresses then bade Weissenberger farewell over the radio, "Theo, I've used up all my ammunition, I'm going to ram! See you in Valhalla!" It is not certain that he really made this dramatic transmission, although it would have corresponded to his state of mind at the time. The wording of the death certificate, signed by *Major* Weissenberger and Oblt. Schuck, *Staffelkapitän* of 3./JG 7, gives no clue as to the precise cause of the crash:

> "Major Ehrler failed to return from a combat sortie on April 6, 1945. A body was found on April 7, 1945 near Stendal and an autopsy revealed that it was that of *Major* Heinrich Ehrler. *Major* Heinrich Ehrler was buried in Stendal cemetery on April 10."

April 7, 1945

April 7, 1945 saw the now famous – or infamous – so-called suicide mission by *Kommando Elbe*. It was an attempt to inflict "unbearable" losses on the bombers and thus force a last-minute "halt to the bomber offensive" through brutal mass operations, including ramming, without regard for the lives of the pilots. It is not our intention to argue the sense or madness of this mission or dispute the courage and self-sacrifice of the pilots involved. One can only understand this desperate operation by considering the prevailing mood in those April days, when the old Germany was dying in an unimaginable slaughter of hundreds of thousands of people. In such conditions many young men could see no future at all. In any case one thing is clear: the young pilots stood no chance whatsoever in their old Bf 109s and Fw 190s. They had received no specialized training to allow them to ram the heavy bombers without losing their own lives. The conditions necessary for success were absent and the operation was thus doomed to failure from the beginning. Seen thus it was irresponsible.

But the question may be raised: if one assessed their chances of success dispassionately, was not every mission by the German Luftwaffe with conventional propeller-driven aircraft during the final months of the war a suicide mission anyway? The loss lists provide the shocking answer.

The outcome was inevitable. The inexperienced volunteers were easy meat for the American fighters; the aircraft of the *Sonderkommando* were intercepted as they approached the bombers, scattered and wiped out.

In one of the bloodiest air battles ever in the skies over Germany more than 80 of the approximately 130 German pilots who had taken off were killed in the Soltau-Lüneburg-Salzwedel area. A few at most may have succeeded in piercing the American fighter screen and attacking the bombers. To this day there is no conclusive answer to the question of the actual losses inflicted on the US 8th Air Force by the *"Rammjäger."* Total heavy bomber losses on April 7, 1945 were fourteen B-17s and four B-24s. Two of these machines were known to have been shot down by Me 262s and three others fell to flak. The ramming unit could thus have accounted for twelve heavy bombers at most.

Twelve destroyed bombers against more than 80 pilots killed. A dismaying ratio.

It is not well-known that efforts were under way at the beginning of 1945 to motivate jet pilots to volunteer for suicide missions. The following is the text of an OKL Abt. Ia/Flieg document on the subject from February 17, 1945:

"Proposal that suicide pilots with jet aircraft be employed to ram the aircraft of enemy formation leaders.

1. Number of suicide pilots trained on Fw 190:
    7 pilots in Einhorn Staffel KG 200.
2. a) Total suicide pilots with training command: 97
    b) Training levels: 4   100 hours
                                      34   41-45 hours
                                      59   6-10 hours
    c) Time required for completion of retraining on
    Fw 190:   115 hours
    d) Time required for retraining on jet: 100 flying hours

3.Training of suicide pilots to achieve mastery of jet aircraft requires so much time that they will arrive too late for the proposed operation in any case.

Recommendation:

a)   Place 7 trained suicide pilots at disposal for proposed operation and retrain on jets.

b)   Complete training of suicide pilots with 45-100 hours so as to at least employ them in Sturmgruppen.

c)   Appeal to trained jet pilots to volunteer for proposed operation.

Volunteers step forward!

It is doubtful whether the pilots of JG 7 were made aware of this appeal. In any case none of the former members of JG 7 can recall one. As well none can remember flying escort missions for the *Rammjäger* as various publications have maintained. On April 7 the unit had 48 machines ready for action. Operations that day were once again directed exclusively against the heavy bombers of the US 8th Air Force, which was employing its vast resources in the ongoing task of destroying the German ground organization. Parchim was bombed again, as was Kaltenkirchen, which had escaped destruction on April 2 as a result of poor weather. This time a dense concentration of bombs fell on the airfield.

JG 7 flew 59 sorties but results were far below expectations. Only four confirmed victories and one probable were recorded: one B-17 over Parchim, one B-24 near Bremen at 1234, one P-38 over the *Autobahn* near Seesen and two Mustangs near Wittenberge. 8th Air Force combat reports confirm these losses. The victorious German pilots are believed to have been Ofw. Göbel, Uffz. Schöppler, Oblt. Schuck and Ofw. Neuhaus (P-51). Fhr. Pfeiffer may also have shot down an enemy aircraft. For the time being an event mentioned in a chronology of the air war in April 1945 by an American air war historian must go unexplained: a battle-damaged Me 262 is said to have collided with a B-24 of the 389th Bomber Group over Lüneburg. Both machines subsequently crashed. German documents list an Me 262 as missing, but it is still uncertain whether this was the aircraft involved in the collision.

April 8, 1945

The German air defenses had little left to throw against the 1,150 heavy bombers of the US 8th Air Force which attacked transport facilities, tank farms and industrial targets in central Germany, focusing on the Gera-Leipzig-Chemnitz area. Most of the flak batteries had been committed to a ground role and the rest of the conventional fighters were for the most part being used as fighter-bombers against the advancing enemy columns. JG 7 reported only a few sorties on April 8. The supply of J2 fuel, a low-grade kerosine which was extracted at an early stage of the hydrogenation process, had been seriously reduced. As a result of this shortage, coupled with the effects of the previous day's bombing raid, which had left the airfield temporarily unusable, only about 15 Me 262s got into the air. They scored four victories. The British, several of whose bomber units appeared over northern Germany, lost two aircraft. Oblt. Stehle shot down a Lancaster, Lt. Weihs a P-38. The other two kills were credited to Uffz. Geisthövel. He destroyed two Mustangs while flying an Me 262 equipped with the most modern aiming device available to the Luftwaffe, an automatic gyro gunsight. These two kills are probably the only ones ever achieved by an Me 262 so equipped.

A specification for the development of the gunsight, which automatically determined the necessary amount of lead by measuring angular velocity and target distance during pursuit, had been issued by the RLM in July 1939. However it was not until mid-1944 that the first examples of the gyro gunsight, designated EZ 40, were delivered to the *E-Stelle Tarnowitz* for testing.

By the end of August 1944 the Askania Firm had assembled the first 15 production examples; on orders of the *General der Jagdflieger* they were installed in Bf 109 fighters of JG 300. At this time the *E-Stelle* took delivery of the third prototype of the EZ 42, which was seen as the definitive version of the gyro gunsight. Extensive testing was carried out in an Fw 190 beginning in early September 1944. The first 15 examples of the pre-production series, which incorporated various design changes, were delivered about two months later. Like the earlier version, they were installed in machines of II./JG 300 for front-line testing.

High hopes were placed on the gyro gunsight, especially when used in high-performance fighters. A meeting took place in early November 1944 between representatives of the Askania Firm and the aircraft manufacturers, during which questions relating to the installation of the gunsight in the Me

163, Me 262, He 162, Go 229, Do 335 and Ar 234 C were discussed. However it was still too early to make any concrete decisions; installation drawings for the relevant designs were not yet available.

On November 24, 1944 technicians of the Askania and Messerschmitt firms met in Oberammergau to plan the installation of the EZ 42 in the Me 262 using drawings which had been prepared in the meantime and a prototype gunsight. A number of design problems came to light which took about two months to overcome. On January 10, 1945 *Hauptdienstleiter* Saur of the Armaments Staff became involved in the matter. He went on record as saying, "the EZ 42 automatic sight is of fundamental importance for increasing accuracy and permitting slant approaches. Its installation in all high-performance fighters, particularly the Me 262, is to be pursued using all means." However, even Saur was unable to accelerate the process of overcoming the design's shortcomings. According to Messerschmitt records the parts for the installation of the "*Adler*" unit in the Me 262 test machine Werk-Nr. 130 167 were not delivered until January 23, 1945. Further necessary modifications meant that only five flights, some with film shot by the BSK 16 gunsight camera, were flown in February 1945. In March, too, the number of test flights was low, due to difficulties with the power supply, predictor installation and gunsight mount. In spite of this Messerschmitt chief pilot Karl Bauer submitted his initial evaluation on March 18, 1945:

> "Shooting with the EZ 42 is not simple and requires much practice. I imagine that a pilot who has learned on the fixed Revi and had success with it will want nothing to do with the EZ 42. There are negative aspects for use in the 8-262 which are created by the aircraft's great speed superiority over existing enemy fighters. The range must constantly be adjusted so quickly while overtaking that accuracy suffers as a result. During longer turning battles, for example Bf 109 versus Mustang, the range decreases slowly. One thus has sufficient time to adjust the controls. Such turning battles will not take place with the 8-262. Using the aircraft's superior speed one will have only a short time to fire in the turn. To have adequate time for precise range measurements, one will have to give up the main advantage of the 8-262, namely its high speed. That means approaching a bomber formation from behind with the engines throttled back. Only thus can range measurements be made with the required accuracy. In summing up it may be said that shooting with the EZ 42 in the 8-262 will demand much practice and the use of new tactics."

It is impossible to determine whether Baur's opinion caused any doubts regarding the "forced beginning of series production." In any case the requirement was still in place on March 25, 1945. The following is from the minutes of discussions held by the Messerschmitt firm: "40 units have been delivered in March thus far, as well a further 240 units will be delivered before the end of March, half each to Lechfeld and Schwäbisch Hall. Thus a preliminary run has been created for series production. In April 80 units will be delivered during the first ten day period, 130 units during the second and 190 during the third." How many were actually handed over to Messerschmitt and installed in series production aircraft, if any, is unknown.

During late February – early March the EZ 42 was demonstrated to III./ JG 7 in a Siebel made available by the Vaerløse Gunnery School. The gunsight was tested by experienced pilots of the *Gruppe* and *Geschwaderstab*. After careful consideration *Major* Sinner turned down an offer to equip the unit's aircraft with the device, 43 of which had supposedly been reserved for JG 7. Unaware of the ongoing testing of the EZ 42 at Lechfeld and Tarnewitz, Sinner, too, became convinced that its use in the jet offered more disadvantages than advantages.

In spite of these reservations several of JG 7's Me 262 fighters were equipped with the gyro gunsight during the final weeks of the war. Whether they were installed as a retrofit or in series aircraft supplied as replacements is thus far unclear. One of the Me 262s so equipped was that of Heiner Geisthövel. He demonstrated the aircraft to a Japanese military delegation at Brandenburg-Briest in late March-early April, but was under strict orders not to mention the new gunsight or explain how it functioned.

The previously-mentioned action is believed to have taken place on April 8:

"I took off alone from Brandenburg-Briest in my Me 262 on a combat sortie into the Cottbus area and ran into a flight of Mustangs. When these spotted me they went into a defensive circle. With my greater speed I flew around outside the circle. I was unable to attack and climbed up into the sun in a cloudless sky. I turned while climbing and came down on the Mustangs, which by now were flying in line astern again, at an angle from in front from a slightly higher altitude. I was not spotted and was able to allow the four to fly through my sight from right to left. I was able to observe hits on two aircraft. My speed was too great to see more. I reversed course but could not find them again. When I had landed I was asked whether I had made contact with the enemy. I told my story and they were able to confirm two Mustangs shot down by me in the Cottbus area by the time of day.

Such a result gave one the feeling of superiority, and yet we were the hunted wild animal. We were too few to conduct larger operations."

April 9, 1945

The US 8th Air Force began a double strike against the German jet units and their ground organization with 1,252 heavy bombers and 846 fighters. The Allies planned 3,000 bomber and 2,000 fighter sorties for April 9 and 10 to eliminate the "jet menace" once and for all.

The first phase of the operation on April 9 was carried out with clockwork precision. 3,108 tonnes of high-explosive and incendiary bombs and aerial mines crushed identified or suspected jet bases in southern Germany. Fürstenfeldbruck and Oberpfaffenhofen, Neuburg and München-Riem, Lechfeld, Leipheim, Memmingen and Landsberg, none escaped destruction. Runways and taxiways were torn up by thousands of craters. Repairs were held up for days by duds and delayed-action munitions. Water and power supplies, as well as telephone and teletype circuits, were cut, hangars, maintenance shops and quarters smashed to rubble. In addition to the heavy losses in personnel, more than 100 parked aircraft were destroyed or damaged beyond repair. Included in this number were many Me 262s of KG 51, KG(J) 54, III./EJG 2 and the Messerschmitt test division. Among the aircraft lost by the latter were the *Heimatschützer* II and the *Heimatschützer* IV, the latter still under construction.

The British were also in action that day. Their night bombers attacked various targets in northern Germany with deadly precision. In Kiel harbour the cruiser *Scheer* broke apart after being hit by heavy-caliber bombs. The cruiser *Hipper* caught fire and the *Emden* was damaged by a near miss.

During the afternoon of April 9 about fifty British bombers were sent to bomb shipyards and harbour facilities at Hamburg. Twenty-nine jet fighters of JG 7 took off to intercept. The jet pilots achieved good success in spite of heavy defensive fire. Oblt. Schall, Gefr. Müller, Lt. Zingler and Uffz. Engler each shot down a Lancaster, while Lt. F.R.G. Müller destroyed a Thunderbolt.

April 10, 1945

At bases of the US 8th Air Force in England the engines of 1,315 heavy bombers roared to life. The bomber crews were prepared for a sortie over Germany. Their mission: carry out the second and decisive phase of the operation against the German jet units. The day's targets: Brandenburg-Briest, Rechlin-Lärz, Oranienburg, Neuruppin, Burg and Parchim. A total of 905 P-47s and P-51s taxied out for takeoff. Their mission: to provide wide-ranging, vertically-staggered coverage of the airspace in the target area as well as subsequent engagement of the "German jets" on the ground and in the air.

JG 7's bases in the Berlin area had been at the highest state of readiness since early morning. All the signs indicated that the long-awaited destructive blow against the *Geschwader* was imminent. The beams of the German radars continually swept the sky, but the hours passed uneventfully. There were no signs of major incursions on the plan position indicators of the two "*Jagdschloss*" installations. The men in the command centers began to think that they might be able to breathe more easily. But then, at about 1300, the first echoes appeared on the long-range display. They were coming. From the north, from the west and from the south. In their hundreds.

The serviceable German fighters – 12 Fw 190 Dora-9s and 55 Me 262s – were scrambled when the bombers were within about 100 kilometers. Sixty-seven German fighters against 2,183 enemy aircraft. The Me 262s of the Stehle *Staffel* based at Burg were the first to scramble and probably the only unit to reach battle altitude as a cohesive unit. Moments after they took off enemy fighters swept over Burg and silenced the anti-aircraft guns. Then the bombers of the 3rd Air Division arrived and the airfield was caught in an inferno. Hundreds of tonnes of bombs transformed the base and surrounding area into a moonscape. The effect of the twenty-minute bombardment was so devastating that Burg was still useless for any type of flying when it was captured by the Americans. All the units based there reported heavy losses in equipment and aircraft. "Father and Son" combinations, Ju 88s and Ju 188s, Fw 190s and Bf 109s, He 111s and He 177s, about 60 machines in all, were reduced to smoldering metal. Among the destroyed aircraft were almost a dozen Me 262s. Three machines of 2./JG 7 undergoing repairs lay under the wreckage of collapsed maintenance hangars. NAG 6 was forced to write off three jets as total losses, and Oblt. Welter's 10./NJG 11 lost four of its night fighters.

At about 1415 – as Burg was being pulverized by the carpet bombing of the American formations – at Parchim the jet fighters of 9. and 10. *Staffeln* were ordered to take off. Weather conditions were unfavorable: a ceiling of 150-200 meters and visibility of no more than 2,000 meters. These conditions represented a deadly danger to the majority of the pilots who had not been trained in instrument flying. But they took off, at intervals of perhaps 30 seconds to reduce the danger of collision in cloud. The first aircraft had already lifted off and entered the curtain of rain, when without warning Mustangs appeared on the scene. The warning "fighter-bombers over the airfield" came too late for at least two of the Me 262s which had just taken off. Fhr. Windisch and Uffz. Vigg had no chance against the maneuverable enemy fighters. The two jet fighters were hit and came down not far from the airfield. Miraculously both pilots survived the crash of their machines. They were hauled from the wreckage with life-threatening injuries and burns – Vigg later lost his sight as a result – and delivered to the hospital.

At about 1430 the bombers opened their bomb doors over Parchim. However, the weather prevented a repetition of the catastrophe at Burg; the majority of the bombs fell on open ground. Losses of personnel and machines were held within limits at Parchim. Nevertheless direct hits were scored on several living quarters, killing a pilot of 10./JG 7 and a number of soldiers.

Approximately 30 Me 262s took off from Oranienburg, Lärz and Brandenburg-Briest to intercept the bombers. The fighter pilots were about to face one of their most difficult missions from which many of them would not return.

The fighter controllers were unable to assemble the various elements and guide them to the bombers as a cohesive force. The accounts of the action by German pilots were all the same: "They were everywhere, whether at 3,000, 6,000 or 9,000 meters, whether over Stendal, Oranienburg or Briest. We were constantly plagued by them. Large, orderly formations, undisturbed approaches or even coordinated attacks were completely out of the question because of the countless Mustangs and Thunderbolts." Split up into pairs and fours, the *Geschwader* was unable to bring its full strength to bear. Events in the air disintegrated into individual actions. In these bitter air battles, constantly harried by enemy fighters, only the most experienced had any chance. It was these pilots who scored the last noteworthy success against the US 8th Air Force. According to German sources the jet fighters scored 16 confirmed and 3 probable victories on April 10. These figures are based on reports submitted by the pilots immediately following the action and forwarded by the *Geschwader* command. Even if they can no longer be verified, they nevertheless appear to be realistic: according to its own records the 8th Air Force lost 23 bombers and 9 fighters. Nine of the heavy bombers lost are known to have been destroyed by Me 262 fighters.

Oblt. Grünberg shot down two B-17s, while Oblt. Stehle, Oblt. Bohatsch, Ofhr. Neuhaus, Fhr. Pfeiffer and *Flieger* Reiher destroyed one each. Oblt. Schall, Lt. Hagenah, Ofw. Griener, Ofw. Lennartz and Lt. Rademacher each accounted for a Mustang. Fw. Pritzl destroyed two P-47s. But it was Oblt.

Schuck who scored the success of the day. Schuck had taken off with seven aircraft of his *Staffel*. Near Magdeburg the jets attacked a formation of American bombers from above and behind. Schuck's first burst of fire tore the wing off a B-17. The Me 262 raced through the formation. The next burst shattered the elevator assembly of one of the heavy bombers, whose crew immediately bailed out. Seconds later the next Fortress was in his gunsight. Schuck fired and pulled up; the enemy aircraft disintegrated. The *Leutnant* was now behind the leading formation. A short burst of cannon fire and the fourth Boeing broke apart. By now running low on fuel, Schuck broke off the engagement and decided to land at Jüterbog. But this was not to be. At an altitude of about 1,000 meters his left engine exploded, tearing off the wing. Schuck reacted in fractions of a second. He jettisoned the canopy hood, released his straps and jumped out. At 300 meters above the ground he pulled the rip cord and landed safely soon afterward.

The successes achieved in no way compensated for the horrible losses in personnel and materiel which JG 7 suffered that day. There was no doubt: the jet *Geschwader* had suffered a decisive defeat.

April 10, 1945 went down in American aviation history as "the day of the great jet massacre." On their return the P-47 and P-51 pilots who had flown escort for the bombers reported the certain destruction of no fewer than 20 Me 262s. Bomber crews claimed at least five more.

Although in most cases claims for German fighters shot down by the American side were many times the actual losses suffered by the Luftwaffe, on April 10 they tallied almost exactly with known German losses of jet fighters. A document compiled by the Wehrmacht Operations Staff dryly lists the catastrophic losses: 5 pilots killed, 14 missing; 13 aircraft lost, 14 missing, 8 damaged.

In spite of efforts by the author it has not been possible to compile a complete list of personnel losses; however the following pilots are known to have died that day: Gefr. Heim, Fw. Schwarz, Oblt. Wever, Oblt. Wagner, Uffz. Köhler and Oblt. Schall. Schall's aircraft rolled into a bomb crater during an emergency landing at Parchim and turned over, burying the *Staffelkapitän* of 10./JG 7 beneath it. The names of the remaining personnel lost are not available. It is known that, among others, Uffz. Anzer, Uffz. Helms, Hptm. Lehmann, Lt. Spangenberg and Lt. Siegfried Müller were killed during the last weeks of the war, and one or more of them may have been among the victims of April 10. Gaps in the memories of the survivors can easily be accounted for. Within the unit there was a continual coming and going. Individual names, especially those of young replacement pilots, were not imprinted in the minds of those present, especially since they were often together for only a few days.

With 27 personnel losses and 27 aircraft totally destroyed, which represented the loss of 56% of the Me 262s in action, JG 7 had suffered a blow from which it was never to recover.

The American air force had fully achieved the objective it had set for itself. The last threat in the skies over Germany had been eliminated for good.

Worthy of note are the conflicting documents regarding the losses suffered by JG 7 on April 10, 1945. *Luftwaffenkommando Reich* operational readiness reports for JG 7 on the evening of April 9 show 73 Me 262s on strength. Two days later, on the evening of April 11, the same source reveals 70 Me 262s still on strength, or a reduction of only three machines. The latter figure cannot be reconciled with the actual losses suffered by the *Geschwader* on April 10, which are also reflected in documents of the Luftwaffe Operations Staff. It seems very unlikely that 24 replacement aircraft were delivered to the unit within a few hours and included in the operational readiness reports. This is one of the unclarified points which still awaits an answer.

During the evening hours of April 10, 1945 the *Geschwader* command of JG 7 was forced to accept the fact that with the almost total destruction of the jet ground organization the defensive battle against the US Army Air Force in the Berlin area was over. Reports from the bases which had been attacked revealed a dismal picture. Due to the situation of the labor force, which was strained to the limit, repairs to the battered airfields and a resumption of operations could not be expected in the near future. The consequence of this was the relocation of JG 7. The rapid implementation of this measure was also dictated by the desperate military situation. The eastern and western fronts had already moved so close to the unit's bases that during the night of April 10/11 the Luftwaffe Operations Staff directed the jet *Geschwader* to several bases in northeastern Bavaria, which was not yet directly threatened: Plattling, Mühldorf and Landau.

On the morning of April 11 the ground elements of 2./JG 7 set out from Burg and those of 9. and 10./JG 7 under Oblt. Külp from Parchim, bound for Deggendorf via Prague. They arrived there on April 15 with orders to prepare the airfield for the continuation of jet operations.

The transfer of the air elements of the *Geschwader*, which had temporarily been assembled at Brandis and Alt-Lönnewitz following the destruction of their home fields, began on April 12. As the planned "Silver Bases" in Bavaria were either not at all or insufficiently prepared, and the weather situation in southern Germany (10/10 cloud) would not allow direct flights, the advance element of the unit was initially ordered to make an intermediate stop at Prague-Ruzyne.

Gerhard Reiher was one of the pilots who took off during the early afternoon of April 12:

> "I took off at 1437. Over Dresden I made contact with about 20 Thunderbolts. They were completely surprised and I was able to shoot one down. I subsequently landed at Ruzyne at 1502."

Reiher was one of the few who transferred to Ruzyne on this first day of the relocation of the *Geschwader*. He recalled that perhaps six to eight machines had landed there by that evening.

The next day a sudden deterioration in the weather over central Germany considerably hindered the move which had barely got under way. It is thought that no aircraft left Alt-Lönnewitz for Prague on April 13, and that only a few pilots from Brandis tried to find their way through the thick cloud cover.

Brandis and Alt-Lönnewitz were also reporting "qbi" on April 14. On the other hand the meteorologists were reporting a significant improvement in the weather over southern Germany. As fuel supplies had allegedly been assured at Plattling, at about 0800 about 15-20 Me 262s prepared to take off from Alt-Lönnewitz. Helmut Lennartz recalled:

> "The weather was miserable. Low cloud almost to the ground. We therefore agreed to take off in flights of four with one to two minutes between aircraft, climb up through the cloud, assemble and fly to Bavaria in formation. As the first to go, I took off and entered cloud. I broke out at about 3,500 to 4,000 meters and waited for my companions. But none came. After a while I set course alone for Plattling. In fact there had been no improvement in the weather over southern Germany. On the contrary, it had worsened steadily. Lower Bavaria was socked in. Even today I am still so angry over the forecast of 3/10 cloud that I would choke the 'weather frog' if he crossed my path. It still strikes me as a miracle that I managed to find the airfield in that awful weather and get down safely. Fhr. Pfeiffer arrived about thirty minutes later, the sole pilot among those who had taken off behind me to reach Plattling. I have no idea where the others went. I assume that they flew low out of fear of the cloud and subsequently crashed at high speed somewhere in the mountains due to the poor visibility."

On April 15 *SS-Obergruppenführer* Kammler, the "Führer's Plenipotentiary for Jet Aircraft," intervened decisively in the transfer of the *Geschwader*. "On orders from the highest authority" he had the Luftwaffe Operations Staff halt the move to southern Germany and direct JG 7 to bases at Eger, Saaz and Prague-Ruzyne. The order was intended to permit the jets to continue to participate in the air defense of Berlin and central Germany, which would have been impossible from more southerly airfields due to the Me 262's limited range.

Among the pilots who took off from Brandis and Alt-Lönnewitz for Prague that day was Lt. F.W. Schenk:

> "Many Me 262s and heroes on the field. The fronts were audibly approaching from both sides. No one wanted to take off on account of poor weather along the route, 10/10 cloud in the mountains. It illustrated the dilemma facing the German fighter arm. Scarcely anyone was able to fly blind. A suggestion by Ofw. Pritzl and myself, to assemble below cloud and then fly to Prague with an instrument-qualified formation leader, daily bread in JG 300, was not well received. As I recall each took off at his own discretion. I never made it to Prague. High above the clouds I suffered a total electrical failure. Over Lower Bavaria I found a hole in the cloud near Plattling. My engines were dead, their fuel exhausted. I pulled the emergency handle to lower the undercarriage and by pure luck managed to land at Plattling. There I met another JG 7 pilot, Fw. Leverenz (whether he landed before or after me and from where he came I no longer know), who later shot down a Lightning near the airfield (on April 17). I telephoned my *Gruppe* in Prague. A little later Weissenberger telephoned and ordered me to prepare the airfield at Plattling for the aircraft coming from Prague. Weissenberger told me that a column of vehicles with the ground personnel was on its way so that servicing people would be available. The ground party arrived soon afterward. With the unit was Oblt. Stahlberg, who lost his life under tragic circumstances in a truck crash on the 'Rusel-Berg' just outside Deggendorf.
>
> Plattling was a secondary airfield. To be sure it possessed a runway but lacked any technical equipment whatsoever. There were no refuelling facilities and no tank trucks. Nearby, however, in Deggendorf, there was a hydrogenation plant with considerable stocks of fuel. Liquid manure spreaders and other tank-equipped vehicles were requisitioned from local farmers to ship the fuel from Deggendorf.
>
> The Deggendorf hydrogenation plant was totally destroyed before this grotesque oxcart train could get under way. As a result there was no

fuel for the Me 262s arriving at Plattling.

Later that same day our airfield was attacked by American P-51s. All the aircraft there, including my and Leverenz' Me 262s (Lennartz, Pfeiffer and several others had flown on to Mühldorf in the meantime) were destroyed.

Orders were issued for all the elements of JG 7 in Bavaria to make their way to Lechfeld, where the unit was to be reformed.

We returned the manure spreaders – which had never before been so clean – to the farmers and began the night journey to Augsburg. Travel by day was impossible due to low-flying Allied aircraft. I no longer remember the date of our departure from Plattling.

We didn't make it to Lechfeld as the Americans had got there ahead of us. The whole procession turned round and drove past Munich into southern Bavaria. The remains of JG 7 assembled in a large field somewhere, chased once or twice into the surrounding woods by low-flying enemy aircraft, and Weissenberger, who had caught up with us sometime or another, delivered an address. He informed us that he had placed the unit at the disposal of the Americans for further action (against the Russians?) – or intended to place it at their disposal.

When this notion proved illusory the units spent a few more days moving through southeastern Bavaria, maintaining loose contact with one another. They wandered back and forth without any thought or planning, trying to decide what to do. JG 7 gave all the members of the unit who could be reached – or only those who so desired – 'certificates of discharge from active military service.' I still have this certificate of discharge, which of course was completely worthless, to this day."

April 16, 1945

The continuing bad weather on April 16 frustrated the hopes of the JG 7 *Geschwader* command to finally complete the transfer of the unit. Low cloud over the foothills and mountains forced many pilots to return to their starting points or make costly landings away from base. Among the pilots who tried to fly to bases in the Prague area late that morning were Lt. Fritz R. G. Müller and Ofw. Arnold of 11./JG 7. Müller recalled:

"Part of the time we flew over American-occupied territory, and I can still remember the endless columns of vehicles with the white star. As the ceiling was becoming steadily lower, we decided to turn back. After reversing course I had neither visual nor radio contact with Arnold. I finally landed alone at Alt-Lönnewitz. I suspect that Arnold was shot down by flak."

Ofw. Arnold is still listed as missing, however the Me 262 in which he scored seven victories while flying from Brandenburg-Briest is one of the few still in mint condition today. Once again Fritz R.G. Müller:

> "Arnold was not flying his own aircraft on his fateful last flight. Like many others at Alt-Lönnewitz it was unserviceable in the maintenance hangar. On April 18 a pilot whose name I cannot remember landed Arnold's Me 262 at Saaz, to where I had transferred in the meantime. As my own bird had gone up in flames during a fighter-bomber attack, I took possession of it on the spot and flew it until the surrender. On May 8, 1945 my wingman and I took off from Ruzyne for Lechfeld, where I handed over the aircraft to Messerschmitt chief pilot Karl Baur, under whose direction selected American pilots had eagerly learned to fly other captured Messerschmitts."

The aircraft made its way to America via France. In the early 1950s it was given to the Smithsonian Institution for inclusion in its collection of historic aircraft. Restored in 1981, today it is on public display at the Air and Space Museum in Washington D.C.

Increasingly, control over the fate of JG 7 slipped from the hands of the *Geschwader* command. Under the direct command of IX *Fliegerkorps (J)* following the transfer to Prague, the unit's commanders all too frequently found themselves running up against instructions from Kammlers, whose proclamations had been declared "Führer orders." Göring, too, sought to protect his interests through *General* Kammhuber, whom he had named as "the *Reichmarschall's* Plenipotentiary for Jet Aircraft" as a countermove. The situation was further complicated by the physical separation of the individual elements of the *Geschwader*. Several of these were sitting in Mühldorf and Plattling without clear orders. The entire command post with Lt. Preusker and the ground elements of 11./JG 7 were still at Brandenburg-Briest. Several pilots, among them Lt. Rademacher, had transferred to Kaltenkirchen[1], and about 15-20 Me 262s, some in need of repairs, were still stuck at Brandis and Alt-Lönnewitz. A small number of machines and elements of the *Geschwader* command with *Major* Weissenberger were at Saaz, and about 25-30 Me 262s had made their way to Ruzyne. Elements of II./JG 7 with *Major* Staiger and Oblt. Glunz were at Osterhofen. Other fragments of the unit were with Hptm. Gottuck at Stephansposching, with Lt. Unger at Langenisarhofen, with *Major* Freytag, Hptm. Reinert, Oblt. Seidel at Osterhofen or with Oblt. Leykauff at Moos.

In view of this confused situation and the catastrophic supply situation, a continuation of the battle on the previous scale was completely out of the question. In spite of this, "responsible" offices pressed ever more energetically for a resumption of operations.

During the afternoon of April 16 a strong force of American fighter-bombers attacked airfields in the Reich Protectorate of Bohemia. It had not taken the Americans long to find out to which airfields the remains of the Luftwaffe had retreated. The Mustangs and Thunderbolts wrought a real massacre on the unprotected and overcrowded airfields. They reported the destruction of 747 German aircraft. This figure is highly inflated, but the loss of 250-300 aircraft represented a large percentage of the machines left to the Luftwaffe. A teletype message from *Luftflottenkommando* 6 to Army Group Center stated:

> "About 150 aircraft were totally destroyed as a result of American air attacks on airfields in the Prague area. A substantial number were so badly damaged that in view of the considerably reduced repair facilities available they are indefinitely or permanently unserviceable. This enemy success was possible only because the enemy aircraft were able to circle over the airfields for some time virtually unmolested and strafe the individually parked aircraft at very low altitude. As much as we recognize the necessity of incorporating the flak units to effectively reinforce the defensive strength of the ground front, it must be pointed out most strenuously, that as a result of such enemy attacks the danger exists of the extensive paralysis or even destruction of our own air units. We can no longer expect even a relatively regular supply of aircraft and replacement parts of all types."

The teletype message's warning of further attacks on the "decisively important jet airfields at Prague-Ruzyne, Saaz and Pilsen" were to be proved correct the following day.

On April 17 about 300 enemy fighters appeared over the airfields once again and strafed the parked German aircraft. The weak airfield defenses at Ruzyne managed to shoot down five of the fighter-bombers, but were unable to prevent the destruction of a number of machines, including one Me 262. Nine other jets suffered 20% damage.

At the same time swarms of P-51s and P-47s circled above Saaz, attacking targets on the ground. Four Me 262s returning from a sortie flew into the midst of the American attack. Under the command of Oblt. Grünberg, the *Schwarm* was warned too late of the danger by the ground station. All four Me 262s were shot down as they approached to land. Grünberg was the only pilot who managed to escape by parachute.

In spite of the enemy air patrols JG 7 had managed to get about 20 Me 262s into action. Some of these were sent against American bombers in the Dresden area. Victories were scored by Hptm. Späte, Oblt. Bohatsch and Oblt. Stehle. There were further engagements with heavy bombers in the Prague area. Fritz R. G. Müller shot down a B-17, while additional kills were credited to Ofw. Göbel, Uffz. Schöppler and Ofw. Pritzl.

It should be mentioned that the account of the last days of combat by JG 7 is largely an attempt at reconstruction. Many of the pilots questioned are no longer in possession of written sources, so the author was forced to rely on their memories. As a result there may be inaccuracies concerning dates on which actions took place and victories and losses were assigned.

The Me 262s also flew sorties in *Rotte* and *Schwarm* strength against heavy bombers over Bohemia on April 18, during which Oblt. Bohatsch may have shot down a B-17.

The threat of the encirclement of Berlin by Russian forces led to the evacuation of Brandenburg-Briest airfield on April 18, 1945. In addition to other air units, elements of JG 7 had been left there on Hitler's express order. Following repairs to the airfield these were to participate in "the final battle for the Reich capital." Carrying special passes from Kammlers, the unit train under *Major* Mikat managed to reach its destination of Prague-Ruzyne during the evening hours of April 20 after a hair-raising journey.

Based on reliable reports it appears that jet fighters were even assembled from major components on hand at Briest and subsequently flown to Saaz, Eger and Ruzyne.

The last flyable jet fighters at Brandis and Alt-Lönnewitz – about 10-12 machines – are believed to have left for airfields in the Prague area around the 18th or 19th. These provided valuable reinforcements for the shrunken unit, which on April 19 once again threw all available forces against the Americans. About 30-35 Me 262s were committed against the 3rd Air Division of the 8th Air Force, which bombed targets in the Aussig and Pirna areas on the way to Dresden.

American accounts of the day's fighting record that fighters sweeping ahead of the bomber force shot down four Me 262s immediately after takeoff from Ruzyne and damaged three more.

Enemy fighters staggered above Prague prevented the jets from forming up into a cohesive unit. Instead the Me 262s attacked the approximately 50-kilometer-long bomber stream in twos, threes and fours from what appeared to the pilots to be the most favorable positions. The fighters lacked ground control, which was vital to a successful interception. The jets scored at least four confirmed kills over Aussig, however they lost several machines to concentrated defensive fire from the bombers (according to American sources). The Germans scored a further success over Pirna. A pair of Me 262s made a frontal attack on a formation of B-17s from out of the sun. One Flying Fortress was destroyed in this engagement and two others badly damaged. This attack appears to have cost the jet fighters another aircraft. The day's successful pilots are believed to have been Hptm. Späte, Uffz. Schöppler, Oblt. Bohatsch, Oblt. Grünberg and Ofw. Göbel.

Despite this brief flicker, April 19 saw the ultimate end of the dedicated defensive effort against the bombers of the U.S. Army Air Force. From that day on the jet fighters of JG 7 were only sent against enemy aircraft in small formations when the occasion arose. From April 25 until the German collapse attacks against ground targets were given priority over air defense.

April 20, 1945

Berlin. Instructions from the Luftwaffe Operations Staff on the future organization of jet fighters:

"1. Effective 21. 4. 45 the O.B. Lfl. 6, Gen.Oberst. Greim, will assume overall command of the Luftwaffe in southern Germany.

2. As per a decision at the highest level operational jet fighters and Headquarters, IX. Flg.Korps (J) will remain in the Prague area for the time being.

3. It is planned that IX. Flg.Korps (J) will be disbanded and that 7. Jagddivision will assume command of jet fighters following transfer to southern Germany. It is intended that several command officers with experience in jet operations will be taken into Headquarters, 7. Jagddivision.

4. Proposed disbandments will be ordered from here. Necessary measures can be implemented immediately. The best pilots of KG (J) 54 and III./KG (J) 6 are to be combined with the two existing Gruppen of JG 7.

5. Agreement in principle with later accommodation of units in southern Germany. However individual decisions are to be made based on developments in the situation."

Prague-Ruzyne: The Führer's birthday parade with flags, music, promotions, awarding of decorations and reading of the order of the day urging the troops to fight on.

"Our Führer and Supreme Commander celebrates his 56th birthday on April 20.

Threatened by the enemy, the German people is fighting with all its strength for the preservation of its race.

German blood soaks German soil; poured out by pure hearts; offered up in faith for Germany's greatness.

Unshakeable in trust in the courage, wisdom and will to win of our Führer, we grip our weapons more firmly, clasp our hands harder. More than ever!

Steadfast and true!

Long live our Führer!

Munich. *Luftflottenkommando* 6. *Führungsabteilung* I receives the following teletype from Prague: "Jet operations 20. 4. impossible due to continuous, strong enemy fighter patrols over operational airfields. Request that a combat-capable Gruppe of JG 27 be left in the Prague area to cover jet takeoffs."

April 22, 1945

Stocks of J2 jet fuel in the area of *Luftgaukommando* VIII:

Eger	0 cubic meters
Prague-Ruzyne	34 cubic meters
Prague-Gbell	0 cubic meters
Saaz	0 cubic meters

Berlin. 2240 hours. OKL. Luftwaffe Operations Staff. Radio message. Urgent: "To LFL KDO 6. Headquarters Ia: Führer instructs units of IX.

Fliegerkorps to temporarily remain in Prague area and undertake operations. OKL General Staff Officer in charge of supply will expedite delivery of J2 with all means."

April 24, 1945

Munich. Lfl.Kdo. 6 to LGK VII Munich: "LGK VII will immediately remove following quantities of fuel from L.T.L. Krailing:

> 360 tons B-4
> 2,500 tons J-2

and half the B-4 and C-3 as well as all the J-2 produced from the mixture components available on the evening of the 23rd. As this is the last aviation fuel available, all agencies are to support the removal, which is to be carried out under the direction of a skilful and capable officer, with all means at their disposal."

Berlin. OKL. Operations Staff. Urgent telegram: "LFL 6 is to commit all available and appropriate forces, including the jet fighters of IX Flg. Korps, by day and night in support of the battle for Berlin."

April 25, 1945

Munich. *Luftflottenkommando* 6. Radio message to Headquarters, IX. Fl. Korps:

> "On orders of the OKL IX. Fl. Korps is temporarily placed under the operational control of VIII. Fl. Korps to support the battle for Berlin. Jets are to be employed against enemy columns advancing on Berlin from the south! Out of necessity air defense sorties must temporarily cease in favor of ground attack missions."

That day the pilots of JG 7 flew what were probably their last sorties against the American heavy bombers and scored several victories. The probable victors were Uffz. Schöppler, Ofw. Göbel, Lt. Kelb, Uffz. Engler and *Major* Späte, who shot down two B-17s on one pass. Uffz. Köster, who had been transferred to JV 44, shot down two Mustangs.

171

There was a tragic incident at Ruzyne that day. A damaged Me 262 landed, touched down rather late and caught fire. Oblt. Sturm jumped onto a motorcycle and raced to the burning machine in order to save the pilot. As he approached the aircraft its ammunition exploded and Sturm suffered serious chest wounds when he was struck by several fragments.

April 26, 1945

Munich Lfl.Kdo. 6. 0500 hours. Radio message to IX. Flg. Korps (J):

> "1. Jagd-Div. is temporarily transferring flying elements of I./KG 51 (estimated 12 Me 262) to Prague-Ruzyne 26. 4.
>
> 2. On arrival Prague-Ruzyne I./KG 51 is placed under operational command of IX. Flg. Korps (J).
>
> 3. IX. Flg. Korps (J) will provide technical support by calling on Me 262 unit.
>
> 4. I./KG 51 operations through IX. Flg. Korps (J) primarily in support of defensive battle Berlin against rear communications of 3rd and 4th Guards Tank Armies.
>
> 5. 7. Jagd-Div. will report departure, IX. Flg. Korps (J) arrival at Prague-Ruzyne."

Luftflottenkommando 6. 0120 hours. Radio message to Headquarters, IX. Flg. Korps (J), Prague via VIII. Flg. Korps:

> "Report immediately:
>
> (a) Deployment of units,
> (b) delivery of Me 262s from KG (J) 6 and JG 7 in Munich area,
> (c) delivery site for 12-13 aircraft of I./KG 51 (less technical personnel), which are to be temporarily placed under operational control of IX. Flg. Korps (J)."

Prague. 1215 hours. Through VIII *Fliegerkorps*, IX. *Fliegerkorps (J)* reports to *Luftflottenkommando* 6 that it has begun "defensive support of

Berlin" as ordered, with mission by 8 "Silver" against Forst-Cottbus *autobahn*.

The deliveries of fuel – on the evening of April 26 Ruzyne still had 243 cubic meters and Saaz 98 cubic meters of J2 – enabled the jet units to carry out large-scale close-support operations. Whenever the air situation permitted, the jet fighters took off from Ruzyne and Saaz to attack movements in the Russian rear. During the twilight hours of April 27, 36 jets of JG 7, III./KG(J) 6 and KG(J) 54 were sent to attack supply columns in the Cottbus area. The low rate of fire of the MK 108 made it only marginally suitable for this type of operation, but this was more than made up for by the explosive power of its ammunition. A total of 65 trucks was left ablaze after two passes.

On the return flight the jets, most of them by now out of ammunition, crossed paths with a large formation of Soviet Il 2s. Only eight to ten of the Me 262s still had enough ammunition to attack the enemy aircraft. Six of the heavily-armored close support aircraft were shot down for two German losses. Unfortunately, the names of the victorious German pilots are unknown.

There were frequent encounters with Russian aircraft in late April. Oblt. Schlüter shot down a Yak 9 near Breslau, and Ofhr. Günter Wittbold destroyed two Il 2s near Bärwalde:

> "The action was over quickly and took place at low altitude. I was actually surprised to meet Russians there. The rear gunner of the first Il 2 never had a chance to fire. I had just completed a 360-degree turn when the second Il 2 flew into my flight path. I didn't notice it until tracer from the dorsal gun began flying about my ears. I hit it with several bursts and the Il 2 broke into a number of pieces."

According to conservative estimates JG 7 shot down about 20 Russian aircraft during the final weeks of the war.

The Russians bolstered their convoys' anti-aircraft and fighter defenses, and these inflicted considerable losses on the units committed on April 28. Although there are no reliable sources available concerning personnel and materiel losses, according to realistic estimates about 10 Me 262s are believed to have been lost in the period April 28-May 1.

The only pilot lost by JG 7 during this period whose identity is known is Lt. Fritz Kelb, who was shot down and killed by light flak near Cottbus on April 30. Kelb was the only Luftwaffe pilot to achieve victories flying the Me 163 rocket fighter as well as the Me 262 jet. While a member of JG 400 he destroyed a B 17 flying a "Power Egg" (Me 163) equipped with the SG

500 *Jägerfaust*. Following his transfer to JG 7 he shot down another B-17 with the Me 262.

Further losses resulted from the almost constant patrols over the jet bases by American fighters. Rudi Geldmacher of 11./JG 7 was shot down as he took off from Ruzyne, probably on April 28. He was taken to the Luftwaffe hospital in Prague with severe burns. Geldmacher died a violent death at the hands of an enraged mob on May 15, 1945.

April 30, 1945

Hitler commits suicide. For many this was cause to call for a halt to further senseless fighting. The following announcement was issued by the commander of *Luftflottenkommando* 6:

> *"Soldiers of Luftflotte 6!*
>
> The Führer has fallen. On his order Großadmiral Dönitz has assumed control of the Reich.
> The struggle against bolshevism goes on.
> It is the task of every officer and NCO to ensure that discipline is maintained. Any appearances of slackening are to be countered with circumspection, energy and speed.
> I call upon you, the soldiers of my air fleet, to remain faithful to your honor as soldiers, bearing in mind your oath of allegiance.
>
> The preservation of the Reich rests on your shoulders!"

May 1945. The Final days

At Prague-Ruzyne the operational activities of the approximately 20 serviceable jets were coming to an end. Deliveries of supplies had virtually ceased; stocks of fuel, ammunition and bombs were nearly exhausted. Nevertheless the flood of orders, decrees and directions continued. One read, "... effective immediately Headquarters, IX. Flg. Korps (J) is charged with the command of all jet units deployed within the area of *Luftflotte* 6 . . ."

New bases were chosen for the jets: "Salzburg is to be evacuated by the units of Lw.Kdo. West immediately. It is anticipated that the airfield will be used for jet operations . . ." Units were reorganized: "JV 44 is hereby redesignated IV./JG 7." There were even death threats: "Every abandoned aircraft and vehicle must be completely drained of fuel. Anyone who organizes or tolerates a black market, uses even the smallest quantities of fuel for purposes not related to the war or allows fuel to fall into enemy hands is a saboteur and will be punished accordingly!"

With typical German thoroughness the chaos was administered until the last second.

The elements of JG 7 in Bavaria went into captivity on May 2/3. Among them was a *Gruppe* with *Major* Düllberg. In February he had been transferred from JG 27 to III./EJG 2 and finally to II./JG 7. On April 22 he directed the evacuation of all flying students from Lechfeld to Mühldorf. Ernst Düllberg recalled:

"The members of JG 7 were handled courteously and very correctly at first. Several hours after our capture an American signals platoon appeared with a long-range short wave radio. We were asked to contact Prague and convince those in authority there to abandon the hopeless struggle and fly the remaining serviceable Me 262s to American-occupied territory."

German radio operators spent two days trying to reach their comrades. In vain. Prague was no longer answering. Luftwaffe and assorted Army units were meanwhile fighting for their lives there. The Czech uprising had begun and the Vlasov Army had changed sides. Günter Wittbold provided a graphic description of the inferno of those final days:

"During the night of May 5/6 the airfield came under surprise fire from 105mm artillery and mortars. Vlasov was now also against us and approached with Tiger tanks. SS troops from the barracks in Prague and whatever other forces were available came to the airfield. Everyone, including me, was sent into shallow trenches at the edge of the field. My weapons were a 98 K rifle and a *Panzerfaust* with no fuse, as well as a 6.35mm pistol. I spent two days and nights in the trench. The Vlasov troops got to within 300 to 400 meters several times but were driven off by our anti-aircraft guns, which fired shells fused for air burst. The last Me 262s flew continuous sorties in the immediate vicinity of the airfield.

"Vlasov had the airfield in a corner from three sides. Motorcyclesidecar combinations evacuated the many wounded while the firing was still going on. We were to hold the airfield at all costs, because about 1,000

Luftwaffe female signals personnel and Red Cross sisters had to be transported out of Prague in the remaining trucks, and these were now on the road. There was a gradual withdrawal on the evening of May 8. I scarcely know how to say where and how I got out. At first on foot, later I caught a ride on a wood-gas truck and sat on the front fender. In a village a bundle of hand grenades exploded beneath the truck. Following a circuitous route and frequently under sniper fire, I reached Saaz on May 10. Later I was sent to the large American POW camp at Eger."

On May 6 Ruzyne airfield came under artillery and mortar fire, which reduced even further the already shrunken number of serviceable jet fighters. About a dozen Me 262s were damaged by direct hits or shrapnel. In view of the shortage of replacement parts there could be no hope of restoring them to service. When, at about midday on May 7, it appeared that the airfield might be overrun by troops of Vlasov's army, the damaged machines were blown up and the others ordered to Saaz. The remaining jets in the Protectorate, about 15-20 Me 262s, were assembled there on the morning of May 8, 1945. As they there were without orders, in the hours prior to the unconditional surrender of the German armed forces the pilots were given permission to fly to the destinations of their choice. As a result this day saw the complete disbandment of the *Geschwader*. Many pilots decided to fly to their homes in territory occupied by the Anglo-Americans. Oblt. Grünberg, for example, took off with four others and flew to Kaltenkirchen, where he set his aircraft, "White 1," down in a field near his home. Today Hans Grünberg still lives near the former base of I./JG 7. Others, whose homes had been overrun by the Red Army, surrendered their Me 262s to the Americans somewhere in southern Germany.

At 1600 on May 8, 1945 fighters of JG 7 fought the last air battle of the war. At about 1520 Oblt. Stehle and his wingman took off to intercept Russian Yak 9 fighters over the Erz Mountains. The two Germans came upon the surprised enemy over Freiburg. The cannon roared for the last time, and for the last time MK 108 rounds shattered the fuselage of an enemy aircraft. To our knowledge this was the last aerial victory by a German fighter pilot in the Second World War. Modifying the title of a well-known book, one could say that Oblt. Stehle was not the first, but he was certainly the last!

Notes:
[1] Little is known about the fate of the elements of the Geschwader which wound up in the north. What is known is that Hermann Buchner was shot down over Luneburg Heath on or around April 20, 1945.

...ner relieved Major Hohagen as
...eur of III./JG 7 on January 24, 1945.

Georg-Peter Eder, first Staffelkapitän of 9./JG 7, at
Parchim.

...z Schall, Staffelkapitän of 10./JG 7 at
...urg.

Lt. Joachim Weber, first Staffelkapitän of 11./JG 7 at
Brandenburg-Briest.

Lt. Heinrich
Lönnecker, 9./JG 7.

Top right:
Oblt. Karl-Heinz
Seeler, 9./JG 7.

Günther Wegmann,
9./JG 7.

Center right:
Hptm. Heinz
Gutmann, 9./JG 7.

Parchim, March
1945. From left: Fhr.
Ehrig, Ofw. Buchner
(10. Staffel, later
transferred to 9.
Staffel), Ofhr. Russel,
Lt. Petermann and
Ofw. Lennartz.

Fhr. Ernst Pfeiffer,
9./JG 7.

Top right:
Oblt. Franz Külp,
10./JG 7.

Center left:
Lt. Friedrich-
Wilhelm Schenk,
10./JG 7.

Group photo of pilots of 11./JG 7. Upper row from left: Fw.
Heinz Eichner, Ofw. August Lübking, Lt. Fritz R.G. Müller;
center row: Uffz. Helmut Detjens, Lt. Joachim Weber; bottom row:
Uffz. Ernest Giefing, Fw. Bergmann (?), Ofw. Heinz Arnold, Uffz.
Heiner Geisthövel, Fhr. Franz Köster.

Ofw. Heinz Arnold.

Ofw. August Lübking.

Lt. Rudi Geldmacher.

Lt. Rudi Rademacher.

Lt. Fritz R.G. Müller (sleeping) and Lt. Alfred Ambs (with pipe).

Old warriors, 37 years later. From left: Helmut Detjens, author, Alfred Ambs and Heiner Geisthövel at a fighter pilots reunion in May 1981.

Pilots of the Stabsschwarm and 11. Staffel

Major Heinrich Ehrler. Transferred to JG 7 follow the Tirpitz tragedy, he was killed in action on April 6, 1945.

Lt. Harry Mayer.

Lt. Herbert Schlüter.

One of Jagdgeschwader 7's bases, probably Parchim or Oranienburg.

A unique photographic document. An Me 262 makes a firing pass at a Liberator.

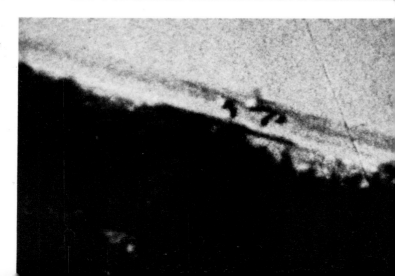

"Rat catching." Stills from the gun camera of an American fighter as it pursues an Me 262 on approach to land.

Top and center:
An aircraft's fate.
"White 8" of
11./JG 7 before a
sortie on April 7,
1945 . . . and on the
scrap heap in June
1944.

Bottom:
Ofw. Hermann
Buchner, a former
close-support pilot
with 6./SG 2, on
the wing of his Me
262 at Parchim.
March 1944.

Pilots of I. Gruppe

Uffz. Günther Engler, 2./JG 7.

Oblt. Walter Schuck, last Staffelkapitän of 3./JG 7.

Oblt. Grünberg, Staffelkapitän of 1./JG 7 and Oblt. Bohatsch (from left).

Uffz. Heinrich Kempken, 7.

3./JG 7. Kaltenkirchen, March 15, 1945. From left: Uffz. Willi Fick, unidentified, unidentified, Flieger Gefr. Heim, Ofhr. Schrey, Uffz. Rach, Ofhr. Kretschmar, Uffz. Geisthövel, Oblt. Wagner, Ofhr. Tönissen, Weiss, Lt. Hoyer and Fw. Gzik.

Aircraft of 11. Staffel photographed at Brandenburg-Briest by an amateur photographer on April 7, 1945.

Parchim, April 7, 1945. The Kommandeur of III. Gruppe, Major Sinner, after being wounded in combat.

Major Heinz Bär (center) and Ofw. Schuhmacher (behind and to the right). Lechfeld, April 1945.

ets of III./EJG 2, c. March 1945.

he "Heimatschützer I." While flying this aircraft during his tour as a
Messerschmitt test pilot, Major Bär established an altitude record for jet aircraft of
4,700 meters.

Installation of the Walter engine in the "Heimatschützer I."

The "Heimatschützer II," Werknummer 170 074. Explosion of the combustion chamber in the right engine during stationary tests on January 25, 1945.

R engine of the Heimatschützer II with rocket
removed.

Kelb (left) and Ofw. Siegfried Rudschinat (right, JG
Kelb was the only German fighter pilot to obtain
g the Me 163 and the Me 262.

Weapons pack (262 F/107) for the A-1a/U1
fighter version: 2 MG 151/20 (2 x 146
rounds), 2 MK 103 (2 x 72 rounds), 2 MK
108 (2 x 65 rounds). Only one example of
this version was completed before the end
of the war.

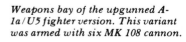

Me 262 A-1a/U4 with MK 214 cannon. Only two of these aircraft were built. Their Werknummern were 170 083 and 111 899.

Weapons bay of the upgunned A-1a/U5 fighter version. This variant was armed with six MK 108 cannon.

Top:
The end. Prague-Gbell,
June 1944.

Center:
Werknummer 111 792 on
the autobahn west of Ulm.

"White 9" of III./EJG 2 at
an aircraft graveyard. A
pile of wreckage was all
that was left of the once-
proud Luftwaffe.

Destroyed Me 262s following a destructive USAAF raid on Neuburg/Donau on April 9, 1945.

Under the red star. An Me 262 captured by the Russians.

Ofw. Heinz Arnold's "Yellow 7," faithfully restored by the Paul Garber Restoration Facility at Silver Hill, Maryland.

Chapter VI
A Look Back

Surrender – JV 44 – The Pilots of JG 7, a Cross-Section of the Entire Luftwaffe – Foreign Jet Fighter Developments – The Legend of the Me 262 as a Possible War-Winning Weapon – Criticism of Previous Literature on the Me 262 Fighter – There Was no Jet Fighter Tragedy and no Stab in the Back – The Me 262, One Armaments Problem of Many – A Word from the Author

May 8, 1945

The unconditional surrender of the German Wehrmacht brought to an end a European tragedy.

For six years every branch of the German armed forces, the Luftwaffe and the German fighter pilots had lived up to their oath of allegiance, enduring deprivation and immense sacrifices in blood. On this May 8 the youngest *Jagdgeschwader* of the Luftwaffe, *Jagdgeschwader* 7, also ceased to exist. The feelings of the German fighter pilots are evident in an extract from the war diary of another *Jagdgeschwader* (JG 4), which surrendered at Leck, in Schleswig-Holstein:

> "6.5.45. We draw up the aircraft, vehicles and all equipment in parade formation. The English will be astonished at the imposing sight on the airfield. The scene of more than 100 machines fills us with proud nostalgia. The latest designs, the Me 262 and He 162, which scarcely saw action, stand between the old, brave Bf 109 G and the Fw 190 assault fighters, which were victorious in thousands of air battles, waiting to be surrendered to the enemy."

> "7.5.45. We are to remove the propellers and rudders from the aircraft and take out all the ammunition. For us pilots the scene on the base is unspeakably sad and painful. To have to see our pride, our arm, our world

standing there so naked! Perhaps 30-40 Me 262s, the fastest fighter in the world, sit side by side in front of a hangar, ready to be handed over . . . We bear the inevitable with dignity and honor."

Such feelings may also have been felt in the ranks of *Jagdgeschwader* 7. All the effort, all the sacrifices had been in vain. In retrospect it is easy to know better and to wonder what drove these men to climb into their aircraft and accept battle with a crushingly superior enemy to the last day in spite of the inevitable outcome. Defiance, desperation, the feeling of technical superiority, sense of duty – all these may have played a role. However, these young men knew one thing for certain: each heavy bomber shot down, prevented from delivering its deadly load, meant life for a number of women and children. And the Allies grimly continued to attack this land in agony: the US 8th Air Force until April 25, 1945, the 15th until May 1, the 9th until May 3, to say nothing of the attacks by RAF Bomber Command and the plague of the fighter-bombers. This was pure terror, in no way justifiable militarily.

In the previous chapters we have described the difficulties *Jagdgeschwader* 7 was forced to grapple with and the success it achieved in spite of them. This was possible only because everyone in this unit, from *Kommodore* and *Gruppenkommandeur* down to the last man on the ground, burned with a desire to achieve success with the new weapon and once again show "them" something. All the more amazing then is a statement by Johannes Steinhoff in his book *In letzter Stunde*:

> "Actually I knew none of the pilots. They hadn't flown a mission, had seen no air combat, and I sensed that there was scarcely any of the impetuous urge to prove oneself and for single combat that had led to the fighters' great success in the first year of the war."

But there must have been something there, otherwise how could the *Geschwader* have achieved the considerable success it did under the most adverse conditions? It may be that resignation, resentment, bitterness and depression may have guided Steinhoff's pen. But are such feelings the appropriate means to motivate a *Geschwader* to unconditional action? In his own way Steinhoff, too, honestly wanted to do his best, otherwise why would he once again risk his life with JV 44 during the last weeks of the war? At this point we will offer a brief comment on a unit surrounded by legend: JV 44, the unit of "conspirators," of "outcasts" and "exiles," the unit of "experts." We quote from Galland's book *Die Ersten und die Letzten*:

"The Knight's Cross was, so to speak, the service uniform of our unit. After a long period of technical and numerical inferiority, they wanted once again to experience the feeling of superiority in the air. They wanted to be numbered among the last fighter pilots of the Luftwaffe as the world's first jet fighter pilots. For this they were willing to once again risk their lives."

It is somewhat surprising that Galland makes only a single passing reference to JG 7 in his book. It may be that he is unaware of the unit's successful actions during March and April. One is entitled, however, to be skeptical about that long-lived, oft-repeated legend that the Knight's Cross was the unit's service uniform. Of the 44 pilots belonging to JV 44 on April 20, 1945, only 12 wore the Knight's Cross; as well there were 16 non-commissioned officers in the unit's ranks.

But back to *Jagdgeschwader 7*. Who were the men who flew with this *Geschwader* and who once again posed a threat to the all-powerful Allies in the air? Were they members of a selected corps of pilots, as Göring had demanded in November 1944? Was JG 7 really an elite unit, as one occasionally reads? The list of the *Geschwader*'s pilots reads like a cross-section of the Luftwaffe. Highly-decorated *"Experten"* flew alongside young pilots who had only recently received their baptism of fire on the invasion front. Retrained bomber pilots flew beside young pilots fresh out of fighter pilot school, former transport pilots alongside veterans of "Wilde Sau" (Wild Boar) night fighter operations, experienced flight instructors with old hands from the close-support units. They came from everywhere. There were *Eismeerjäger* like Weissenberger, Ehrler, Schuck, Arnold, Reinhold and Lübking. There were daredevils from the *Sturmgruppen* like Stahlberg, Gossow, Pritzl and Todt. From the *Grünherz Geschwader* came Rudorffer, Rademacher, Schnörrer and Späte, from JG 52 Schall, Petermann and Tangermann, from JG 27 Sinner, Sturm and Ullrich. There were the former *Zerstörer* pilots Stehle, Weber, Wörner and Büschen. This sampling should convince the reader of the diverse background from which the unit's pilots came.

It speaks volumes about the high morale of all the participants, from the men in the headquarters, the technicians and the signals people right up to the pilots, that in spite of the difficulties they were able to forge a unit of high fighting quality. The men of *Jagdgeschwader 7* earned the enemy's highest respect. Right to the end they displayed an unshakable will to fight and gave the enemy a convincing demonstration of what the ingenuity and hard work of the German engineers was capable of producing, even under adverse conditions.

It is true that the enemy had not been inactive in the field of jet fighters. In 1944 American projects, like the P-59 Airacomet and the P-80 Shooting Star, had not yet overcome their teething problems. The P-80 made its first flight on January 9, 1944, but did not enter unit service until just prior to the end of the war and then in small numbers.

The British progressed somewhat farther with their Gloster Meteor. Development of this aircraft had begun before the war, however its first flight did not take place until March 1943. The RAF's 616 Squadron became the first unit to equip with the jet fighter, in July 1944. Initially used at home against the V 1, the first Meteor landed on the continent in mid-February 1945. In April they began flying missions against German airfields, but there were no encounters with German aircraft. The Meteor thus had no opportunity to demonstrate its value as a fighter. The de Havilland Vampire entered series production shortly before the end of the war. Those who know how long it took the British aircraft industry, which suffered from no material shortages whatsoever, to produce an operationally-capable jet fighter are somewhat more cautious in their judgement of the difficulties and failures in the development story of the Me 262 than the literature of the past. It was undoubtedly one of the greatest accomplishments of the German aircraft industry and the responsible offices of the RLM that, in spite of unimaginable difficulties, they succeeded in producing the world's first operational jet fighter and made aviation history.

All due admiration should not, however, prevent us from returning to the legends surrounding the Me 262's potential as a weapon capable of changing the course of the war.

We will begin with General Galland's hastily-written book *Die Ersten und die Letzten*. "It's as if angels were pushing," he said after his first flight in a prototype of the Me 262. This feeling of exhilaration is understandable. One must take exception, however, when he writes: ". . . Production of the Me 262 had already been delayed about a year by as the result of an order from the Führer in autumn 1940 to suspend development."

The facts tell a different story. On November 1, 1940, Messerschmitt submitted a proposal for Project III. The first airframe was completed at the end of January 1941, the first prototype flew in April and a production contract for a total of 25 Me 262s was issued in July of that same year. Delays in production were the result of the non-availability of suitable power plants.

Galland:

"Production was delayed at least a further six months by Hitler's order, in July 1943, not to make any preparations for series production."

The fact is that in June 1943 Messerschmitt projected delivery of the first pre-production series aircraft for January 1944. As a result of a series of verifiable delays caused by problems in the delivery of materials, the destruction of important production facilities and other unexpected difficulties, the first pre-production aircraft were not delivered until early April 1944. Hitler can be blamed for much, but he bears no guilt in the so-called "jet fighter tragedy."
Galland:

> "I still believe today that it was not exaggerated optimism to expect a decisive turn in the German air defense from the mass employment of the Me 262 even at that time . . . It doesn't bear thinking about that we could have had these jet fighters years before!"

At that time! Years before! When? Even if the Me 262, especially its power plants, had been ready for series production in May 1943, and without any of the troublesome consequences of Hitler's interventions, which were nowhere near as disruptive as has been claimed, the Me 262 could not have been available in large numbers until at least 1945. By then the Russians were already on the Oder and the Anglo-Americans were at the gates of the Ruhr.

Galland's misinterpretations are understandable as the resignation of an armaments General who had been the sole voice crying in the desert for a timely strengthening of his arm in preparation for the coming air battle over Germany. But in these quotes we find bundled together all the legends and half-truths which are happily repeated in literature and research on the air war. It is useless to ask who copied from whom. Common to all is a certain tendency toward irrationality.

Next we turn to *Oberst* Werner Baumbach, whose book *Zu Spät*, appeared in 1949. In it he wrote, "It is important to remember that the Allied bomber offensive would certainly have been stopped if production of jet fighters had started six months earlier." This claim should be put to rest once and for all. In June 1943 Messerschmitt planned to manufacture 430 Me 262s by October 1944. In reality it was about 340 machines. If we assume that all of these machines would have found their way to the fighter arm, and subtract the aircraft required by Messerschmitt, which was responsible for testing and training, and those lost through accidents and enemy action, then the first *Geschwader* complete with *Stab* and three *Gruppen* could not have been formed until November 1944 and would not have been operational until some time later. We leave it to the imagination of the reader to decide whether this *Geschwader* would have been enough to stop the Allied bombing offensive at that late stage of the war.

However, Baumbach's hypothesis is harmless compared to that put forward by *General* Karl Koller, who was Chief of the Luftwaffe Operations Staff until August 1944, in his book *Der letzte Monat*, which appeared in 1949:

> "It also happened that the Me 262 jet fighter, development of which was quite far advanced, was more or less put on ice and was thus delayed about two years. The Me 262 could have been our salvation in the air war."

When? Quite far advanced? More or less put on ice? Delayed about two years? Koller's "exact" statements call into question the accuracy of the former Luftwaffe Chief of Staff's memory.

One can only shake his head on reading Koller's imaginative version of events:

> The Me 262 arrived too late and in far too limited quantities. Because – and this is the most incredible thing – when the first machines were delivered in April 1945 Hitler ordered this thoroughbred fighter converted into a fighter-bomber. This made necessary changes to the cockpit, the installation of bomb-aiming equipment, bomb racks and release mechanisms and the construction of a sturdier undercarriage able to bear the weight of a 1,000 kg bomb without collapsing. Anyone with even a limited knowledge of the subject can understand the significance of introducing such a change after the beginning of series production. The result was a delay in production, which under the existing circumstances one can only characterize as criminal. Hitler forbade delivery of the aircraft to the fighters, and in tyrannical stubbornness held fast in the face of all arguments."

There is hardly anything in this account which tallies with the facts. One must ask oneself whether these are consciously written untruths or whether the former Chief of the General Staff really was so innocent as to believe what he wrote. Either notion is deplorable, because no conversion was necessary to enable the Me 262 to carry bombs; it had been designed to do so from the beginning. As well, the aircraft never carried a 1,000 kg bomb in service. Its normal load was either one SC 500 or two SC 250 bombs, for which the undercarriage was completely adequate following some minor strengthening.

General Koller claims to have sent a telegram to Hitler and Göring during an inspection trip to the invasion front in August 1944: "Send the Me 262 to the front as a fighter immediately!"

This is so silly and fantastic that it leaves one speechless. The two trials units, *Erprobungskommandos Thierfelder* and *Schenk*, had at most twenty aircraft between them at that time and no experience in fighter operations. Furthermore the Western Theater lacked both suitable airfields and a ground organization capable of supporting and controlling this new-generation fighter.

In the face of so much nonsense and misinformation from high places, it is no wonder that *Generalfeldmarschall* Kesselring blew from the same horn in *Soldat bis zum letzten Tag*:

> "Today there is no denying that the jet fighter would probably have changed the face of the air war over Germany, and probably even the outcome of the war."

Walter Lüdde-Neurath offered a modified version in his 1980 book *Regierung Dönitz*:

> "Development of the jet fighter was initially held up through Göring's lack of interest . . . In the summer of 1944 Hitler himself discarded his last trump card. Contrary to the strong representations by the OKW, Luftwaffe and the armaments industry, he ordered the pure fighter which had been developed converted into a fighter-bomber. According to statements by leading experts, service employment of the aircraft was delayed at least six, if not twelve months."

In 1973 Herbert Molloy-Mason also made a significant contribution to the Me 262 theme in his book *The Luftwaffe 1918-1945*:

> "If the jet aircraft had appeared early enough and in sufficient numbers, the American daylight raids would have been stopped until the introduction of effective countermeasures."

The author fails to speculate what these countermeasures might have been, and continues:

"In early 1944, when series production was finally about to begin, Hitler intervened and ordered the machines, which were urgently needed as fighters, converted to fighter-bombers. This although whole units could have been equipped with the Arado 234, which had been designed as a bomber from the beginning, after a sufficient number of engines had been delivered. Hitler's insane decree was later withdrawn, but once again a failure of leadership had deprived a technically-superior German product of its success. The Me 262 was committed to action too late to alter the outcome of the war."

There is nothing too stupid to be printed. Mason's recipe is so disturbingly simple that it is simply unimaginable that no one thought of it before him.

Someone pulls a number of engines from the hat and he has conjured up whole units of jet bombers. It wouldn't have been that simple.

Albert Speer is surprisingly modest in his book *Erinnerungen* which appeared in 1976. But he too succumbs to the fascination of the wonder weapon:

"Because the General staffs expected a decisive turn in the air war from this fighter aircraft alone (June 1944! the author) . . . After the war I heard from Galland that a lack of interest on the part of the supreme command had caused a delay of about a year and a half . . . Furthermore Hitler (on 22. 3. 45! the author) wanted our jet fighter, the Me 262, converted to fighter aircraft as quickly as possible. He thus involuntarily confirmed the tactical mistakes he had stubbornly made against the advice of all the experts a year and a half earlier."

Cajus Bekker, usually not so easily duped, concluded in *Angriffshöhe 4000*:

"The jet fighter, developed before the war, then ignored for years, even categorically forbidden by the Supreme Commander of the Wehrmacht and finally thrown rashly into battle – this jet fighter perhaps demonstrated German efficiency even in the most difficult times, but at the end of the war it changed nothing."

The memory of *Oberst* Nikolaus von Below (*Als Hitlers Adjutant*, 1980) is also somewhat clouded:

"Hitler had Professor Messerschmitt come on Sept. 7, 1943, and asked him about the state of development of the jet aircraft. To everyone's *surprise* he asked whether the aircraft was suitable for use as a bomber, to which Messerschmitt replied in the affirmative . . . (At Insterburg) Hitler summoned Messerschmitt and suddenly asked whether this aircraft could also be built as a bomber. Messerschmitt answered that it could . . . But the Luftwaffe could only offer the aircraft as a fighter-bomber as additional equipment for carrying and aiming bombs was required for the high-speed bomber role. Hitler accepted this out of necessity . . . After inspecting the aircraft at Insterburg Hitler drew false conclusions about the production of jet aircraft. He was of the opinion that the first machines equipped to drop bombs could reach the front as early February 1944. This could not be done. A new engine had to be produced, completion of which could not be expected until May 1944. Hitler still knew nothing of this. He had been misinformed and no one saw cause to correct this."

Fiction and the truth also lie close together in this version.

Naturally *General* Steinhoff's *In letzter Stunde* can not be left out:

> "The superstition of the wonder weapon struck me as a transparent trick. In the end I commanded one of these wonder weapons – a whole Geschwader of jet fighters – and I knew only too well that its use was not decisive."

A powerful passage. The *Geschwader* which he had led for six weeks consisted of a single *Jagdgruppe* and never saw action before he was relieved.

Although *Oberst* Steinhoff knew very well that the use of jet fighters was not decisive, he changed his opinion diametrically a few dozen sentences later:

> "We (JV 44, the author) had proved convincingly that the concentrated employment of jet fighters could have stopped the bomber streams. Galland's theory, that 80 Me's brought to bear on the enemy would have stopped the daylight incursions, was logical."

A puzzling, fatal blindness. JV 44 began operating in *Rotte* or *Schwarm* strength at a time when JG 7, which had been in action since February 1945, was conducting operations with between 30 and 50 aircraft. Even with these numbers the unit inflicted little better than pinpricks on the American 8th and 15 Air Forces and stopping their attacks was never in question. A simple calculation would have convinced Steinhoff. On the day in question nine Me

262s of JV 44 scored six confirmed and two probable victories. Purely hypothetically then, eighty Me 262s could have shot down 54 bombers at best. Measured against the 8th Air Forces average operational strength of 1,200 bombers, this would have constituted a loss rate of 4.5%. At this point in time that would not have been enough to scare away the USAAF, instead it would probably have led to even greater concentrations.

One could continue the quotes if one chose to. We find them from Deichmann, Grabmann and Suchenwirth, from the Historical Division of the US Army and the *Bundeswehr*'s Command Academy, from Mano Ziegler and so on and so on . . .

We wish to end this illustrious parade with the man with whom we began the revue. In an interview in the magazine *Bild am Sonntag*, 7. 3. 1982, Galland said:

> "I was also unable to push through use of the revolutionary Me 262 jet aircraft as a fighter in good time. But today I know that it was just as well for us! Certainly 500 Me 262s would have stopped the American bombers, but that would only have lengthened the war . . ."

Steinhoff hoped to achieve a miracle with 80 Me 262s; at least Galland's notion is somewhat more realistic. But there still remains a puzzle: where, in spite of all his best efforts, did he expect to obtain 500 Me 262s during the years 1943/44, and at what point in time?

Guilt for the delay in committing the Me 262 as a fighter is unanimously sought in Hitler's decision to initially use the aircraft as a high-speed bomber. Let us rather stick to the facts. In the preceding chapters we have attempted to trace the development history of the Me 262. Once again the most important points:

> 1. When Späte and Galland first flew one of the prototypes in early 1943 the aircraft was in no way ready for front-line service for reasons which are well-known. Even Messerschmitt did not foresee completion of the first pre-production aircraft before January 1944 and the start of large-scale production before November 1944.

> 2. Hitler's August 1943 order, not to stop production of the Me 209, could not have had a negative effect on output of the Me 262 until late 1944. In any case it was withdrawn again soon afterward.

> 3. Hitler's order that the Me 262 be capable of dropping bombs could

not have come as a surprise, as an order had existed since February 1943 that every aircraft must be capable of being employed as a fighter-bomber. Messerschmitt had thus conceived the Me 262 as a bomb carrier from as early on as March 1943.

4. There could be no question of delays in work on the Me 262 as the result of Hitler's interference at least until early 1944, if at all, as construction of the pre-production series did not begin until the beginning of 1944 and it was not until May 25, 1944 that Hitler ordered that all Me 262s coming off the production line were to be delivered to bomber units.

5. *Hauptmann* Thierfelder's Me 262 fighter test detachment was formed in December 1943 and trained with V-Series aircraft until April 1944. The first production machines appeared in May 1944. The first kill by an Me 262 occurred on July 26, 1944.

The KdE report on the (limited) front-line suitability of the Me 262 A as a fighter aircraft followed on September 12. *Einsatzkommando Nowotny* was formed in mid-September 1944.

In parallel the bomber developments:

6. The first bomber pilots began converting to the Me 262 on June 20, 1944. On July 20, 1944 *Kommando Schenk* transferred to France with nine Me 262s and flew its first sorties there. In September 1944 I. *Gruppe* and elements of II. *Gruppe* of KG 51 were retrained on the Me 262 and began operations in October 1944. III. *Gruppe* of *Jagdgeschwader* 7 was formed on November 19, 1944.

Fighter or bomber, one thing is clear: in spite of the highest level of patronage, a powerful high-speed bomber unit (approx. 30-40 Me 262s) was not combat-ready until October 1944. At the same time the Nowotny fighter test detachment consisted of about 20 Me 262s. Had the *Schnellbomber* episode not come about, at the end of 1944 the fighters would have had at most 40 more Me 262s at their disposal.

Even the keenest optimist will not wish to claim that this handful of jet fighters would have been in a position to change the face of the war in the air at a time when the enemy had already reached the frontiers of Germany in the east and west.

The fact that from December 1944 some of the Me 262s produced were not made available to JG 7, but were assigned instead to KG (J) 54 (a total of 145 aircraft) and III./KG (J) 6 (about 6 aircraft) – bomber units converted to the fighter role – had no effect on the overall military situation. Due to a shortage of aircraft, plans to equip KG (J) 6, 27, 30, 40 and 55 with the Me 262 did not materialize. Without the loss of these aircraft JG 7 could no doubt have been fully equipped and its operations would certainly have been more effective, but basically it was just a shifting of aircraft within units.

What remains then of the so-called "jet fighter tragedy?" The fighter units equipped with the Me 262 (JG 7, KG (J) 54 and JV 44) were deprived only of the high-speed bombers of KG 51 – at best that would have meant a doubling of available Me 262s in 1945. We agree then with *General* Galland's sentences in his book *Die Ersten und die Letzten*:

> "We could thus have put 100 to 150 jet fighters into the air during the last days of the war. Even though they could not affect the outcome, it would have demonstrated the possibilities this technical advance opened up to us . . ."

We cannot follow Galland, however, when he continues, ". . . and what grave mistakes the supreme command also made in this area." In view of all the projects in the field of armaments, which for whatever reason failed to materialize or appeared too late, the jet fighter was just one problem of many. It is natural that each branch of the service views its problems as the most important and critical to the war effort. But all these futuristic weapons had their limits where the possibilities of German industry ended. They were limited simply by raw materials and labor forces. Filling a gap here meant creating one somewhere else. Everything else belongs to the realm of speculation.

Let us content ourselves with the verifiable facts. Fact is, the Me 262 was a magnificent aircraft and its design and production under the most adverse of conditions ranks as one of the greatest feats of German technology and industry. And for the former members of *Jagdgeschwader* 7 we end this work with the words of *General* Steinhoff from his book *In letzter Stunde*:

> "To my surprise I found pilots with a new self-confidence. Distinguished by the privilege of being considered fit to be pilots in this the only jet fighter unit, and fully conscious of being far superior to the enemy with this aircraft, there was a resurgence of the desire for action which had characterized the Luftwaffe at the beginning of the war."

After these conciliatory words all that remains is the request that the fallen of the *Geschwader* be kept in honored remembrance. Whether heroes or victims, one thing is certain: they were pioneers in the history of aviation.

In closing a word on my own behalf. The author freely admits that he handed over this book, the result of years of investigative work, for publication with mixed emotions, because he knew that it would initiate considerable controversy. He understands fully that many a man who flew the Me 262 during the last months of the war will not recognize "his" aircraft. In him lives the memory of exultation at finally being able to go into battle in an aircraft which was technically far superior to the enemy after years of hopeless inferiority during which he was, as it were, fair game for hordes of Spitfires, Mustangs, Thunderbolts and Tempests. To such a man the Me 262 must have seemed like a kind of "life insurance." On the other side there is the fully documented high loss rate, with or without enemy action, which cannot be avoided. At 15%, losses in action among the Me 262s which made contact with the enemy – if the 56.5% of the unlucky 10.4.45 are left out – are surprisingly high. In the eight weeks from the end of February to mid-April 1945, which marked the high point of its activities, JG 7 lost 51 pilots killed and 12 badly wounded, most of whose names are known. This meant that the operational strength of one-and-a-half *Gruppen* was lost and had to be replaced. This rate of loss is not much lower than that of the conventional fighter units with piston-engined aircraft.

As always, the truth lies somewhere in the middle. There is no doubt that the Me 262 presented no insurmountable difficulties to a good pilot, especially one with many years of practical experience. It is also beyond question that the majority of pilots took this aircraft into action with a minimum of familiarization time, and that the "experts" simply did not have the time to pass on some of their wealth of experience to the newcomers. Walter Hagenah, one of the successful *Sturmjäger* of the *Udet Geschwader*, hit the nail on the head when he said:

"I had little difficulty converting to the Me 262. But there were also less-experienced pilots trying it around me, and for them the problem was much greater. We had pilots with a total flying time of barely 100 hours. They could take off and land the aircraft but I am firmly convinced that they were not ready for operations. It was criminal to send them into battle with such limited training. These young people did their best, but they had to pay a high price for their lack of flying experience."

That there were individuals who achieved success even with a minimum of training time is a credit to the Me 262. That it did not achieve more is due on one hand to the unfavorable hour, and on the other to the fact that there was insufficient time to completely eliminate all the tactical and technical problems presented by such a revolutionary aircraft.

The author believes that with his book he has made an important contribution to the discussion of the Me 262 as a fighter aircraft. It is precisely because he became so deeply involved with the Me 262 during years of investigative work that he is able to depict its development and its advantages as well its shortcomings without bias.

Appendixes

Appendix A

JG 7 Pilots

This list makes no claim to completeness. Included are all the names known to the author, even if they belonged to the Geschwader for only a brief time. The numbers of victories and combat missions listed refer to the period *before* the pilot was transferred to JG 7. I have forgone listing the kills achieved with JG 7 as it was impossible to record all victories or provide accurate dates (Schuck, Eder, Rudorffer, among others). It was also considered inadvisable to try and differentiate between confirmed and unconfirmed kills and between aircraft forced to leave formation and those seriously damaged so long after the events took place. † Indicates date of death.

Name	Rank	Year of Birth	Previous Unit	Number of Missions	Combat Victories	Notes
Alf, Rudolf	Ofw.		JG 2		ca. 12	†26.11.44
Ambs, Alfred	Lt.	1923	JG 104		-	Wounded 24.3.45
Anschütz, Helmut	Ofw.	1915	Trans.	64	-	
Anzer, Fritz	Uffz.	1921				†4.45
Arnold, Heinz	Ofw.		JG 5		42	†17.4.45
Ast, Hans-Joachim	Ofhr.					†14.1.45
Auerbach, Rolf	Uffz.	1919	NJG?	36	-	
Barden, Ewald	Fw.	1920	EK 388	109	-	
Baten, Kurt	Fw.	1919	JG 1	370	24	
Baudach, Helmut	Ofw.	1918	JG 2		ca.15	†22.2.45
Beck, Max	Lt.	1910				
Beckert, Otto	Uffz.	1923	JG 54	9	1	
Bergmann	Fw.					
Berndt, Hans-Joachim	Uffz.	1922		2	-	
Biermeier, Alois	Fw.					Wounded 19.2.45
Bischoff, Günther	Hptm.	1918	JG 300	123	4	
Bodes, Hans	Ofw.	1921	Trans.	20	-	
Böckel	Ofw.				12	
Böttge, Erwin	Uffz.	1924		6	-	
Bohatsch, Walter	Oblt.		JG 3		13	
Bongart, Peter	Uffz.	1917	Recon.	11	-	
Bott, Hans	Lt.		JG 400		1	
Braun, Hans	Lt.		JG 4			
Brill, Karl	Lt.	1919	JG 54		52	
Brüse, Wendelin	Uffz.					
Büschen, Wilhelm	Lt.	1919	JG 6, ZG 26	170	9	
Büttner, Erich	Ofw.		EK 262			†20.3.45

JG 7

Name	Rank	Year of Birth	Previous Unit	Number of Missions	Combat Victories	Notes
Buchner, Hermann	Ofw.	1919	SG 2	600	46	Knight's Cross
Burkhardt, Lutz-Wilhelm	Hptm.	1919	JG 77, 1	245	61	Knight's Cross
Burkschat	Ofw.	1916	Jabo			
Burchardt	Uffz.					
Caatz	Uffz.					
Chlond, Herbert	Uffz	1923		14	4	
Christer	Fhr.					
Degener, Karl	Fw.	1921	JG 6	201	12	
Detjens, Helmut	Uffz.	1924	JG 4		1	
Döhler	Major					
Dorn, Hans	Lt.					
Drfla, Hubert	Fw.	1920	JG 3	230	18	
Düllberg, Ernst	Major	1913	JG 27, 76	650	50	Knight's Cross
Eden, Georg-Peter	Major	1921	JG 51, 2, 1, 26	ca.700	53	Oak Leaves Wounded 16.2.45
Eden, Hermann	Lt.	1921				
Ehrig, Friedrich	Fhr.	1921		39	-	
Ehrler, Heinrich	Major	1917	JG 5		201	Oak Leaves †6.4.45
Eichorn, Erwin	Fw.		JG 2			†29.12.44
Eichner, Heinz	Fw.					†22.3.45
Elschner	Uffz.					
Engel, Heinrich	Lt.	1920				
Engel, Wolfgang	Uffz.	1924		5	1	
Engler, Günther	Uffz.		JG 3		ca.5	
Fährmann, Gottfried	Lt.		JG 77			to JV 44
Freytag, Siegfried	Major	1919	JG 77	879	102	Knight's Cross
Frodl, Franz	Obersting.					
Frohs	Ofw.					
Führmann, Hein	Lt.	1917	JG 54	8	-	
Gartmann, Benvenuto	Fw.	1909		54	-	
Gehlker, Fritz	Ofhr.					†20.3.45
Geisthövel, Heiner	Fw.				3	
Geldmacher, Ernst-Rudolf	Lt.					†14.5.45
Giefing, Ernst	Uffz.					Wounded 24.3.45
Glogner, Rolf	Lt.	1922	JG 52,	400	3	
Glunz, Adolf	Oblt.	1918	JG 52, 26	574	72	Oak Leaves
Göbel, Hubert	Lt.	1920	JG 301		1	
Gödde, Ernst	Fw.	1918		2	-	
Götz	Ofw.					
Gomann, Heinz	Fw.	1920	JG 26	118	13	
Gossow, Heinz	Fw.	1917	KG 33, JG 301	409	9	Knight's Cross
Gottuck, Hans	Hptm.	1917	JG 300	21	7	

194

Appendixes

Name	Rank	Year of Birth	Previous Unit	Number of Missions	Combat Victories	Notes
Griener, Alfred			JG 52, 11		9	
Grigo, Kurt	Oblt.	1915	KG ?	310	2	
Grözinger, Ludwig	Major	1914	KG 53			Knight's Cross Died 15.2.45
Groß, Hanns	Ofw.					
Grünberg, Hans	Oblt.	1917	JG 3	ca.500	77	Knight's Cross
Gutmann, Heinz	Hptm.	1921	KG 53			Knight's Cross †3.3.45
Gzik, Eberhard	Fw.	1921	JG 300 Kdo. Stamp		3	
Haack, Heinz	Stfw.	1923	EK 388		-	
Haas, Reinhard	Lt.	1917	Recon.	304	-	
Hagenah, Walter	Lt.	1919	JG 3, 11	135	16	
Hankammer, Karl-Heinz	Ofhr.	1924	JG 54	48	2	
Hanning, Norbert	Oblt.		JG 54		42	
Harbort, Rudi	Lt.	1923		53	4	
Heckmann, Günther	Lt.	1920	JG 51, 1	260	20	
Heckmann, Hubert	Uffz.	1924	JG 1	34	5	
Heckmann, Otto	Uffz.					†4.4.45
Heidenreich, Hanns	Fw.	1920	JG 51	500	11	
Heim	Gefr.					†10.4.45
Heiser, Helmut	Ofw.	1915	JG 300		ca.15	
Helms	Uffz.					†1945
Hener, Rudolf	Fw.	1919	JG 3	34	5	
Herrmann, Fritz Erhard	Oblt.		ZG 26, EK 335	150	2	
Heuer, Robert	Fw.		JG 51, 3		6	
Hickethier, Walter	Ofw.	1912	Trans.	261	-	
Hochleitner, Helmut	Fhr.	1922			-	
Hocker, Ernst-Otto	Oblt.		JG 300	28	-	
Hölscher, August	Uffz.	1922	JG 301	12	5	
Hohagen, Erich	Major	1915	JG 51, 2	ca.500	55	Knight's Cross to JV 44
Holzinger, Franz	Fw.	1921	JG 54	140	10	
Hoster, Hans	Lt.	1923	JG 4	30	2	
Hoyer, Hans	Lt.		JG 3			
Humburg, Heinz	Ofw.	1915	JG 26	83	6	
Jänsen, Jan	Gfr.	1925			-	
Jänke, Hans-Jochen	Oblt.	1920	JG 1	60	5	
Jahner, Heinz	Lt.	1917	Recon.	36	1	
Jahnke, Walter	Lt.	1914	JG 52, 11	653	58	
Jansen, Heinrich	FjFw.	1921				
Jelinski, Günther	Ofhr.	1922		3	-	
Jötten, Günther	Fhr.	1924				
Jurzitza, Karlheinz	Fhr.	1920				
Kaiser, Erich	Ofw.		JG 3, 1			

JG 7

Name	Rank	Year of Birth	Previous Unit	Number of Missions	Combat Victories	Notes
Kaiser-Dieckhoff, Hans	Lt.					
Karsten	Lt.					
Kaser, Herbert	Fhr.					
Kelb, Fritz	Lt.		JG 400		1	†30.4.45
Kempken, Heinrich	FjFw.	1922	SG 3, JG 54		2	
Kindermann, Joachim Hans	Lt.	1921	KG ?	33	-	
Klausen, hans	Ofw.					†17.2.45
Knauth	Hptm.		KG?			
Kögler, Hans	Uffz.	1921		28	-	
Köhler	Uffz.					†1945
König, Harald	Uffz.		JG 3			
Köster, Peter	Uffz.					to JV 44
Kolbe, Kurt	Uffz.					†21.3.45
v. Kortzfleisch	Lt.					
Kostrzewa, Gerhard	Hptm.	1912	Recon.	26	-	
Kraft, Karl	Lt.	1919	JG 1	82	5	
Kretzschmar, Georg	Ofhr.	1917		1	-	
Kreutzberg	Ofw.					
Kriegshammer	Hptm.					
Kühlein, Elias	Lt.	1918	JG 51	600	36	
Kühn, Heinz	Uffz.					†19.1.45
Külp, Franz	Oblt.	1919	JG 27	140	5	Wounded 24.3.45
Landsenbacher	FjFw.				10	
Langer, Hans	Fw.		JG 51		ca.10	
Lehmann	Hptm.		KG ?			†1945?
Lehmann, Wolfgang			2.H 55			
Lehner, Alfred	Lt.		JG 5		35	†4.4.45
Leikhoff	Oblt.					
Leisner, Otto	Ofhr.	1924	JG 300	53	3	
Leitner	Oblt.					
Lennartz, Helmut	Fw.		JG 11		5	
Leverenz	Fw.					
Leykauf, Erwin	Oblt.	1918	JG 54	551	33	
Lönnecker, Heinrich	Lt.		JG 300			†1.1.45
Löschenkohl, Ferdinand	FjFw.	1910	JG 3	12	11	
Löschner	Ofw.					
Loose, Fritz	Oblt.	1915	ZG ?	320	7	
Lübking, August	Ofw.	1918	JG 5		37	†22.3.45
Luchs, Hugo	Lt.					
Mai	Lt.					
Mattuschka, Heinz-Berthold	Ofw.					†19.3.45
Mayer, Harry	Lt.	1924				†19.3.45
Nayer, Karl	Uffz.	1922				
Mehn, Hans	Uffz.			19	1	†20.3.45
Meinhardt, Erich	Uffz.	1923				
Meinhold	Gefr.					
Mertz, Willi	Gfr.	1925				

Name	Rank	Year of Birth	Previous Unit	Number of Missions	Combat Victories	Notes
Mikat, Erich	Hptm.		JG 5			
Mischkot, Bruno	Lt.	1920	JG 54, 26	60	2	†1945
Müller, Erwin	Lt.	1920	JG 77	378	18	
Müller, Fritz R.	Lt.		JG 53		16	
Müller-Welt, Herbert	Uffz.	1922	JG 54	12	1	
Müller, Herbert	Uffz.	1918	JG 301	139	6	
Müller, Hermann	Lt.	1920	JG 27	44	10	
Müller, Paul	Gfr.					
Müller, Siegfried	Lt.	1924	JG 3	137	17	†1945
Müller, Wolfgang	Lt.	1920	Trans.	7	-	
Mühlbauer, Kurt	Uffz.	1920	KG 40, 261	30	-	
Mutke, Guido	Fhr.					
Naumann, Johannes	Major	1917	JG 26, 6	450	34	Knight's Cross
Neugebauer	Ofhr.					
Neuhaus, Josef	Ofhr.	1918	ZG 26		13	
Neumann, Klaus	FjOfw.	1923	JG 51, 3	195	32	Knight's Cross to JV 44
Neumar	Oblt.					
Notter, Hermann	Gefr.	1916				
Nordbruch, Karl	Oblt.	1920	KG ?	120	-	
Pauleweit, Fritz	Ogfr.	1923	Trans.	3	-	
Pelletier	Uffz.					
Petermann, Viktor	Lt.	1916	JG 52	374	64	Knight's Cross left arm amputated
Pfeiffer, Ernst	Fhr.	1924				
Philipp, Richard	Oblt.	1918		100	5	
Pickruhn, Hartmann	Lt.	1920	JG 54			
Pings, Rudolf	Uffz.	1921	EK 388	26	-	
Prettner, Erik	Lt.					
Prigge, Rolf	Ofhr.		JG 27		2	transferred back to previous unit
Pritzl, Otto	Fw.	1922	JG 51, 3		10	
Rach, Hein	Uffz.		JG 3			
Rademacher, Rudi	Lt.	1913	JG 54	ca.500	102	Knight's Cross
Rauchensteiner	Fw.					
Raupach, Richard	Ofhr.	1922	JG 54		23	
Recker, Helmut	Ofw.					†22.3.45
Reiher, Gerhard	Ofw.		JG 52, 3		1	
Reinert, Ernst-Wilhelm	Hptm.	1919	JG 77, 27	715	174	Crossed Swords
Reinhold, Gerhard	Ofw.	1919	JG 5	250	41	†4.4.45
Reinke, Fritz	Ofw.	1911	ZG ?	1	2	
Renner, Friedrich	Uffz.					†6.12.44
Rentsch, Wolfgang	Lt.	1923	JG 3	82	9	
v. Rettberg, Günther	Lt.		Trans.			†25.3.45
Rezepka, Hans-Friedrich	Uffz.	1921		86	3	

Name	Rank	Year of Birth	Previous Unit	Number of Missions	Combat Victories	Notes
Ricker	Fw.					
Röwe, Willy	Lt.	1914	Trans.	538	4	
Rudorffer, Erich	Major	1917	JG 2, 54	ca.950	212	Crossed Swords
Rüffler, Helmut	Ofw.	1918	JG 3	ca.650	63	Knight's Cross to JG 51
Rütt, Hans	Fw.	1924		90	-	
Russel, Heinz	Ofhr.	1925		9	1	†9.3.45
Sachsenberg, Heinz	Lt.	1922	JG 52	520	104	Knight's Cross to JV 44
Seeler, Karlheinz	Oblt.	1920	JG 300	137	8	†18.3.45
Seidl, Alfred	Oblt.	1919	JG 53, 3	614	30	
Seip, Georg			JG 300			
Sinner, Rudolf	Major	1915	JG 27, 54	305	37	wounded 4.4.45
Späte, Wolfgang	Major	1911	JG 54, 400	320	94	Oak Leaves
Spangenberg	Lt.					†4.45
Stahlberg, Erwin	Oblt.	1917	JG 300	136	9	
Staiger, Hermann	Major	1915	JG 51, 26, 1	ca.400	63	Knight's Cross
Stedtfeld, Günther	Oblt.		JG 51	237	25	
Stehle, Fritz	Oblt.		ZG 26		15	
Steinhoff, Johannes	Oberst	1913	JG 52, 77	980	170	Crossed Swords to JV 44
Stromm	Uffz.					
Sturm, Gustav	Lt.	1921	JG 27, 51	130	16	wounded 4.45
Suwelack, Gert	Hptm.	1920	JG 27		5	
Schätzle	Oblt.		KG ?			†25.3.45
Schall, Franz	Hptm.	1918	JG 52	525	117	Knight's Cross †10.4.45
Scheibe, Rudolf	Fw.					
Schenk, Friedr. Wilhelm	Lt.	1922	JG 300		1	
Schiebeler, Kurt	Uffz.	1920	JG 54, 400			6
Schielicke, Siegfried	Uffz.	1925	Ind.Schutz		1	-
Schießke, Horst	Fw.	1923		30	2	
Schlick, Horst	Lt.	1921	JG 77	480	32	
Schlüter, Dietrich	Oblt.	1919	Trans.	176	-	
Schlüter, Herbert	Lt.	1917	JG 300		15	
Schmidt, Bruno	Fhr.	1920	JG 54			
Schmitt, Dieter	Uffz.	1924	JG 54	4	-	
Schmude, Karlheinz	Lt.		JG 54		31	
Schneider, Werner	Uffz.	1918	JG 54	87	-	
Schneller, Wilhelm	Uffz.					†15.12.44
Schnörrer, Karl	Lt.	1919	JG 54	520	35	Knight's Cross wounded 30.3.45
Schnurr, Karl	Ofhr.					†23.1.45
Schöppler, Anton	Uffz.		JG 5		6	
Scholz, Helmut	Ofw.	1916	Seeflg.		1	
Schrangl, Hans	Oblt.	1910	JG 11	83	13	

Name	Rank	Year of Birth	Previous Unit	Number of Missions	Combat Victories	Notes
Schreiber, Alfred	Lt.		ZG 26			†26.11.44
Schrey, Günther	Ofhr.		JG 3			†18.3.45
Schuck, Walter	Oblt.	1920	JG 5	ca.400	198	Oak Leaves
Schulte, Erich	Lt.	1919		100	1	†30.3.45
Schwarz, Christoph	Fw.					†10.4.45
Tabbat, Adolf	Fw.	1921	JG 26	64	6	
Tangermann, Kurt	Lt.	1921	JG 52, 54	304	36	
Tappe, Siegfried	Oblt.	1918	JG 301	54	-	
Taube, Fritz	Uffz.	1919	Trans.	145	-	†25.3.45
Tegtmeier, Fritz	Lt.	1912	JG 54	530	146	Knight's Cross
Theis, Hans	Fw.	1920	JG 300	25	10	
Thimm, Arno	Ofw.		JG 54	60	4	wounded 15.4.45
Timmermann, Hans	Lt.					
Todt, Hans	Ofw.	1919	JG 301	50	11	
Toennissen, Harald	Ofhr.		JG 3			
Tollsdorf	Hptm.		LN-Truppe			
Trübsbach, Wolf	Oblt.					
Ullrich, Günther	Fhr.	1925	JG 27	21	2	†25.3.45
Unger, Willi	Lt.	1920	JG 3		22	Knight's Cross
Vigg, Louis-Peter	Uffz.	1922				wounded 10.4.45
Wagner, Walter	Oblt.		JG 3			†10.4.45
Waldhöfer	Uffz.					
Waldmann, Hans	Oblt.	1922	JG 52, 3	525	132	Oak Leaves †18.3.45
Weber, Joachim	Lt.	1919	ZG 26			†21.3.45
Wegmann, Günther	Oblt.		ZG 26		6	wounded 18.3.45
Weihs, Hadi	Lt.	1918	JG 105		-	
Weißenberger, Theodor	Major	1914	JG 5	ca.500	22	Oak Leaves
Wenzel, Werner	Hptm.				18	
Werner, Hans	Uffz.					†15.2.45
Wever, Walter	Oblt.	1923	JG 51	250	44	†10.4.45 Knight's Cross
Wienberg, Otto	Ofw.	1914	Glider	30	-	
Wilkenloh, Wilhelm	Fw.					†23.12.44
Windisch, Walter	Ofhr.	1924	JG 52	8	2	wounded 10.4.45
Wittbold, Günther	Ofhr.		JG 4	7		
Wörner, Ernst	Oblt.		ZG 26			wounded 24.3.45
Wolf, Hermann	Lt.	1919	JG 52, 11	586	57	
Wurm, Heinz	Fw.					†14.1.45
Zander, (Helmut?)	Ofw.					
Zeller, Joachim	FjFw.	1922	JG 26	46	7	
Zimmermann, Konstantin	Fw.	1919		11	-	
Zingler, Rudolf	Lt.	1920		7	1	

Me 262 Three-view Drawings

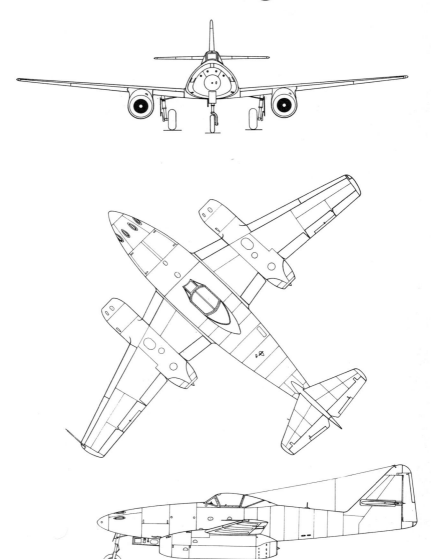

Three-view Drawing of the Me 262 B-1a Two-seat Trainer

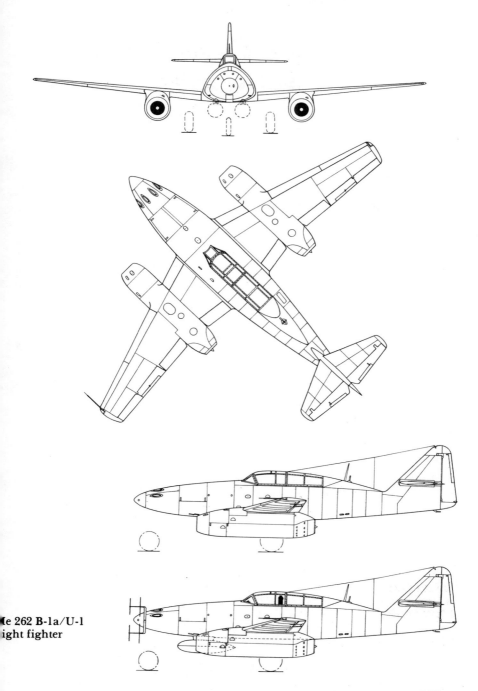

Me 262 B-1a/U-1
night fighter

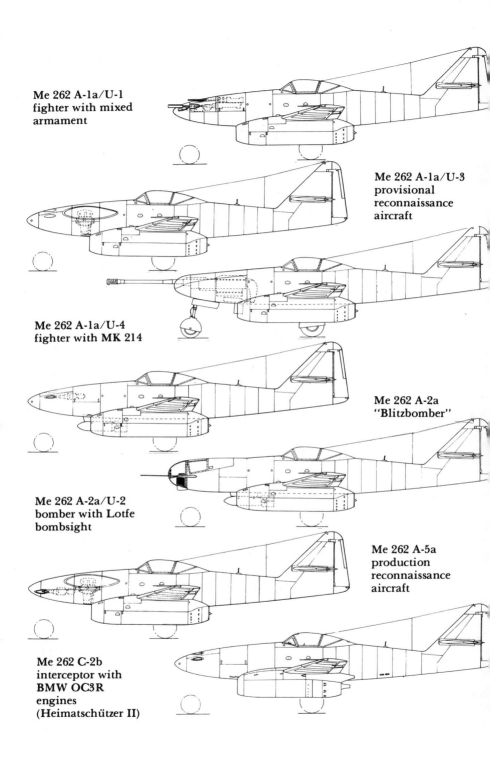

Me 262 A-1a/U-1
fighter with mixed
armament

Me 262 A-1a/U-3
provisional
reconnaissance
aircraft

Me 262 A-1a/U-4
fighter with MK 214

Me 262 A-2a
"Blitzbomber"

Me 262 A-2a/U-2
bomber with Lotfe
bombsight

Me 262 A-5a
production
reconnaissance
aircraft

Me 262 C-2b
interceptor with
BMW OC3R
engines
(Heimatschützer II)

Appendix C

Time Table

Progress of the War	Development of Me 262	Other Developments
		1937/38 Initial design work on Gloster E 28/39
	1. 4. 39 Beginning of project work by Messerschmitt	27. 8. 39 First flight of He 178
1. 9. 39 Outbreak of war, Polish Campaign		Sept. 1939 Beginning of project work on Gloster Meteor
	7. 6. 39 Messerschmitt submits Project Tender P 65 to the RLM	
	9. 11. 39 Improved Project Tender I	
	ca. 15. 1. 40 Work starts on the first mock-up	
	1. 3. 40 Contract issued for the construction of three prototypes	
10. 5. 40 French Campaign	15. 5. 40 Project Tender II	
	11. 10. 40 Junkers begins testing the T 1 jet engine	22. 9. 40 First flight of He 280
	1. 11. 40 Project Tender III	Winter 1940/41 Project work begins on Arado 234
	late January 1941 First Me 262 airframe completed	
6. 4. 41 Balkan Campaign	18. 4. 41 First flight of the Me 262 V1 with Jumo 210	2. 4. 41 First flight of He 280 with HeS 8a jet engines
		15. 5. 41 First flight of Gloster Whittle E 28/39 (total of 2 built)
22. 6. 41 Attack on Russia		
	25. 7. 41 Contract for construction of 5 V-Series and 20 O-Series aircraft	
8. 12. 41 Japanese attack on Pearl Harbor		

Progress of the War	Development of Me 262	Other Developments

Progress of the War		Development of Me 262		Other Developments	
11. 12. 41	Germany declares war on the United States				
		early March 1942	BMW delivers the first Type 3302 jet engine		
		30. 3. 42	First flight with BMW engines		
Summer 1942	Germany at the peak of its military success (Africa, the Caucasus, U-Boat war)				
1. 7. 42	The first American B-17 four-engine bomber lands in England				
		18. 7. 42	First flight of Me 262 V3 with Junkers T 1 engines		
		11. 8. 42	Me 262 V3 crashes		
		12. 8. 42	RLM issues contract for 5 further V-Series aircraft		
17. 8. 42	First mission over Europe by the US 8th Air Force				
		1. 10. 42	First flight of Me 262 V2	1. 10. 42	First flight of Bell P-59 Airacomet (design work begun in 1940)
8. 12. 42	Allied landings in North Africa	2. 12. 42	RLM issues contract for total of 30 pre-production aircraft by the end of 1943	2. 12. 42	First controlled nuclear fission in the USA
		10. 12. 42	Me 262 and He 280 assigned priority level		
27. 1. 43	First attack by the 8th Air Force against a target in Germany				
2. 2. 43	The German Sixth Army surrenders at Stalingrad	February 1943	Führer Order: every fighter must also be capable of performing in the fighter-bomber role		
		20. 3. 43	Me 262 V3 rebuilt		

Appendixes

Progress of the War	Development of Me 262	Other Developments
18. 2. 43 Goebbels announces "total war"		5. 3. 43 First flight of the Gloster Meteor (325 built by end of war)
	17. 4. 43 Me 262 flown by Hptm. Späte	
		27. 3. 43 He 280 dropped from development program (total of 9 built)
	18. 4. 43 Crash of Me 262 V2	
15. 4. 43 First combat between American P-47 fighters and Fw 190s		
12. 5. 43 Surrender of Army Group Afrika	17. 5. 43 Testing continues with Me 262 V3 and V4	
	22. 5. 43 General Galland flies the Me 262 V4 for the first time	
	25. 5. 43 GFM Milch orders series production of the Me 262	
		30. 7. 43 First flight of Arado 234 V1
Summer 1943 The German U-Boat offensive collapses	17. 6. 43 Messerschmitt submits plans for pre-production and production series: completion of 1st pre-production aircraft in January 1944, 430 aircraft by October 1944, series production from November 1944	
10. 7. 43 Allied landings on Sicily		
24. 7. to 3. 8. 43 Operation "Gomorrah" against Hamburg	25. 7. 43 Crash of Me 262 V4	
28. 7. 43 American fighters are equipped with long-range fuel tanks	4. 8. 43 Crash of Me 262 V5	
17. 8. 43 8th Air Force attacks Schweinfurt		
8. 9. 43 Italy surrenders		
9. 9. 43 The Allies land in		

Progress of the War	Development of Me 262	Other Developments
Italy		26. 9. 43 First flight of de Havilland Vampire (project begun in 1942)
14. 10. 43 Second attack on Schweinfurt	17. 10. 43 Completion of Me 262 V6 with retractable nosewheel undercarriage (crashed 9. 3. 44)	
		30. 10. 43 Production of Bell P-59 Airacomet cancelled (total of 65 built)
	2. 11. 43 Regensburg. Göring discusses possibilities of using the Me 262 as a fighter-bomber	
	26. 11. 43 At Insterburg Hitler orders production of Me 262 as a fighter-bomber. (This is quietly ignored.)	
13. 12. 43 First mission by P-51 escort fighters to Kiel		
	9. 12. 43 Formation of Me 262 Test Detach ment	
		9. 1. 44 First flight of Lockheed P-80 Shooting Star (projected in 1942)
20. to 25. 2. 44 "Big Week"		
3. 3. 44 American fighters over Berlin for first time		
6. 3. 44 First major raid on Berlin by the 8th Air Force		
2. 4. 44 The first B-29 Superfortress lands in India		
	25. 5. 44 Hitler once again emphatically demands that the Me 262 is to be employed initially solely as a carrier of bombs	
6. 6. 44 The Allies invade France		June 1944 Production of Ar 234 B-1 jet bomber begins (total of 214 built)

Progress of the War	Development of Me 262	Other Developments
13. 6. 44 First V1 launched against England		
	20. 6. 44 The first bomber pilots of KG 51 begin training on the Me 262	
	22. 6. 44 Hitler orders that the Me 262 is to be built as a bomber until the Ar 234 is available in sufficient numbers	
		12. 7. 44 The RAF's 616 Squadron receives its first Gloster Meteor
17. 7. 44 The USAAF uses napalm bombs for the first time on the invasion front		
20. 7. 44 Assassination attempt on Hitler	20. 7. 44 EKdo Schenk moves to France with 9 Me 262s	
	26. 7. 44 First aerial victory by an Me 262	
28. 7. 44 First combat sortie by Me 163 rocket fighter		
		4. 8. 44 Gloster Meteors shoot down two V1 "flying bombs"
	20. 8. 44 Hitler authorizes every 20th Me 262 to be assigned to the *Jagdwaffe*. Formation of operational test detachment at Läz	
25. 8. 44 Paris captured by the Allies		
8. 9. 44 First launching of a V2 rocket against England		
10. 9. 44 Allied troops reach the German border in the west		
	12. 9. 44 KdE report: Me 262 A suitable (with limitations) for use as a front-line fighter	
	20. 9. 44 Hitler agrees to transfer main weight of Me 262	

Progress of the War	Development of Me 262	Other Developments
	production to fighters	
	Formation of *Einsatzkommando Nowotny* and KG (J) 54	
16. 10. 44 Russian troops enter East Prussia	October 1944 First missions by KG 51 equipped with Me 262 high-speed bombers	
	4. 11. 44 Hitler authorizes total production of Me 262 as fighters	
	19. 11. 44 *Jagdgeschwader* 7 is formed from the expanded *Kommando Nowotny*	
24. 11. 44 First B-29 raid on Tokyo		
	12. 12. 44 First Me 262 night victory by EKdo Welter	
23. 1. 45 The Russians reach the Oder		
3. 2. 45 First area raid on Berlin by the US 8th Air Force		
	12. 2. 45 III./JG 7 operational	
13. to 15. 2. 45 Allied air raids destroy Dresden		
		25. 2. 45 First flight of Bell XP-83 (projected in 1942, 2 built)
9. to 10. 3. 45 US bombers attack Tokyo and Nagoya with napalm bombs		
11. 3. 45 The RAF drops 4,700 tonnes of bombs on Essen		
12. 3. 45 The RAF drops 4,851 tonnes of bombs on Dortmund		
		early 1945 Lockheed P-80 employed by USAAF for first time in Italy (50 built by end of war)
18. 3. 45 The 8th Air Force	18. 3. 45 First operational	

Progress of the War		Development of Me 262		Other Developments	
	drops 4,000 tonnes of bombs on Berlin		use of R4M		
24. 3. 45	British troops cross the Rhine				
				20. 4. 45	First flight of first production de Havilland Vampire (10 built by end of the war)
8. 5. 45	Germany surrenders	8. 5. 45	1,433 Me 262s delivered by end of war	16. 7. 45	Explosion of first atomic bomb at Los Alamos

Appendix D

Anglo-American

Date	AAF	Primary Target	Bomber Strength	Fighter Strength	Bomb-load	B-17	B-24	P-51	P-47	P-3
1.1.45	8.	Kassel, Koblenz, Dollbergen	850	725	1821	9	2	4	–	
	9.					–	–	–	7	
2.1.45	8.	Bad Kreuznach, Lebach, Koblenz	1011	503	2802	5	–	4	–	
	9.					–	–	–	6	
3.1.45	8.	Fulda, Köln, St. Vith, Aschaffenburg	1168	589	3044	–	1	4	–	
	RAF	Dortmund	480							
5.1.45	8.	Koblenz, Frankfurt, Hanau	1032	584	2153	3	–	1	–	
	9.					–	–	–	5	
6.1.45	8.	Köln, Koblenz, Worms	816	622	2223	1	–	2	–	
7.1.45	8.	Hamm, Bittburg, Köln, Rastatt	1073	700	2907	2	1	1	–	
	9.					–	–	–	–	
8.1.45	8.	Frankfurt, Speyer	736	269	1554	3	–	–	–	
	15.	Linz	300			–	1	–	–	
10.1.45	8.	Köln, Karlsruhe	1119	362	2197	20	–	2	–	
	9.					–	–	–	2	
13.1.45	8.	Mainz, Worms	958	469	2439	9	2	2	–	
	9.					–	–	–	4	
	RAF		150							
14.1.45	8.	Derben, Magdeburg, Salzgitter	911	860	2327	19	–	9	2	
	9.					–	–	–	10	
	RAF	Saarbrücken	200							
15.1.45	8.	Ingolstadt, Augsburg, Reutlingen	640	782	1547	–	1	2	–	
	9.					–	–	–	2	
	15.	Wien	400			1	10	1	–	
16.1.45	8.	Magdeburg, Dresden, Dessau	627	693	1435	–	4	2	–	
	9.					–	–	–	4	
17.1.45	8.	Hamburg, Paderborn	700	362	1894	6	4	7	–	
18.1.45	8.	Kaiserslautern	120	117	322	–	–	3	–	
19.1.45	9.					–	–	–	4	

Daylight Bomber Raids

Me 262	In Com-bat	Missions by JG 7 — Confirmed Victories					Probable Victories		Own Losses			
		B-17	B-24	P-51	P-47	Other	Bombers	Fighters	Me 262	KIA	WIA	MIA
									2	1		
									1	–		
		1							2	1		
		1										
									1	1		

211

JG 7

Date	AAF	Primary Target	Bomber Strength	Fighter Strength	Bomb-load	B-17	B-24	P-51	P-47	P-3
20.1.45	8.	Rheine, Heilbronn, Mannheim	772	455	1770	6	–	3	–	–
	15.	Linz, Salzburg, Rosenheim	345			2	12	1	–	
21.1.45	8.	Aschaffenburg, Mannheim, Heilbronn	912	523	2092	9	–	–	–	–
	9.					–	–	–	1	
	15.	Wien	170			3	–	2	–	
22.1.45	8.	Sterkrade	206	258	473	6	–	1	–	–
	9.					–	–	1	11	
23.1.45	8.	Neuß	209	171	312	2	–	–	–	–
	9.					–	–	–	3	
24.1.45	8.	–		70	–	–	–	1	–	–
	9.					–	–	–	1	
25.1.45	8.	–		122	–	–	–	1	–	–
	9.					–	–	–	2	
26.1.45	9.					–	–	–	1	
28.1.45	8.	Köln, Kaiserstuhl, Moers	1006	249	2201	4	8	–	–	–
	RAF	Köln	150							
29.1.45	8.	Siegen, Kassel, Hamm, Münster	1158	700	3114	3	1	2	–	–
	9.					–	–	1	4	
30.1.45	9.					–	–	1	–	–
31.1.45	15.	Graz, Moosbierbaum	670			–	13	1	1	
1.2.45	8.	Mannheim, Wesel	699	328	1178	1	–	–	–	–
	15.	Moosbierbaum, Graz	300			2	1	–	–	
	RAF	Deutz								
2.2.45	9.					–	–	–	6	
3.2.45	8.	Berlin, Magdeburg	1437	948	3279	28	3	7	1	–
	9.					–	–	–	1	
5.2.45	8.					–	1	–	–	–
	15.	Regensburg, Rosenheim, Salzburg, Straubing	730			1	2	1	–	
6.2.45	8.	Chemnitz, Gotha, Magdeburg	1383	904	2675	9	2	4	–	–
	9.					–	–	–	2	
7.2.45	15.	Moosbierbaum, Wien	680			5	18	1	–	
	RAF	Essen	250							
8.2.45	9.					–	–	–	2	
	15.	Wien, Graz	500			2	–	–	–	
9.2.45	8.	Magdeburg, Weimar, Lützkendorf, Paderborn, Dülmen, Bielefeld	1296	871	2965	7	3	7	–	–
	9.					–	–	–	1	
	15.	Moosbierbaum	49							
10.2.45	8.	Dülmen	164	237	457	–	–	2	–	–

262	In	Missions by JG 7 Confirmed Victories					Probable Victories			Own Losses			
nmited	Com- bat	B-17	B-24	P-51	P-47	Other	Bomb- ers	Fight- ers	Me 262	KIA	WIA	MIA

1 Spitf.

3   –   2

5   1
4 engine
bomber

JG 7

Date	AAF	Primary Target	Bomber Strength	Fighter Strength	Bomb-load	B-17	B-24	P-51	P-47	P-3
	9.					–	–	–	3	–
1.2.45	8.	Dülmen	127	316	336	–	–	1	–	–
	9.					–	–	1	1	–
13.2.45	9.					–	–	–	9	1
	15.	Wien, Graz	640			3	3	–	–	1
14.2.45	8.	Dreden, Chemnitz, Magdeburg, Prag	1377	962	3202	8	2	8	1 Spitf.	–
	9.					–	–	1	5	1
	15.	Moosbierbaum, Wien, Graz	500			1	1	–	–	1
15.2.45	8.	Cottbus, Dresden, Magdeburg	1131	1075	2652	2	2	1	–	
	9.					–	–	–	2	
	15.	Korneuburg, Wien, Wn-Neustadt, Graz	650			1	1	–	–	–
	RAF	Rheine, Münster	70							
16.2.45	8.	Hamm, Osnabrück, Dortmund	1042	197	2735	8	2	–	–	–
	9.					–	–	–	5	–
	15.	Regensburg, Landsberg, Neubiberg, Rosenheim	630			4	5	2	–	2
	RAF	Wesel	50							
17.2.45	8.	Frankfurt	895	183	812	3	2	1	–	–
	15.	Linz, Wels, Steyr	500			–	1	–	–	–
18.2.45	15.	Linz	160			–	–	–	–	–
	RAF	Wesel	150							
19.2.45	8.	Osnabrück, Meschede, Bochum, Münster, Rheine	1135	560	3085	–	1	8	–	–
	9.					–	–	–	1	–
	15.	Wien, Klagenfurt, Graz	500			–	4	2	–	2
20.2.45	8.	Nürnberg	1264	726	2177	5	1	13	–	–
	9.					–	–	–	1	–
	15.	Wien	520			2	1	–	–	–
21.2.45	8.	Nürnberg	1262	792	2890	1	1	7	–	1
	9.					–	–	1	2	1
	15.	Wien, Wiener-Neustadt	500			3	8	–	–	–
22.2.45	8.	Ansbach, Halberstadt, Peine, Hildesheim, Stendal, Salzwedel, Wittenberge	1428	862	3895	3	4	13	–	–
	9.					–	–	3	8	2
	15.	Österreich, Süddeutschland	350			–	2	8	–	1
	RAF	Ruhrgebiet, Altenbeken	200							
23.2.45	8.	Ansbach, Plauen,	1274	705	3317	–	2	6	–	–

262 mited	In Com- bat	Missions by JG 7 Confirmed Victories					Probable Victories		Own Losses			
		B-17	B-24	P-51	P-47	Other	Bomb- ers	Fight- ers	Me 262	KIA	WIA	MIA
						1 P 51 (Recon.)						
At least 3									1	−		1
34		2	3	−					5	1		

JG 7

Date	AAF	Primary Target	Bomber Strength	Fighter Strength	Bomb-load	B-17	B-24	P-51	P-47	P-3
		Paderborn, Weimar								
9.						–	–	5	8	
15.		Villach, Klagenfurt	380			1	1	–	–	–
	RAF	Ruhrgebiet	400							
24. 2. 45	8.	Hamburg, Misburg, Bremen	1114	592	2775	1	1	11		–
9.						–	–	1	2	
15.		Graz, Klagenfurt	500			–	–	–	–	–
	RAF	Dortmund, Rheine	400							
25. 2. 45	8.	München, Friedrichshafen, Aschaffenburg	1197	755	3181	5	–	10	–	
9.						–	–	1	8	
15.		Amstetten, Linz, Villach	600			5	3	3	–	–
26. 2. 45	8.	Berlin	1207	726	2886	4	2	4	–	–
	RAF	Dortmund	150							
27. 2. 45	8.	Halle, Leipzig	1107 745	2729	1	2	3	–	–	
15.		Augsburg, Salzburg	540			4	9	–	1	
	RAF	Mainz, Recklinghausen	450							
28. 2. 45	8.	Soest, Hagen, Kassel	1104	737	2882	–	1	5		
9.						–	–	–	3	–
15.		Lienz, Bozen, Brixen	680			–	9	1	–	1
1. 3. 45	8.	Bruchsal, Ingolstadt, Heilbronn, Ulm	1228	488	3354	–	–	7	–	–
9.						–	–	–	8	2
15.		Moosbierbaum, St. Pölten, Amstetten	630			–	10	1	–	2
	RAF	Mannheim, Dortmund	420							
2. 3. 45	8.	Chemnitz, Dresden, Magdeburg	1232	774	2590	11	3	13	–	–
9.						–	–	1	5	2
15.		Linz, St. Pölten, Amstetten	470			1	5	–	–	–
	RAF	Köln, Neuwied, Andernach	500							
3. 3. 45	8.	Hannover, Magdeburg, Chemnitz, Braunschweig	1102	743	2895	5	4	9	–	–
9.						–	–	1	4	–
15.						–	–	2	–	–
4. 3. 45	8.	Ulm, Ingolstadt	1028	522	1712	–	1	1	–	–
15.		Graz, Wiener-Neustadt	630			2	2	–	–	2
	RAF	Dortmund, Bochum								
5. 3. 45	8.	Chemnitz, Hamburg	429	689	992	1	–	–	–	–
	RAF	Gelsenkirchen	120							
6. 3. 45	RAF	Salzbergen	150							

Missions by JG 7

262 imited	In Com- bat	Confirmed Victories					Probable Victories		Own Losses			
		B-17	B-24	P-51	P-47	Other	Bomb- ers	Fight- ers	Me 262	KIA	WIA	MIA
			1	1								
		1										
29	20	4	2	1	2		1 Damaged, forced to leave formation		3	1		

Date	AAF	Primary Target	Bomber Strength	Fighter Strength	Bomb-load	B-17	B-24	P-51	P-47	P-3
7.3.45	8.	Soest, Siegen, Datteln	946	322	2610	–	1	1	–	
8.3.45	8.	Siegen, Dortmund, Frankfurt, Essen	1353	326	3770	–	–	–	–	
	15.	Ungarn, Marburg/Drau	550				–	5	–	–
9.3.45	8.	Frankfurt, Kassel, Münster, Rheine	1045	443	2428	8	1	–	–	
	9.					–	–	1	4	
	15.	Graz, Klagenfurt	372			1	2	–	–	
	RAF	Dortmund, Dtm.-Ems-K.	200							
10.3.45	8.	Arnsberg, Paderborn, Bielefeld, Dortmund, Soest	1374	670	2958	–	–	2	–	
	9.					–	–	–	5	
11.3.45	8.	Kiel, Hamburg, Bremen	1256	814	3021	1	–	3	–	
	9.					–	–	–	5	
	RAF	Oberhausen, Essen	1055		4700					
12.3.45.	8.	Swinemünde, Wetzlar, Marburg, Siegen, Betzdorf	1355	797	3003	1	–	5	–	
	9.					–	–	–	2	
	15.	Wien, Wn-Neust., Graz	790			1	2	1	–	
	RAF	Dortmund	1000		4851					
13.3.45	9.					–	–	–	6	
	RAF	Wuppertal	400							
	15.	Regensburg	572			2	–	2	–	
14.3.45	8.	Hannover, Vlotho, Löhne, Gütersloh, Gießen	1262	804	3499	3	–	1	1	
	9.					–	–	1	10	
	15.	Wiener-Neust., Graz	634			2	3	3	–	
	RAF	Recklinghausen, Dortmund	150							
15.3.45	8.	Zossen, Oranienburg	1353	833	3348	12	4	5	–	
	9.					–	–	1	5	
	15.	Ruhland, Kolin, Moosbierbaum, Wien, Wn-Nstd., St. Pölten	680			4	2	–	–	
		Bochum	350							
						–	–	2	12	
		Korneuburg, Wien, Moosbierbaum	720			5	2	4	–	
17.3.45		Ruhland, Bitterfeld, Plauen, Böhlen, Münster, Hannover	1328	820	3464	8	–	3	–	
						–	–	–	2	

Missions by JG 7

...262 mited	In Com- bat	Confirmed Victories					Probable Victories		Me 262	Own Losses		
		B-17	B-24	P-51	P-47	Other	Bomb- ers	Fight- ers		KIA	WIA	MIA
15				2 (Recon.?)								
,t least 3				1 P51 Recon.								
				2	3							
				1								
				4								

Date	AAF	Primary Target	Bomber Strength	Fighter Strength	Bomb-load	B-17	B-24	P-51	P-47	P-3
18.3.45	8.	Berlin	1329	733	3374	25	2	8	–	–
	9.					–	–	2	7	1
	15.					–	–	3	–	4
	RAF	Dortmund	150							
19.3.45	8.	Zwickau, Plauen, Jena, Neuburg	1273	675	3143	8	1	10	–	–
	9.					–	–	–	12	–
	15.	Landshut, Passau, Mühldorf	800			–	1	2	–	3
	RAF	Arnsberg, Bochum	100							
20.3.45	8.	Hamburg, Hemmingstedt	451	355	1176	4	1	2	–	–
	9.					–	–	1	6	–
	15.	Korneuburg, Wels, St. Pölten, Steyr	760			4	–	1	–	–
21.3.45	8.	Plauen, Hardorf, Hesepe, Achmer, Rheine, Hopsten	1408	806	3115	8	–	10	–	–
	9.					–	–	1	7	–
	15.	Neuburg, Villach, Wien	660			1	2	–	–	–
	RAF	Bremen, Münster	150							
22.3.45	8.	Ahlhorn, Rheinland, Kitzingen, Frankfurt	1331	662	3069	4	–	3	–	–
	9.					–	–	–	3	–
	15.	Ruhland, Wien, Graz, Wels	680			11	21	–	–	–
	RAF	Hildesheim, Ruhrgeb.	500							
23.3.45	8.	Münster, Recklinghausen, Holzwickede, Coesfeld, Gladbeck	1276	499	3140	5	3	–	–	–
	9.					–	–	1	10	–
	15.	Ruhland, Wien, St. Pölten	658			2	7	1	–	–
24.3.45	8.	Vechta, Steenwijk, Varelbusch, Plantlünne, Störmede, Ziegenhain, Twente, Frontunterst.	1749	1375	4775	7	17	9	–	–
	9.					–	–	–	5	–
	15.	Berlin, München, Neuburg, Plattling, Erding	660			9	1	5	–	–
25.3.45	8.	Hitzacker, Ölziele	1009	341	484	–	5	1	–	–
	9.					–	–	–	10	–
	15.	Prag, Wels, Eger	650			–	2	–	–	4
	RAF	Hannover, Osnabrück								
26.3.45	8.	Plauen, Zeitz	337	527	893	4	–	–	–	–
	9.					–	–	–	5	–
	15.	Wiener-Neustadt	500			–	6	4	–	–

Me 262 committed	In Combat	Missions by JG 7 — Confirmed Victories				Probable Victories		Own Losses			
		B-17	B-24	P-51 P-47	Other	Bombers	Fighters	Me 262	KIA	WIA	MIA
37	28	12	–	1		6 forced to leave formation	–	5	3	–	1
45	30	5	–	1		3 forced to leave formation	–	2	2	–	–
29	24	8	1	–		1		3	2	–	1
31	25	13	–	1		–	1	4	2	–	2
27	27	13 4 engine bomber				1	2	4	3		1
14	11	2 4 engine bomber		2 Brit.	1 P-38 Recon.	1	–		–		
31	26	10 4 engine bomber				3					
25	20	–	5	2	1		5	4	–	–	

Date	AAF	Primary Target	Bomber Strength	Fighter Strength	Bomb-load	B-17	B-24	P-51	P-47	P-3
27.3.45	9.					–	–	–	2	–
	RAF	Bremen, Unna, Paderborn	750							
28.3.45	8.	Berlin, Hannover	965	390	2521	7	–	–	–	–
	9.					–	–	–	5	–
30.3.45	8.	Hamburg, Bremen, Wilhelmshaven	1402	899	3720	7	–	4	–	–
	9.					–	–	1	–	–
	15.	Wien, Graz	60			–	–	–	–	–
31.3.45	8.	Zeitz, Brandenburg, Braunschweig, Halle	1348	889	3618	4	4	4	–	–
	9.					–	–	4	6	
	15.	Linz, Villach	540			–	4	3	–	(
	RAF	Hamburg	460							
1.4.45	9.					–	–	1	5	
	15.	St. Pölten, Graz, Marburg	400			3	–	2	–	–
2.4.45	8.	Dänemark abgebrochen				–	1	1	–	–
	9.					–	–	–	4	–
	15.	Graz, St. Pölten, Krems	600			–	2	3	–	
3.4.45	8.	Kiel	752	691	2230	2	–	5	–	–
	9.					–	–	–	1	–
	RAF	Nordhausen	150							
4.4.45	8.	Parchim, Faßberg, Kiel	1431	866	2686	4	6	4	–	–
	9.					–	–	2	3	–
	RAF·	Erfurt, Nordhausen	150							
5.4.45	8.	Ingolstadt, Plauen, Nürnberg	1358	662	2815	7	5	1	–	–
	9.					–	–	–	5	–
6.4.45	8.	Halle, Leipzig	659	666	1629	4	–	1	–	–
	·9.					–	–	–	3	–
7.4.45	8.	Kaltenkirchen, Parchim, Hitzacker, Wesendorf, Lüneburg, Güstrow	1314	898	3451	14	4	5	–	–
	9.					–	–	1	6	1
	15.	Innsbruck, Klagenfurt	128			–	–	–	–	–
8.4.45	8.	Halberstadt, Stendal, Fürth, Grafenwöhr	1173	794	3179	10	–	1	–	–
	9.					–	–	–	3	1
9.4.45	8.	München, Schleißheim, Lechfeld, Neuburg, Landsberg, F.-bruck	1252	846	3109	9	2	5	–	–
	9.					–	–	–	7	–
	RAF	Hamburg	50							
10.4.45	8.	Oranienburg, Brandenburg, Rechlin, Burg, Neuruppin	1315	905	3402	22	1	8	1	–
	9.					–	–	–	4	1
	RAF	Leipzig	120							

Me 262 committed	In Combat	Missions by JG 7 — Confirmed Victories					Probable Victories		Own Losses			
		B-17	B-24	P-51	P-47	Other	Bombers	Fighters	Me 262	KIA	WIA	MIA
						1 Lancaster						
		1		2								
31	19	3	–	3		1 Moskito	2	–	3	1	–	1
38	29	3 4 engine bomber	2	–	–				4	1	2	–
						14 Lancaster u. Halifex	1	–				
47	44	7 4 engine bomber			1	1		3		8	4	1
		2								1	1	–
									1	–	1	
59		1-2	1	2	–	1 P 38			1	–	1	
15				2	–	1 Lancaster 1 P 38						
29					1	4 Lancaster	2	2				
55	48	10	–	5	2	–	2	–	27	5	14	5

JG 7

Date	AAF	Primary Target	Bomber Strength	Fighter Strength	Bomb-load	B-17	B-24	P-51	P-47	P-38
11. 4. 45	8.	Kraiburg, München, Landshut, Ingolstadt, Donauwörth, Regensburg	1303	913	3364	1	–	–	–	–
	9.					–	–	3	11	1
	RAF	Bayreuth	200							
12. 4. 45	9.					–	–	–	2	–
13. 4. 45	8.	Neumünster	212	399	577	2	–	7	1	–
	9.					–	–	–	4	1
	RAF	Stettin, Kiel, Lübeck	500							
14. 4. 45	8.	Bordeaux	1167	40	3318	1	2	–	–	–
	9.					–	–	3	4	–
	RAF	Potsdam	200							
15. 4. 45	8.	Royan, Bordeaux	1348	136	2855	–	–	1	–	–
	9.					–	–	–	2	–
16. 4. 45	8.	Landshut, Regensburg, Bordeaux	1252	913	3449	–	1	34	1	–
	9.					–	–	–	7	–
17. 4. 45	8.	Dresden, Rudnitz	1054	816	2724	8	–	18	–	–
	9.					–	–	–	6	1
18. 4. 45	8.	Kolin, Straubing, Passau, Rosenheim	767	808	2088	2	–	2	–	–
	9.					–	–	–	3	1
	RAF	Helgoland								
19. 4. 45	8.	Elsterwerda, Pirna, Aussig, Falkenberg	605	584	1524	5	–	3	–	–
	9.					–	–	1	3	–
	15.	Linz, Rosenheim, Klagenfurt	619			–	–	–	–	–
	RAF	Helgoland								
20. 4. 45	8.	Nauen, Brandenburg, Oranienburg, Zwiesel, Mühldorf	837	890	1954	1	–	1	–	–
	9.					–	–	1	3	1
	15.	Innsbruck, Italien	700			8	–	–	–	–
21. 4. 45	8.	München, Landsberg	532	444	828	2	1	2	–	–
	9.					–	–	–	1	–
	15.	Rosenheim, Spittal	240							
22. 4. 45	9.					–	–	–	2	–
24. 4. 45	9.					–	–	–	3	–
25. 4. 45	8.	Pilsen, Salzburg, Traunstein	589	584	1386	10	–	1	–	–
	9.					–	–	3	7	–
	15.	Linz, Wels, Prag	467			4	11	–	–	–
26. 4. 45	9.					–	–	1	4	–
	15.	Lienz, Spittal, Klagenfurt	107			–	1	1	–	–
27. 4. 45	9.					–	–	–	2	–
29. 4. 45	9.					–	–	–	5	–
30. 4. 45	9.					–	–	–	1	–
1. 5. 45	15.	Salzburg	27			–	–	–	–	–
3. 5. 45	9.					–	–	–	1	–

262 ...mited	In Com-bat	Missions by JG 7 Confirmed Victories					Probable Victories		Own Losses			
		B-17	B-24	P-51	P-47	Other	Bomb-ers	Fight-ers	Me 262	KIA	WIA	MIA
		–	–	–	1	–	–	–				
									At least 1	1	–	
a. 30		6	–	–	–	–	1	–	At least 4	3	–	–
a. 10		1	–	–	–	–	–	–				
a. 30		5	–	–	–	–	–	–	At least 4			
ca. 10		7	–	–	–	–	–	–				
ca. 36		–	–	–	–	6 IL 2	–	–				

225

Sources

Acknowledgements

During my many years of work on this book I had the good fortune to meet many outstanding men and establish friendships with them. It would be unfair to give prominence to one or the other. They always gave me encouragement and good advice and contributed their knowledge, documents and photos unselfishly. Writing a book such as this is beyond the ability of one person, therefore all those named here may look upon the book as a joint effort as befits a Geschwader history. I am extremely sorry if I have left out anyone.

Ambs, Alfred
Aders, Gebhard

Barbas, Bernd
Bär, Elfriede
Becker, Karl-Heinz
Becker, Kurt Peter
Bell, Kurt
Birkholz, Heinz
Bob, Hans Ekkehard
Bohatsch, Walter
Braunegg, Herward, Dr.
Brüse, Wendelin

Christl, Georg
Creek, Eddie J.
Clauter, Ulrich

Dahl, Walter
Diener, Horst
Detjens, Helmut
Düllberg, Ernst

Ebert, Hans J.
Eder, Georg Peter
Engler, Margot

Frodl, Franz †

Fuchs, Hermann
Flade, Cilly,
    nee Weißenberger

Grimminger, Hans
Girbig, Werner
Galland, Adolf
Geyer, Horst
Göbel, Maria
Grünberg, Hans
Gzik, Eberhard
Geisthövel, Heiner
Giefing, Ernest

Horten, Walter
Hellmold, Wilhelm
Heckmann, Günther
Hahn, Fritz
Hofmann, Ludwig †
Held, Werner
Haase, Ernst
Hitchcock, Thomas
Heuer, Robert

Kempken, Heinrich
Köster, Franz
Kiefer, Karl
Külp, Franz

Leykauf, Erwin
Lux, Eugen
Lennartz, Helmut
Lehmann, Ole †
Langsdorff, Gero von
Lyons, Michael
Lorant, Jean Yves

Müller-Nahlbach, Hans
Müller, Fritz R.G.
Mikat, Erich
Müller, Erwin
Meyer, Michael

Neppach, Fritz
Nowarra, H.J.

Ott, Günther
Oldenstätt, Fritz

Nonnenmacher, Emil
Naumann, Johannes
Neuhaus, Josef

Preusker, Viktor E., Dr.
Prigge, Rolf
Pritzl, Otto
Petrick, Peter
Pawlas, Karl R.
Pfeiffer, Ernst, Dr.

Rudorffer, Erich
Radinger, Willy
Rey, Günther
Reiher, Gerhard
Rudschinat, Siegfried

Schumacher, Leo
Sinner, Rudolf
Schliephake, Hanfried
Schlüter, Herbert
Schnörrer, Karl †
Schnez, Albert
Scholl, Herbert
Smith, Richard
Stehle, Fritz
Schultze, Walter
Schenk, Wolfgang
Späte, Wolfgang
Schenk, Friedrich W.
Schöppler, Anton

Trenkle, Fritz
Tetzner, Hellmut

Wegmann, Günther
Wölfer, Joachim
Weißenberger, Karl
Windisch, Walter

Zucker, Walter

Sources:

Archival material from the author's archives:

Messerschmitt and Obb. Research Institute:

Transcripts
Test programs
Memoranda
Project submissions
Testing reports
Conference minutes

Specifications
Firing reports
Testing programs
Reports by travelling staff
Document notes
Performance reports

Handling characteristics reports
Inspection reports
Complaint reports
Crash and accident reports
Experience summaries
Discussion notes
T-A reports
Production overviews
Partial reports
Loss figures
Development sheets
Situation reports
Installation conferences
Teletype messages
Type conferences
Operating instructions
Acceptance and rejection flight reports
Pilot's notes
Modification notices
Statistical reports
Production manuals
Aerodynamic operating instructions
Aircraft handbook
Type reports
Performance calculations
Monthly testing reports
Flight reports

Loading chart
Servicing manuals
Servicing instructions
Performance figures
General correspondence

Junkers:

Special power plant reports 1-361
Activity reports
Monthly reports
Conference minutes
Installation charts
Flight testing reports
Operating instructions Jumo 004
Engine manual Jumo 004
Inspection instructions
Type assessment
Final reports

BMW:

Installation charts
Conference minutes
Monthly activity reports
Development department reports

Documents from the following offices, research institutes, flying units, etc.:

Luftwaffe Operations Staff
Quartermaster General
Fighter Staff
Armaments Staff
OKL (Head of Technical Air Armaments)
Reich Minister for Armaments and War Production
Luftflottenkommando 6
Luftflottenkommando Reich
VIII. *Flieger-Korps*
Luftgaukommando VIII
General der Jagdflieger
General der Kampfflieger

Erprobungskommando Thierfelder
Kommando Nowotny
Jagdgeschwader 7
III./*Erg.Jagdgeschwader* 2
KG(J) 54
Jagdgeschwader 10
Flugzeugüberführungsgeschwader 1
Outlying Station Parchim
E-Stelle Werneuchen
E-Stelle Karlshagen
E-Stelle Rechlin
E-Stelle Tarnewitz
Aircraft Development High Commission

Special Committee for Bad-weather and
Night Fighting
Askania (gunsights)
Arado
Rheinmetall-Borsig (weapons)
Mauser (weapons)
Blohm & Voss
Leuna-Werke (fuel development)
Heinkel
C. Lorenz (radio equipment)
Fluggeräte Elma (Me 262 undercarriage)
DWM Research Institute (R4M)
Brünn Armaments Factory (R4M)
Telefunken A.G. (radio equipment)
Deutsche Lufthansa
Hermann Göring Werke (multi-barrelled

weapons)
Mittelbau Engineering Team
German Institute for Aeronautical Re-
search
German Academy of Aeronautical Re-
search
German Research Institute for Gliding
Flight
Ernst Udet
Göttingen Aeronautical Research Insti-
tute
US Army Air Forces (Air Material
Command) Engineering Division)
A.D.I. (K.) Reports
Operation "Seahorse" File

Also used was the following archival material from the Federal German archives at
Freiburg and Koblenz:

RL 2/III 735, 2/VI 15, 101, 120, 164: RL 11/15: RL 3 1-64: RL 7 523, 528-530, 534-
536, 540, 542, 544-547, 558, 581: RL 7 583, 589-592: RL 10 256, 257, 259, 264,
366, 390, 479, 539, 542, 552, 560, 588, 598: RL 21/81: RL 36/ 41, 45, 46, 52, 54,
55, 57, 60-64, 86, 88, 119, 258, 439, 440, 444: R 3 1503-1511, 1563, 1570, 1576-
1579, 1590, 1633, 1634, 1664-1687, 1729-1732, 1751, 1773, 1936

National Air and Space Museum (Smithsonian Institution), Washington, D.C.
Imperial War Museum, London
Central Information Office Aachen-Cornelimünster
Deutsches Museum, Munich

Bibliography

Baumbach, W: *Zu Spät*, Munich 1949

Bekker, C.: *Angriffshöhe 4000*, Hamburg 1954

Below, N. von: *Als Hitlers Adjutant 1937-1945*, Mainz 1980

Bracke, G.: *Gegen vielfache Übermacht*, Stuttgart 1977

Constable/Tolliver: *Horrido*, New York 1968

Ethell/Price: *The German Jets in Combat*, London 1981

Freeman, R.: *Mighty Eighth War Diary*, London 1981

Galland, A.: *Die Ersten und die Letzten*, Darmstadt 1953

Henkel, W.: *Eismeerpatrouille*, Düsseldorf 1978

Irving, D.: *The Tragedy of the German Air Force*, Ullstein 1970

Kesselring, A.: *Soldat bis zum letzten Tag*, Bonn 1953

Koller, K.: *Der letzte Monat*, Mannheim 1949

Lüdde-Neurath: *Regierung Dönitz*, Leoni 1980

Molloy-Mason, H.: *Die Luftwaffe 1918-1945*, Vienna 1973

Russ/Ness: *German Jets and the US Army Air Force*, private publication 1963

Schramm, P.: *Die Niederlage 1945*, Munich 1962

Speer, A.: *Erinnerungen*, Ullstein 1969

Steinhoff, J.: *In letzter Stunde*, Munich 1974

University of Chicago Press: *Army Air Forces in WW II*, 1953

Ziegler, M.: *Turbinenjäger Me 262*, Stuttgart 1977

Also from the publisher

THE LEGION CONDOR

A History of the Luftwaffe
in the Spanish Civil War • 1936-1939

Karl Ries/Hans Ring

Size: 8 1/2" x 11"   288 pages   hard cover
ISBN: 0-88740-339-5 $37.50

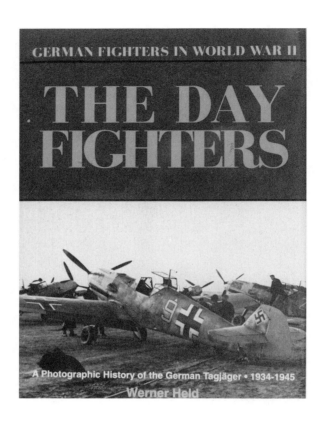

A Photographic History of the German Tagjäger • 1934-1945

Werner Held

GERMAN FIGHTERS IN WWII
THE DAY FIGHTERS

Werner Held

Size: 7 3/4" x 10 1/2"   224 pages   hard cover
ISBN: 0-88740-355-7 $29.95

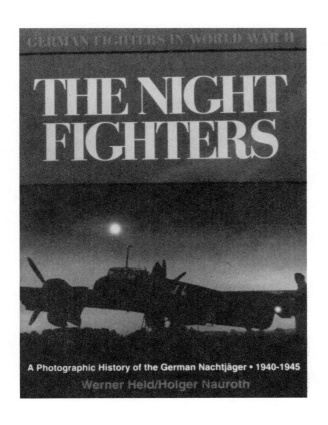

A Photographic History of the German Nachtjäger • 1940-1945
Werner Held/Holger Nauroth

GERMAN FIGHTERS IN WWII
THE NIGHT FIGHTERS

Werner Held/Holger Nauroth

Size: 7 3/4" x 10 1/2"   232 pages   hard cover
ISBN: 0-88740-356-5 $29.95

GERMAN FIGHTER ACE

ERICH HARTMANN

Ursula Hartmann/Manfred Jäger

Size: 8 1/2" x 11"   296 pages   hard cover
ISBN: 0-88740-396-4 $35.00

STUKA PILOT

HANS-ULRICH RUDEL

Günther Just

Size: 8 1/2" x 11"   288 pages   hard cover
ISBN: 0-88740-252-6 $29.95

THE LUFTWAFFE IN THE NORTH AFRICAN CAMPAIGN

Werner Held/Ernst Obermaier

Size: 7 3/4" x 10 1/2"   238 pages   hard cover
ISBN: 0-88740-343-3 $29.95